# THE LOST ZODIAC OF THE DRUIDS

**GREGORY A. CLOUTER** studied Archaeology and Church History at the University College of Lampeter. He was the founder of the Penwith Field Archaeology Group and is currently working on placement at the Cornwall Archeological Unit in Truro.

THE GUNDSTRUP CAULDRON

# THE LOST ZODIAC OF THE DRUIDS

GREGORY A. CLOUTER

ISBN 1-84333-635-9

A catalogue record for this book is available
from the British Library

Published in 2003 by
Vega
64 Brewery Road
London, N7 9NT

A member of Chrysalis Books plc
Visit our website at www.chrysalisbooks.co.uk

Editor: Lisa Morris
Jacket designer: Design Revolution
Designer: Roland Codd
Illustrations: Gregory A. Clouter and Shahid Mahmood
Index: Indexing Specialists Ltd
Printed in Great Britain
by Creative Print and Design Wales, Ebbw Vale

# CONTENTS

# INTRODUCTION

The study of Celtic mythology is based on evidence derived from three various sources: descriptions that have come down to us from the classical authorities of Greece and Rome; indigenous sources originating from the insular traditions of Wales and Ireland; and material clues left in the archaeological record.

When looking at the classical sources one must always be aware of the presence of a biased attitude between the authors and the subject of their descriptions, namely the known civilized world and the mysterious and barbarous tribes of the Keltoi and Galatae who dwelt on its periphery. The primary source upon which several of the earlier writers drew their material was that of the account of the Greek philosopher Posidonus, who described his experiences whilst travelling through Gaul at the turn of the 2nd century BC.

However it is to Caesar that we owe much of our understanding of the Celtic priesthood known as the Druids. His description of the order was based on what he experienced and learned through intelligence during his campaigns in Gaul in the mid-1st century BC (De Bello Gallico). Despite his comprehensive treatise on the political and religious authority of the Druids, he omits information concerning the religious beliefs of the Celts in general, a point which Caesar himself alludes to when he informs us that the Druids did not commit their teachings to writing but preferred tutorial by oral transmission to maintain the secrecy of their doctrines. But Caesar does record that the Celts worshipped a pantheon that he recognized to be similar to that which was venerated in the Graeco-Roman world. Much controversy has surrounded the existence of a pan-Celtic pantheon in that no such evidence remains within the contexts of either the insular sources or the archaeological record. Nevertheless, the re-occurrence of names mentioned in both Irish and Welsh sources are also found in the contexts of Romano-Celtic epigraphy, e.g. Nuada/Nudd/Nodons. With this in mind we must also consider the possibility that Caesar's list of the Gallic pantheon was not merely an attempt to artificially describe the Celtic gods in terms by which his readership would understand them, but truly contains elements of a purely Celtic tradition. For instance Caesar described the principal god of the Celts as Mercury, while in the Greek and Roman pantheon this position was reserved for the sky god Zeus/Jupiter, who is relegated to fourth position on the Gaulish list. We must also take into account that the six deities mentioned by Caesar later occur throughout the iconography of the Roman occupied Celtic world. That such a universally applied system of equations was based singularly upon Caesar's interpretation would be highly unlikely but rather reflects elements of a tradition shared between the two cultures emanating from a common Indo-European source.

Roman authors writing during the 1st century AD tended to concentrate on the bloodier aspects of Druidic ritual practice. This indicates a concordance with the religious policies of Tiberius and Claudius in eradicating the renegade elements of Druidism, which continued to be exercised in rural communities outside of the Roman administration. These included authors like Pliny, Tacitus and Lucan. Despite the evident propaganda contained in their testimonies, they are contemporary accounts that describe factual information, leaving the historian with the unenviable task of discerning the truth from the sensational.

The second source of evidence comes from the insular traditions of Ireland and Wales, which although written by Celts, date from a period when Christianity had already become established as the dominant religion. These would thus be suspect as first hand testimony, containing elements of doctrinal re-editing by the clerics who first put them down on to paper. Nevertheless, many of the narratives described unquestionably date back to an earlier oral source from the Late Iron Age. This becomes remarkably apparent when comparing the myths of Ireland and Wales together, where, although a number of deities appear on both sides of the Irish sea, the narratives associated with them have little in common. Hence we find the Irish Lugh Lamfhada ('of the long arm') appearing in Wales as Lleu Llaw Gyffes ('of the skilful hand'). Both share epithets alluding to the god's skill as a marksman. Another surname applied to Lugh was Samildanach ('the many skilled') indicating that this was one and the same as the Celtic Mercury described by Caesar as 'inventor of all the arts', known in Continental epigraphy as Lugos. Similarly the Irish god Nuada Argatlamh ('the wave of the silver arm') is intimately linked with his Welsh counterpart Lludd Llaw Ereint ('of the silver hand'). Lludd is otherwise known as Nudd and is found in the epigraphy of Britain as Mars Nodens at his principal shrine in Lydney, Gloucestershire. The Celtic Apollo encountered by Caesar in Gaul was frequently invoked under the name of Belenus, cognate with his insular names Bile (Ireland) and Beli (Wales). Caesar refers to only one goddess in his rendition of the Celtic pantheon, whom he equates with Minerva by function, supplying 'the first principles of arts and crafts'. In Ireland she appears as the triple Brighid, the three daughters of the Daghda, patroness of poetry healing and smithcraft. The element 'Brig' alludes to her exalted status, a compound in her name Brigantia in Britain and Brigindo in Gaul. In Romano-Celtic iconography the goddess is often invoked as a trinity in the widespread cult of the Matres or Matronae. A reverence that emphasizes her sacred nature with the number three; a number of profound significance to the Druids who used the triad as a teaching medium.

The Celtic Jupiter was known in Ireland as the Dagdha ('the good god') and was portrayed with his distinctive attributes of the inexhaustible cauldron and wheeled fork, symbolic of the lightening bolt. In Gaul his most common epithets were: Taranus, 'the thunderer' (often depicted as a horseman bearing a wheel); and Sucellus, 'of nourishing juice' (always depicted holding a hammer and a bowl or cup reminiscent of the Dagdha's cauldron).

As I shall attempt to argue in this book, the cauldron itself represented the celestial vault, which was also perceived by the Vedic Aryans as an upturned bowl. In understanding this principle symbolic meaning of the cauldron in Celtic religious tradition fundamentally enables us to look at the mythological narrative depicted on the Gundstrup cauldron (see frontispiece) with a new perspective.

The Celtic Dis described by Caesar is more elusive to identify in both the insular sources and the epigraphic record. In Roman mythology Dis was a relatively minor deity of the underworld associated with the beneficial aspects of the earth. Caesar only informs us of the Druidic tradition that he was an ancestor god. One clue to his identity comes from the classical writer Lucian of Samosata who encounter a Gaulish god called Ogmios depicted leading a retinue of followers by a fine chain linking his mouth with their ears. A religious metaphor describing the psycho-pomp nature of the god who leads the souls of the dead to the underworld. Ogmios literally meaning 'keen of mouth'. The Irish equivalent to this god was Oghma who was similarly associated with the gift of speech where he was given the epithet Cermait ('honey mouthed') and was accredited with the invention of the mystical ogham alphabet. His Welsh counterpart can be identified with Arawn ('silver tongued') god of Annwn or 'the deep'.

In Ireland the sources are contained in three cycles of prose all written in their present condition during the 12th century AD, although the language used suggests that they were first written between the 6th-8th centuries.

These works included: The Mythological Cycle; consisting of The Book of Invasions (Leabhar Gabhala) and The History of Places (Dinnschachas); The Ulster Cycle, which describes the exploits of the champions of Ulster known as the order of the red branch (dated to the 5th century); and The Fenian Cycle, narrating the enigmatic character Fion and the mercenary order of warriors called the Fiana.

In Wales the mythological repertoire is contained in the Four Branches of the Mabinogi or 'The Tales of the Son', so called because the end of each section ends with the phrase 'So ends this branch of the Mabinogi'. The 'son' being a divine character described in all four branches, this probably refers to Mabon, 'the divine son' and his relationship to the rival houses of the goddess Donn and the god Llyr. In their earliest extant the Mabinogi dates back to circa 13th century in the White Book of Rhydderch.

Despite the late date of the existing manuscripts from both Ireland and Wales, the fact that they still contained elements of genuine pagan belief and symbolism suggests that they were based on an oral tradition which remained preserved in the institutions which succeeded the

Druids in both countries, namely among the filidh in Ireland and the bards in Wales.

The archaeological evidence for Celtic religious belief falls primarily into two categories; the material evidence prior to and after the Roman occupation. Under the Roman administration the material culture that expressed Celtic religious belief systems were manifestly re-interpreted to a style that was both coherent and acceptable to the cult of the emperor. This influence both effected ritual observance, with the development of the distinctive Romano-Celtic temple, and the equation of indigenous gods with their closest classical counterparts – Interpretatio Romana.

The evidence from inscriptions name over four hundred different deities, three hundred of which are only named once, leaving the profound problem of recognizing a pantheon as described by Caesar. What we do find is that more than one native name is frequently applied to a single Roman god, indicating that one specific deity was known by a number of different names emphasizing his attributes most particularly venerated within certain tribal territories.

Our greatest problem comes from the lack of evidence during the free Celtic period. The fact that the Druids only passed on their traditions orally left their classical contemporaries ignorant of the fundamental principles of their doctrines. Indeed, only two doctrinal points were recorded by the Romans, that the Gauls believed that they were all descended from a common ancestor, Dis (Caesar) and that the spirit of man and the universe was immortal although at some time or other they will both be destroyed by fire and water (Strabo). These two points indicate a common system of belief shared with the Indo-Aryans of North India. In the Rig Veda the god of the underworld, Yama, (similar to the pronunciation of Oghma) was likewise considered the ancestral deity of mankind and that after death the body was dispersed to the elements prior to a form of rebirth, also alluded to by the classical writers as an integral part of Druidic teaching.

Only two complete documents of recognized Druidic authorship have come down to us from the period before the advent of Rome. One of them is the enigmatic Gundstrup cauldron, found ritually dismantled and deposited on an island in a bog in Denmark. The other is from fragments of the so-called Coligny calendar from Bourg-en-Bresse in France. Both date from circa 1st century BC. The contemporary nature of the two artefacts and their relatively close proximity of manufacture both culturally and spatially relate them in terms of being religious tools used specifically by Gaulish Druids. If some correspondence between the two items can be identified then perhaps we can be directed onto the path of understanding the basic tenets of Druidic philosophy.

We know that the Coligny calendar records the measuring of time by calibrating lunar and solar years. The movement of the moon across the night sky was therefore of paramount importance to the Druids in calculating the timing of ritual activities. Both Caesar and Lucan allude to the Druidic practice of observing the movement of stars, which they considered to represent 'the gods and deities of the sky'. Hence the Druids would have reckoned astronomical time by the movement of the moon through the constellations of the ecliptic rather than the sun. As the full moon fell at the middle of the lunar month (as indicated on the Coligny calendar), the significance of the constellations to the Druids was in direct opposition to the seasonal interpretation of them in the Mediterranean world. The names and order of the months on the Coligny calendar describe the constellations in which the full moon rose during the procession of the year.

Yet, how does the Gundstrup cauldron relate to the Coligny calendar? The cauldron consists of thirteen plates, five inner, seven (of an original eight) outer plates and a base plate. The plates were deliberately dismantled at the time of their deposition, leaving any attempt at interpreting the elaborate pictorial scenes to be a nearly impossible task, since their original order seemed to be irrecoverably lost to posterity. However, if the cauldron does represent a mythological map of the night sky, then by simple deductive analysis the original sequential order of the plates may be determined. This could possibly be achieved by identifying any points of similarity in composition shared between the stars of the ecliptic and the depictions on the cauldron. The mythological star-narrative could then be related to the names and meanings of the lunar months contained in the Coligny calendar. Hopefully this perhaps over simplified form of comparative analysis may lead us into new directions in understanding the philosophy of Druidism.

GREGORY A. CLOUTER

Cornwall, 2003

CHAPTER ONE

# THE CAULDRON AND THE KING

In 1891 the chance discovery of a mysterious silver cauldron was made by peat cutters working on a dry island in the Raevesmore peat bog near Gundstrup in Jutland, Denmark. The context in which the vessel was found suggests that it was of great religious importance to those who carefully deposited it into the earth. Part of this ritual deposition included the deliberate dismantling of the 13 plates that formed the sides of the cauldron. These were then neatly stacked inside the bowl of the vessel prior to its final burial, an act reminiscent of similar votive offerings made throughout the Celtic world during the Late Iron Age.

## Introduction to the Gundstrup Cauldron

Ever since the cauldron's discovery the interpretation and meaning behind the richly decorated plates has, until now, remained unresolved. It is however, generally agreed among scholars that the symbolism and artistic style is unmistakably Celtic and that the composition represents an almost complete surviving record of a mythological narrative.

Fortunately the quality and detail exhibited in the artwork is such that a number of suppositions may be proposed concerning the vessel's date and place of origin. The armour and weaponry depicted are consistent with styles current in Gaul in the Late La Tène. These include: hexagonal shields; round pommelled swords; and animal crested helmets. The 1st-century Greek historian Diodorus Siculus mentions identical helmets in his description of Gaul. Further clues also support a particularly Gaulish origin for the cauldron, such as the representations of ceremonial objects like the carnyx (the boar headed trumpet) and the torc (a twisted gold necklace). The presence of the ram-horned serpent and the stag-antlered god (two hybrid creatures found in other examples of Gaulish religious iconography of the same period) also confirms this association. Some of the smaller details contained within the artwork offer more precise clues to approximately where in Gaul the cauldron was manufactured. The clothes worn by the figures on the cauldron are woollen garments consisting of a hip length coat and knee length breeches. The 2nd-century Greek geographer Strabo conveniently records that the Belgic tribes of north-east Gaul wore an identical fashion.

## The Function of the Cauldron

The cauldron should best be envisaged as a high status cult vessel. This high status is emphasized by the use of precious metals during its manufacture – being made from 96 per cent silver gilded in gold. The variation in artistic style further suggests that at least three silversmiths were engaged on the work, working in unison to a pre-determined pattern. It may be surmised that the cauldron was a cult vessel in terms of the religious symbolism displayed on the plates, where we not only find the aforementioned ram-horned serpent and stag antlered god, but also the distinctive image of the Celtic sky god with his emblematic wheel. In addition to these motifs are a number of scenes depicting ritual activities, such as a bull sacrifice and the immersion of a man into a vat. The use of precious metals and the commissioning of at least three expert silversmiths working to a defined pattern, all indicate that the cauldron was designed with a specific ceremonial function in mind. The immense proportions of the object may itself be a clue, standing 35 centimetres high with a diameter of 63 centimetres. This only leaves us to wonder what ritual would have required a receptacle with the cubic capacity of nearly 130 litres and what were the intended contents. Could it have been wine or mead for ceremonial libations, or perhaps just water for purification rites? The portrayal of a large figure plunging a smaller victim into a vat on one of the inner plates might actually describe a part of the ritual endemic to its use.

The insular sources of Ireland and Wales shed some insight into the regenerative powers attached to an otherworldly cauldron by the Celts. Much like other examples of Celtic religious expressionism, the qualities of this cauldron took on a triune nature. In the Irish Book of Invasions we are informed of a magic cauldron called 'the undry' belonging to the god Dagdha which could supply a limitless amount of food known as 'greal'. Alternatively in Wales the cauldron is described in the Hans Taliesin as the property of the goddess Ceridwen; in it was brewed 'awen' or poetic inspiration. In the Tale of Branwen from the Mabinogi, the cauldron takes on the magical quality of restoring the dead to life.

The cauldron was therefore a prestigious ceremonial cult vessel, designed and manufactured in 1st-century BC Gaul for a specific Druidic ritual, which probably embraced the pan-Celtic theme of a divine receptacle of regeneration. The immense size of the cauldron reflects the contemporary use of the Anathemata among the Greeks. These were usually large tripod vessels, richly decorated in precious materials and were placed at the heart of religious sanctuaries. The key to unlocking the cauldron's enigmatic narrative principally lies in rearranging the 13 plates into an ordered sequence to form the model of an identical religious formula found in the insular sources. I believe that such a comparative model exists in the pan-Celtic concept of sacral kingship.

## Sacral Kingship

The ideal of political unity among the Celtic tribes of both the Continent and the British Isles was never appreciably realized. Even in the face of foreign invasion, the particular interests of the tribe remained of paramount importance. There was, however, a cohesive power that maintained a sense of religious and cultural unity throughout the Celtic world – the sacerdotal order of the Druids.

The office of the king was the highest secular position within the tribe but even this was wholly dependent upon a formula of religious obligations, imposed and regulated only through the authority of the Druids. This was the Celtic concept of sacral kingship. A strict code of ritual observance was enforced on the king, from his nomination as claimant, through to ultimately determining his suitability to remain in power. Evidence drawn from the insular sources, especially from Ireland, describes five distinct ritual procedures that I have identified as corresponding with the narrative of the five inner plates of the cauldron.

In 1892, the Danish archaeologist Muller suggested a sequence for the inner plates based upon preliminary observations of rivet holes and solder mark alignments. However, as this ordering system is reliant on evidence that is far from conclusive, the original sequence remains open to question (see *Figure 1*).

### PLATE II: THE TARBHFESS

According to Irish tradition, any member of the royal family within four generations was an eligible candidate for succession. This extended family group was known as the derbhfhine. The selection of an heir was determined by prophetic ritual, whereby the Druid would receive a prognosis from the gods through a visionary sleep known as the Tarbhfess or 'bull feast'. In the tale The Destruction of Da Derga's Hostel we find the following account of the ritual:

> *A bull was killed by them (the druids) and thereof one man eat his fill and drank its broth, and a spell of truth was chanted over him in his bed. Whomsoever he would see in his sleep would be king...*

Thus it would seem that the Druid who performed the ritual had the sole power to interpret the visions he had seen during the trance-induced sleep, with a free hand to interpret the abstract dream with the personal qualities of his eventual nomination. These visionary qualities may go some way in explaining the origins of the unusual conditions placed on the king in the form of 'prohibitions' or geas. The geise (singular) was a prohibition given to an individual when a position of social distinction had been attained. In many instances, the geas seem to focus on totemic animals, which the king was forbidden to harm at the risk of his own person.

MULLER, 1890s

Based on solder alignments suggesting a clockwise reading for the plates:

(I) The Cernunnos plate, A

(II) The Goddess plate, B

(III) The Wheel plate, C

(IV) The Bull Sacrifice plate, D

(V) The Immersion Sacrifice plate, E

OLMSTED, 1960s

Based on the interpretation of the narrative corresponding with the Irish tale of the Tain Bo. Also read from left to right:

(I) Meave rides chariot, B

(II) Sedanta and Culain's hound, A

(III) CuChulain confronts Fergus, C

(IV) CuChulain drowns foes, E

(V) Fergus stops killing of bull, D

CLOUTER, 2000

Based on the identification of a mythological narrative describing the rites of Sacral Kingship depicted in the constellations of the night sky:

(I) Orion/Taurus and the Tarbhfess, D

(II) Gemini/Cancer and the royal trials, C

(III) Leo-Ophiucus and the divine hunt, A

(IV) Sagittarius-Aquarius and the oblation, E

(V) Pisces/Cetus and the Truth of Kings, B

**FIG. 1.** *Suggested sequences for the inner plates of the Gundstrup cauldron*

The following description adequately summarizes the diverse and abstract nature of some of these prohibitions:

> *...the sun might not rise on the king of Ireland in his bed at Tara; he was forbidden to alight on Wednesday at Magh Breagh, to traverse Magh Cuillinn after sunset, to incite the horse at Fan-Chomair, to go in a ship upon the water the Monday after Beltene, and to leave the track of his army upon Ath Maighne the Tuesday after All-Hallows. The king of Leinster might not go round Tuath Laighean left-hand-wise on Wednesday, nor sleep between the Dothair (Dodder) and the Duibhlinn with his head inclining to one side, nor encamp for nine days on the plains of Cualann, nor travel the road of Duibhlinn on Monday, nor ride a dirty black-heeled horse across Magh Maistean. The king of Munster was prohibited from enjoying the feast of Loch Lein from one Monday to another; from banqueting by night in the beginning of the harvest at Geim at Leitreacha; from encamping for nine days upon the Siuir; and from holding a border meeting at Gabhran. The king of Connaught might not conclude a treaty respecting his ancient palace of Cruachan after making peace on All-Hallows day, nor go in a speckled garment on a grey speckled steed to the heath of Dal Chais, nor repair to an assembly of women at Seaghais, nor sit in autumn on the sepulchral mounds of the wife of Maine, nor contend in running with the rider of a grey one-eyed horse at Ath Gallta between two posts. The king of Ulster was forbidden to attend the horse fair at Rath Line among the youths of Dal Ariadhe, to listen to the fluttering of the flocks of birds of Linn Sailleach after sunset, to celebrate the feast of the bull of Daire-mic-Daire, to go into Magh Cogha in the month of March, and to drink of the water of Bo Neimhidh between two darknesses.*
>
> *Fraser, The Golden Bough*

Plate II stands out among the other inner plates with the depiction of a bull sacrifice repeated in triplicate. The similarity in theme between the imagery of this plate and the ritual of the Tarbhfess is self-evident. The repeated image indicates the importance of this plate, which was not shared with any of the others. It describes the beginning of the cauldron's narrative, just as the Tarbhfess instigated the rites of sacral kingship (see *Figure 2*).

**FIG. 2.** *Plate II of the Gundstrup cauldron depicting the bull sacrifice of the Tarbhfess*

## PLATE III: THE TRIALS OF CONFIRMATION

After the Tarbhfess, the nominee had to endure a series of trials to test his suitability and confirm his selection. This comprised of four trials performed with due ceremony at the Feis Temhra or 'the feast of Tara', at the inaugural seat of the high king of Ireland.

The first trial involved the candidate mounting the royal chariot, said to reject the weight of the unworthy. Having achieved this, the candidate would then don the royal mantle, a loose-fitting, sleeveless cloak that presumably measured the girth or the height of the nominee. The classical sources describe a similar practice whereby the fitness of Celtic warriors was measured by using a belt of a fixed waist. When he had passed the size requirements, the candidate had to drive a chariot between two stones, described as being 'a hand's breadth apart' but which mysteriously opened to allow the passage of the true king. The trial was apparently devised to test the dexterity of the nominee as a charioteer in steering the vehicle through a confined portal. The series of trials were completed when the candidate touched the famous stone of Fial that screamed aloud in recognition of the rightful king.

The depiction on plate III shows the large bust figure of a god handing over a wheel to a smaller, full-length acolyte wearing a bull-horned helmet. The helmet identifies this figure with the candidate nominated from the Tarbhfess, while the chariot wheel represents two of the trials that took place during the feast of Tara. Hence the sky god shows his approval of the candidate by handing over the wheel, the focal point of plate III (see *Figure 3*).

**FIG. 3.** *Plate III of the Gundstrup cauldron depicting the trials of Kingship.*

## PLATE IV: THE REVEALING OF THE GODDESS

Prior to the symbolic marriage between the king and the goddess of sovereignty, there is a tradition recorded from both Irish and Welsh sources describing an otherworldly hunt that must be undertaken before the goddess can reveal herself to her future consort. The underlying metaphor to this myth follows a uniform pattern: the pursuit of a beast from the underworld, usually in the form of a stag or a boar, which leads to the location of the goddess. She is then either miraculously transformed from a hideous crone to a beautiful maiden, or released from an enchanted captivity.

In two Irish tales, Niall of the Nine Hostages and Lughaidh Laoighdhe, a party of hunters pursue their quarry, which leads them to an ugly hag. The rightful king is identified when he agrees to copulate with the old woman. This myth is paralleled in the Welsh tale Culwych and Olwen from the Mabinogi. The future king and hero ('boar runner') has to undergo a series of impossible tasks, culminating in a fabulous boar hunt before the goddess is released by her father.

The imagery of plate IV incorporates several distinct scenes of wild animals: two bulls; two battling lions; a lion chasing a man riding on the back of a salmon; and the antlered god in the company of a deer and a hound, holding aloft a torc and the ram-horned serpent. We may summarise the scene by describing the torc as representing the coronation ring, symbolic of the royal oath the king is obliged to take during his betrothal to the goddess of sovereignty (see *Figure 4*).

**FIG. 4.** *Plate IV of the Gundstrup cauldron depicting the 'divine hunt'.*

## PLATE V: THE INAUGURATION AND MARRIAGE

The principle central to the concept of sacral kingship was that the king could only reign as consort to the goddess of sovereignty, the personification of the land itself. In Ireland the symbolic marriage was known as the Banais Righi, literally 'the woman feast of kingship', a ceremony comprising two essential elements.

The first part consisted of the taking of a libation. In Ireland Medbh, the proto-historical queen of Connaught, was the embodiment of the goddess of sovereignty par excellence. Her name is cognate with the word 'mead' and stems from the Indo-European 'medhu', which meant 'sweet drink'. It was said that she would not allow a king to rule in Ireland unless he consorted with her first. The libation is described in the story of Conn of the Hundred Battles, where the goddess served up a red liquor in a golden goblet filled from an enchanted vat.

The second part of the inauguration rite was a symbolic act of copulation between the king and the goddess. Gerald of Wales, writing in the 12th century, gives a factual account of the coronation ceremony of one Kenelcunil, the petty king of Tyrconnel in Ulster. In this ritual the king undergoes several acts, which link the image of the goddess with a mare. First he mimicked a symbolic birth from a white mare, crawling around on all fours as if he were a foal. Then he copulated with the mare, after which she was slaughtered and cooked in a cauldron wherein the king bathed. The meat was then shared among the gathered assembly.

The association between the goddess and a mare was a widespread phenomenon. In Wales, Rhiannon ('Great Queen') is closely linked with horses (she rode a white horse that was impossible to catch) and as a punishment had to ferry people on her back from a mounting platform to the city gates. In Ireland she is the goddess Macha ('She Steed'). One story recounts how she won a horse race on foot while pregnant, then gave birth to twins before expiring. In

Gaul she was known as Epona ('She Horse'). The widespread distribution of her epigraphy attests to her popularity not only throughout Gaul but to the farthermost military outposts of the Roman Empire. Her popularity even penetrated Rome itself, where she was granted an official festival on 18 December, an unprecedented case of imperial recognition of a Celtic deity. The only known written account of her comes from the anonymous scribe known as the Pseudo-Plutarch:

> *A certain Phoulonivos Stellos, who hated women, had intercourse with a mare, in time she brought forth a beautiful maiden whom she named Epona, a goddess of horses.*

A myth appears to emerge connecting the birth of the goddess from a mare sired by the Celtic sky god, often depicted in native iconography as riding a horse, contrary to the image of his classical counterpart, Jupiter. Plate V can therefore be seen to contain the two constituent parts of the marriage ceremony. The larger figure immersing the smaller one is reminiscent of the libation, while the copulation is represented by the mounted horsemen, who ride the goddess in her symbolic image of the mare (see *Figure 5*).

**FIG. 5.** *Plate V of the Gundstrup cauldron depicting the preparation of the sacred mead.*

## PLATE VI: THE TRUTH OF RULERS

Once the king had been inaugurated, his suitability to rule was constantly scrutinized according to the concept of the Fir Flaithemhan or 'The Truth of Rulers'. This ideal was intrinsically bound with the geas as interpreted through the prophetic Tarbhfess ritual. Hence the king's behaviour was contained within a code of conduct predetermined by a Druid from his earliest recognition as potential king.

If the king kept true to his geas, his realm would prosper in peace with good weather and bountiful harvests. The condition of the kingdom was thus entirely linked with the conduct and health of the king, who was bound to uphold his geas and honour his selection as the consort of the goddess. If, however, any of the geas were broken, the realm would become blemished, the crops would fail and war would replace peace. The removal of the king and his replacement was then the only way to re-establish harmony with the goddess. 'The Truth of Rulers' describes seven circumstances whereby a king was to be considered unfit to remain in office:

> *Without truth, without law, defeat in battle, famine, milk-less cows, spoiled fruit*
> *And scarcity of crops.*

Plate VI depicts the goddess seated on her chariot in her greatest splendour as the bringer of fertility, from where she observes the conduct of her mortal husband, dispensing her approval with ordered seasonal weather, abundant crops and a fruitful reign. This image of the goddess drawn along in a chariot is closely paralleled by the description of Gregory of Tours in his account of the processional ceremonies of the goddess Berecynthia at Augustodunum (Autun) in Gaul during the 2nd century. Here, the goddess is carried on a cart through the neighbouring fields and vineyards, amid salutations and prayers to grant the people an abundant harvest (see *Figure 6*).

**FIG. 6.** *Plate VI of the Gundstrup cauldron depicting the goddess of sovereignty.*

CHAPTER TWO

# THE TRIPLE DEATH

If the depictions on the Gundstrup cauldron are to be interpreted as representing a chronological sequence of the rituals surrounding sacral kingship, we may deduce that these ceremonies would recur in cycles, an annual formula for the re-enactment of sacrifices bound to the agenda of a religious calendar.

## Natural Philosophers

The essential principle of sacral kingship was to maintain the worthiness of the king to rule in his capacity as the symbolic consort of the goddess of sovereignty. Thus, through the concept of 'The Truth of Rulers' the suitability of the king was directly associated with the prosperity of his realm. This condition was dependent on the weather and its effects on the agricultural economy at critical times of the year. The balance between the natural order of the seasons and desired or expected weather is crucial when considering the Celtic perception of the forces of nature and the powers who wielded them, the gods.

The different seasons of the year were associated with the arrival of specific elemental forces, which in the eyes of the Druids were expected to follow an anticipated sequential cycle. This preordained weather lore was the material manifestation behind the cosmological teachings of the Druids, explaining the elemental forces in terms of a seasonal mythological narrative. A divine account, which was re-enacted through ritual sacrifice at particular times of the year using the power of the elements themselves as the medium of execution.

The question as to whether the Druids ever possessed a belief in the elemental ordering of the seasons can only be answered by assessing the existence of a doctrine concerning natural philosophy. In Greek terms, natural philosophy was the scientific investigation into the nature of the physical world, attempting to explain the creation and destruction of matter and the universe through the combination and separation of the four elements; fire, water, earth and air.

In the classical sources both Caesar and Strabo refer to the Druids specifically as natural philosophers, with Strabo also making the distinction that they studied moral philosophy as well. Indeed, it is to Strabo that we are owed our only reference to a Druidic teaching concerning natural philosophy:

*... that men's souls, and also the universe, are indestructible, although both fire and water will at some time or other prevail over them.*

*Strabo, Geography IV, 4.C*

This passage has often been rejected as representing a true Druidic doctrine on the grounds that Strabo relied heavily on the material of the writer Posidonius, who was a Stoic, and that destruction of matter by fire and water was a basic tenet of that school of philosophy. However, as we shall later see, the Druidic tradition of a cataclysmic event is preserved in the 6th-century AD poems attributed to the Welsh bard Taliesin.

Strabo also relates an interesting account concerning the Celts of the Adriatic, who sent envoys to Alexander the Great. They showed no fear in his presence but when questioned about what they feared the most, they replied that they feared nothing except that the sky might fall on their heads.

The same theme is repeated in the Irish tale of the Tain Bo, where Connor MacNessa, king of Ulster, stirs his warriors into action with an oath containing characteristics of a prescribed religious formula in the form of a profession, the so-called 'pledge of the elements:

*The heaven is above us and the earth beneath us and the sea round about us; but surely, unless the heavens fall upon us and the earth splits to swallow us up and the sea overwhelm the earth...*

The most striking feature of the elemental oath is that it appears to have been structured as a triadic riddle. The 2nd century writer Diogenes Laertius mentions the riddles and dark sayings of the Druids, and infers their use of teaching in triads when he described their precepts as:

*... to honour the gods, to do no evil and to practice bravery.*

*Lives of the Philosophers I, Prologue 6*

Among the insular Celts we also come across the preferred method of relating records in the structure of triadic riddles, grouping together similar events, different heroes of likened attributes and even a single character, in threes. The Druidic preoccupation with the sacred nature of three extended to their symbolic descriptions of the Celtic Mercury and the goddess, who were often described in terms of multiples of three – for example, the cult of the triple Matres and the three-faced god of the Gaulish Remi. The link between the triadic riddle of 'the pledge of the elements' and the performance of ritual sacrifice to propitiate the gods is revealed in the lore surrounding 'the triple death' in the insular sources.

## Elemental Executions

The rituals inherent in the application of sacral kingship were performed to retain the elements within their natural seasonal order. A clue to how these rites were performed is found on plate V of the Gundstrup cauldron, with the depiction of the immersion sacrifice. This single image appears to correspond directly with the evidence recorded by two medieval commentators on the Roman poet Lucan.

Lucan wrote his epic poem Pharsalia in the middle of the 1st century AD. The work describes the historical events surrounding the civil war between Caesar and Pompey, from the battle of Pharsalus to the capture of Alexandria. As evidence the work of Lucan is of the highest testimony – since his preoccupation with truthful detail discredited his work among his fellow poets. When describing the people who lived between the Ligurians and the Treveri in eastern Gaul, he denounced them as:

> *You who by cruel blood outpoured think to appease the merciless Teutates, the horrid Esus with his barbarous altars, and Taranis, whose worship is no gentler than the Scythian Diana.*
>
> *Pharsalia I, 422-463*

Further details concerning these sacrifices are given in the marginal notes to the texts scribed by two 9th-century AD commentators to Lucan's work. Both writers appear to have had other sources at their disposal that are now unfortunately lost. Although the commentators differ slightly in their equation of the Gaulish gods with their Roman counterparts (the first commentator correctly identifying Esus with Mercury, Taranis with Jupiter and Teutates with Mars), they both agree to the ritual composition of the three sacrifices.

The victims offered to Esus were hung or suspended from a tree and systematically stabbed. Those sacrificed to Taranis were burned alive inside the hollow trunk of a felled tree, trimmed to the shape of a log. While to appease Teutates, the victims were plunged head-first into a vat or bathtub, which was filled to the brim with water. The latter account is remarkable in its resemblance to the imagery of the sacrifice depicted on plate V of the Gundstrup cauldron.

It would therefore appear that the three gods mentioned by Lucan had more in common than merely the barbarity of their sacrifices. Lucan was renowned for his exactitude to detail, and his description of the three gods together, suggests that he was aware of a tradition that connected them in a single triad – the common form of a Druidic teaching.

Sacrifice is the offering of a gift in exchange for either the granting of a divine favour or as an appeasement against the destructive power of a god: the principle of reciprocity. To maintain the cosmic order and the elemental balance of the seasons, a system of propitiatory rites were developed to appeal to or appease a particular god and thus avoid an elemental catastrophe. Maximus of Tyre, a Greek rhetorician writing in the 2nd century AD, comments on the reciprocal nature of Celtic sacrifice:

> *In war if their ranks anywhere seemed to waver they would massacre those warriors as an offering to the war god or if they suffered under any public calamity, they would devote to death a separate victim to each of the deities under whose displeasure they imagined themselves to have befallen.*

Caesar also informs us of a similar notion of appeasement:

> *They (the druids), in effect that, unless for a man's life a man's life be paid, the majesty of the immortal gods may not be appeased.*
>
> *De Bello Gallico VI, 6*

When comparing the elemental oath of Connor MacNessa with the three sacrifices described by Lucan, we are left with the following elemental apocalypses:

> *The heavens falling down – the fire sacrifice to Taranis, emblematic of the thunderbolt or heavenly fire.*
>
> *The earth taken from under the feet – the hanging sacrifice to Esus.*
>
> *The inundation of the earth by the sea – the immersion sacrifice to Teutates.*

We can now discern the rudimentary principles behind the Druidic understanding of natural philosophy: The earth is the central creative principle in the universe that lies beneath the feet of the mortal, within which resides the god of the underworld. Through the intercession of Esus, the renewal of life is achieved every spring with the sprinkling of the blood of his raised victims. The obvious antithesis to this would be the appeasement of death itself in the metaphor of the earth opening up and swallowing the living.

The first commentator's equation of Esus with Mercury appears logical when we consider his Roman namesake was the messenger of the gods, who alone could transgress the boundaries between the worlds of the living and the dead.

The heavenly fire may be interpreted as the thunderbolt of the Celtic sky god, the seed of which is found in the solar disc, the celestial wheel and chief attribute of Taranis. The allusion to the sky falling down may be made in reference to the winter solstice, when the sun has reached its lowest point on the horizon. The burning sacrifice would then be given for the renewal of a stronger sun.

The elemental opposite to fire is water and the greatest need for moisture falls during the period of the summer solstice. The immersion sacrifice to Teutates was offered to encourage midsummer rains to nourish the growing crops and protect them from the intense and often parching heat of the sun. In the elemental oath, the sea is described as surrounding the earth, the cosmic boundary between the land of the living and the Celtic otherworld. This is the line of demarcation along the horizon where the sun, moon and stars rise and set. It is also the realm of the Celtic Mars, guardian of cattle and the bringer of fertility to the fields.

## Sacrifice by Proxy

The king was set apart from the more mundane duties that could afford him harm. A detachment that even extended to times of war, when he was replaced by an elected war leader, known in Ireland as the Tuaicnid Catha or 'the smiter in battle'.

Insular sources recount the tradition associating the triple death with the demise of a king as a result of breaking his personal prohibitions. His death is inevitable since his conduct as king had become irreversibly blemished. The theme of the king and the three-fold death is strongly reminiscent of the triple sacrifice in the rites of sacral kingship. However, it is difficult to envisage the periodical sacrifice of a king to maintain the balance of the elements, for it was on his behalf that the bloodthirsty rites were performed in the first place. Presumably the chosen victims would then be symbolic representatives of the king, taking his place in a kind of sacrifice by proxy.

This resembles the Greek practice of Pharmakos ('scapegoat'). An account written by the 4th-century AD grammarian Servius Honoratus describes how in Gaul the status of privilege was granted to an individual of the lowest social position for a period of one year. The chosen individual would be kept at the expense of the local people. In return for this high living he had to voluntarily offer himself up for sacrifice to the gods to resolve a certain problem. Caesar records an alternative source of supply for victims if volunteers were not so forthcoming:

> *They (the druids) believe that the execution of those who have been caught in the act of theft or robbery or some other is more pleasing to the immortal gods, but when the supply of such fails they resort to the execution even of the innocent.*
>
> *De Bello Gallico VI, 6*

The three-fold death is described in the Welsh Tale of Lleu (Lleu was the British name for

Lug/Esus). In this story Lleu was protected by a series of prohibitions whereby he could not be killed either indoors or outdoors, whether mounted or on foot. His wife Blodeuwed ('flowerface') conspired with her lover Goronwy Pyber, to overcome Lleu's enchanted defences. The name Goronwy is the Welsh equivalent to the Gaulish Cernunnos (through the Latin verb cernuus or 'headfirst'). Beneath a thatched canopy beside a riverbank Goronwy placed a washtub with a roebuck standing next to it. Blodeuwed then persuaded Lleu to stand with one foot on the bathtub and the other on the roebuck's back while her lover threw a spear mortally wounding the hero. Lleu then transformed into an eagle, and flew off to perch on the top of an enchanted oak tree.

Goronwy and Lleu therefore correspond with the two Gaulish gods: Esus 'the raised one', god of the air (hence the execution of his victims by hanging) and Cernunnos, god of the earth, corresponding to the god whom Caesar equated with Dis. The myth thus describes a seasonal rivalry between Esus and Cernunnos over the goddess. The triple death is described in terms of Lleu hanging precariously on the tub and the back of the roebuck while being ritually stabbed by Goronwy. These are both components of the sacrifice offered to Esus as mentioned by Lucan's commentators. Lleu's transformation into an eagle and subsequent flight to the top of an oak links him with the Celtic sky god.

In Ireland the stories relating to the triple death refer to the demise of semi-historical kings rather then mythological characters. Two tales in particular share a ritualistic formula whereby the king is surrounded and trapped inside a burning house then, when wounded, he seeks reprieve from the flames by sheltering inside a vat of liquor. In the tale of Diarmaid Mac Cerbhaill, the king is initially wounded by a 'spear in the breast that pierced him through and so broke his spine'. The surrounding host then begin to burn down the house about him:

> *Diarmaid himself entered the ale vat, and anon the hall's roof tree fell on his head so that he died.*
>
> *Standish O'Grady, Silva Gadelica*

Similarly another Irish king, Muirchertach Mac Erca, is burned after being drowned in a vat on the eve of Samhain. In the tale The Destruction of Da Derga's Hostel the same chain of events occur surrounding the death of the king Connor Mor. As Connor enters the hostel he is suddenly stricken with a sense of his own impending doom when he realizes that all his prohibitions had been broken. The surrounding enemy attempt to burn the building down. Those left alive inside manage to extinguish the flames with every drop of liquid available. At this moment Connor acquires a debilitating thirst, so one of the king's champions breaks out of the besieged hostel to procure water for his king. On his return he finds all of his comrades dead and the king decapitated. The hero pours the water into the mouth of the king's head, which is then revivified and sings its praises to an able servant.

## The King's Head

The insular sources provide several references to the mystical properties associated with the head of a king. This possibly suggests that the stories were based on a religious precedent comprising of three parts: the decapitation of the head, the singing head, and its later burial or concealment.

After befalling the three-fold death (representing sacrifice through the elements), the king was decapitated. The Irish texts inform us that this occurred at Samhain, the end of the old year and the beginning of the new. Samhain corresponds with the Gaulish month of Samonos, 'the month of seeding', falling in the lunar month October/November.

If the 'seed' represents the head of the king, then the timing of the decapitation and the burial of it during the Celtic New Year suggests a ritual concerned with religious renewal. It would therefore follow that the Celts believed that the head was the repository of the spirit. The veneration of the head is a form of ancestor worship: the belief that bone relics, particularly the skull, contained the spirit and the attributes of the one that possessed it in life. Thus the holder of the skull would receive talismanic power from merely possessing it. Both classical and insular sources bear witness to the widespread practice of headhunting among the Celts:

> *They cut off the heads of enemies slain in battle and attach them to the necks of their horses. The blood stained spoils they hand over to their attendants and carry off as booty, while striking up a paean and singing a song of victory, and they nail up these FIRST FRUITS upon their houses just as do those who lay low any wild animals in certain kinds of hunting. They embalm the heads of their distinguished enemies in cedar oil and preserve them carefully in a chest, and display them with pride to strangers...*
>
> *Diodorus Siculus*

In Ireland these trophy heads were known as 'Macha's acorn crop' – that is, the possession of the goddess in her horse aspect, equated with Epona on the Continent. The use of the terms 'acorn crop' and 'first fruits' suggests a common perception that the head was the repository of the soul, just as fruit houses the seed.

After decapitation, the head of the king was said to acquire the gift of speech, a tradition referred to in the Tale of Branwen from the Mabinogi. The king of the Britons is called Bran Bendigeit, 'the blessed', who after sustaining a mortal injury from a poisoned arrow, informed his companions to cut off his head after he had expired, assuring them it would continue to speak to them as if it were still alive. This was known as Ysbydawt Urdaul Benn or 'the entertainment of the noble head'.

Bran's epithet, Bendigeit, may in fact be a later medieval corruption of Pendictet, or 'the speaking head', in allusion to the principal mythological attribute of the god prior to the advent of Christianity, the original meaning lost by the time the tale was put into writing by later Christian writers.

The final ritual act involved the subsequent burial of the head, a talismanic procedure transferring the power of the dead king to the land, thus protecting his realm after death. Evidence for such burials are known as occurring in Ireland from the 4th to the 6th centuries AD. Two examples of talismanic burials are those of the high king Laoighaire (within the ramparts of Tara) and Eoghan Bel (on the border of his kingdom of Connaught). Both were buried armed and facing the direction of their traditional enemy.

In the Welsh Triads we are informed that this practice was known as Cudd, 'concealment'. Triad 37 describes three concealments. Two refer to the deposition of the relics of semi-historical kings – the burial of Bran's head on the white hill in London and the distribution of the bones of Gwerthefyr in the chief ports of Britain, defending the realm from the incursions of the Saxon invader.

The third concealment is of an entirely different nature as it describes the burial of two mythological serpents at Dinas Emrys (in Wales) by king Lludd. Also, unlike the other two concealments, the serpents were considered to be the oppressors rather than the protectors and it is their burial that preserves the kingdom. The Triad relates to the story of Lludd and Llevelys, where the dragons or serpents appear as one of the three plagues that afflicted the kingdom every May Eve (Beltene). At this time a frightful scream could be heard throughout the kingdom that rendered the land infertile. Llevelys revealed that the source of the noise came from two battling dragons situated in the geographical centre of the kingdom. In Nennius's Historia Regum Brittorum he replaces the term draconis with duo vermes, a generic term for serpents. The link between the two serpents and the ritual act of concealment I believe suggests a religious prototype for the tradition of talismanic burials based on a specific mythological event. An event which may well be depicted on the 1st-century AD Paris column, in the relief showing the god Smertrius holding aloft a headless serpent.

The association between the head and protection is found in the territory of the Celto-Ligurian tribe, the Salii (in the south of Gaul). At their oppidum near Entremont, a sanctuary complex was situated on the high ground overlooking the settlement. Part of this complex consists of the so-called 'hall of the heads', the entrance to which was guarded by a pillar decorated with 12 severed heads, each carved with simple slit eyes and only five possessing a mouth. The closed-eye expression is thought to represent death (see Figure 7). The imagery of severed heads being placed at the entrance to a sanctuary is repeated at nearby Roquepertuse. Here the gateway comprised a portico of four pillars, each one containing carved niches for human heads to be exhibited.

**FIG. 7.** *The Pillar of Heads, Entrement.*

Also peculiar to the Salii was the artistic motif of a crossed-legged warrior, often helmeted and wearing breastplates, holding a human head. This image is found at Entremont, Roquepertuse and Glanum, and represents a god associated with the cult of the head specific to that tribe. This same imagery is repeated in the rest of Gaul in the cult of Cernunnos, who was similarly portrayed in a distinctive cross-legged posture. The cult of Cernunnos was concentrated in the region of central Gaul, later expanding west around Charante, and north and east to the Belgic tribal territories. However, while the Salii's cross-legged warrior holds a human head, Cernunnos is usually depicted holding either one or two ram-horned serpents. If the two variant traditions are to be reconciled to the same mythological story, some connection between the ram-horned serpent and the symbol of the human head must be discerned.

Just as the head of Bran is reflected in the imagery of the Salii warrior god holding the human head, so the battling serpents are depicted in the symbolism of Cernunnos holding the twin ram-horned serpents. It is interesting to note that the link between the serpent and the head is not as spurious as it may seem, since the relief from Vendoeuvres depicts Cernunnos accompanied by two youths balanced on two serpents, which have human heads in place of ram horns (see Figure 8).

**FIG. 8.** *The Vendoeuvres Relief.*

## The Serpent's Egg

If the decapitation of the king's head was the last ritual act of the triple sacrifice, we would expect it to occur at the end of the year during Samhain/Samonos. This represented a time of religious renewal, reflected in the term 'seeding', with metaphors such as 'first fruits' and 'acorn crop' applied to the severed head. The correlation between the head and the serpent resurfaces in the concept of the serpent's egg of which the early 1st-century writer Pliny relates:

> *There is also another kind of egg, of much renown in the Gallic provinces, but ignored by the Greeks. In the summer, numberless snakes entwine themselves into a ball, held together by a secretion from their bodies and by their spittle. This is called anguinum. The druids say that hissing serpents throw this up into the air, and that it must be*

*caught in a cloak, and not allowed to touch the ground; and that one must instantly take to flight on horseback, as the serpents will pursue until some stream cuts them off. It may be tested, they say, by seeing if it floats against the current of a river, even though it be set in gold. But as it is the way of magicians to cast a cunning veil about their frauds, they pretend that these eggs can only be taken on a certain day of the moon, as though it rested with mankind to make the moon and the serpents accord as to the moment of the operation. I myself, however, have seen one of these eggs, it was round, and about as large as a smallish apple; the shell was cartilaginous, and pocked like the arm of a polypus. The druids esteem it highly. It is said to ensure success in law suits and a favourable reception with princes; but this is false, because a man of the Vocontii, who was also a Roman knight, kept one of these eggs in his bosom during a trial, and was put to death by the emperor Claudius, as far as I can see, for that reason alone.*

*Natural Histories XXIX, 52*

Pliny's remark that the serpents eggs were round and pocked is interesting in that if they are related to the cult of the head, they may represent a reference to the use of 'brain balls' on the Continent. Brain balls are mentioned in the Irish sources as magical sling stones made from mixing brains with lime. They were then hardened and fashioned into slingshots.

In the tale of Connor MacNessa the death of the king is attributed to a brain ball made from the brain of his archenemy Mesgerda, thus fulfilling a prophecy. When Connor first acquired the brain ball, he held it in such high regard that he kept it in his treasure house. This brain ball was said to have been fashioned by Conall Cernach (a hero whose name is reminiscent of the god Cernunnos), giving us another link between the head and the serpent. The Irish name for a brain ball, nurchar, and the term for serpent, Iurcher, are almost identical, with the prefix 'nu' added to denote 'lump'. Hence in Gaelic a brain ball was 'the lump of the serpent'.

There is one outstanding mythological precedent for a divine slingshot, mentioned in the Irish Book of Invasions. It concerns the cosmic battle between the Tuatha Dé Dananns (the gods of light) and the Fomorions (the gods of darkness). The Second Battle of Mag Tured was fought significantly at Samhain. During the final stages of the battle, the god Lugh (Lug/Esus) gained the upper hand against the Fomorions when he defeated Balor 'of the baleful eye'. He was called such because he possessed one enormous poisonous eye, which with one look could consume an entire rank of the Danaans, and his eyelid was so heavy that it took four attendants to lift it. When Balor turned his gaze towards Lugh, the hero cast a magical slingshot with such effect that it pierced Balor's eye and head, killing a column of the enemy behind him. Lugh's epithet, Lamfhada 'of the long arm', possibly applies to his prowess with the use of a sling. Taken on a cosmic level, Lugh's slingshot represents the disc of the sun itself, the movement of the orb across the arc of the sky being the symbolic egg of the serpent;

The solar attributes of the serpent's egg is further alluded to by the 6th-century Welsh poet Aneirin:

> *Loud was the clattering of shields around the ancient cauldron in frantic mirth; and lively was the aspect of him, who, in his prowess, had snatched over the ford that involved ball which casts its rays to a distance, the splendid product of the adder, shot forth by serpents.*

CHAPTER THREE

# THE OAK WISE ONES

Before attempting an interpretation of the Gundstrup cauldron's narrative, it would be helpful to offer an introduction to the background of the Celtic priesthood which would have used the vessel during the operation of their religious offices – namely the Druids. As previously mentioned, the Druids were intrinsically linked with the rites of sacral kingship, the one singular pan-Celtic concept of which we are informed in the insular sources. The contemporary accounts of the Graeco-Roman authors give us a clinical description of the three grades of Gallic priest and the religious functions attributed to each, exactly corresponding to the classification recorded within Irish and Welsh tradition. Thereafter we must be aware of common misconceptions that arise in the classical sources, born from unfamiliarity with Druidic religious practices emphasizing the barbaric nature of Celtic worship. This reflects misinformation as a tool of propaganda. Despite the more obvious irregularities contained in the classical texts, they do however, offer us an irreplaceable corpus of knowledge.

## The Druid

The first and most famous category of Celtic priest was the Druid, the 'vid' element being etymologically descended from the Indo-European stem 'wid', denoting wisdom and knowledge. The meaning of the prefix 'dru' is still open to question, however. The original early Celtic form of Druid was 'derwfjes', which became the Gaulish 'Druides' or 'druvid'. One idea suggests that it comes from the adjective 'derwos' or 'truth'. Another theory indicates that it is based on the old Celtic form of 'dru', the name of the oak tree, which is also related to the Greek 'drus'. It is interesting that Pliny remarks on the fact that the name Druid is possibly derived from the Greek name of the oak and makes the point that the tree, and branches of it, was an essential requirement for the performance of their rituals. Our best source of information comes from Caesar's account of the conquest of Gaul (De Bello Gallico). This was based on the intelligence he had acquired over the nine years he campaigned in the country; information gathered from among the Gaulish chieftains who accompanied him in his retinue of political hostages:

> *Throughout Gaul there are two classes of person of definite account and dignity. As for the common folk, they are treated almost as slaves, venturing naught of themselves, never taken into counsel. The most part of them, oppressed as they are either by debt or by the heavy weight of tribute or by the wrongdoing of the more powerful men, commit themselves in slavery to the nobles, who have, in fact, the same rights over them as masters over slaves. Of the two classes above-mentioned, one consists of druids, the other of knights. The former are concerned with divine worship, the due performance of sacrifices, public and private and the interpretation of ritual questions; a great number of young men gather about them for the sake of instruction and hold them in great honour. In fact, it is they who decide in almost all disputes, public and private; and if any crime has been committed or murder done or there is any dispute about succession or boundaries, they also decide it, determining rewards and penalties; if any person or people does not abide by their decision, they ban such from sacrifice, which is their heaviest penalty. Those that are so banned are reckoned as impious and criminal; all men move out of their path and shun their approach and conversation, for fear they may get some harm from their contact and no justice is done if they seek it, no distinction falls to their share. Of all these druids one is chief, who has the highest authority among them. At his death, either any other that is pre-eminent in position succeeds or if there be several of equal standing, they strive for the primacy by the vote of the druids or sometimes even with armed force. These druids, at a certain time of the year, meet within the borders of the Carnutes, whose territory is reckoned as the centre of all Gaul and sit in conclave in a sacred spot. Thither assemble from every side all that have disputes and they obey the decisions and judgments of the druids. It is believed that their rule of life was discovered in Britain and transferred thence to Gaul; and today those who would study the subject more accurately journey, as a rule, to Britain to learn it.*
>
> *De Bello Gallico VI, 13*

In the above account, Caesar makes several observations about the Druids. First, they were a highly organized sacerdotal order whose status was equal to the social position of knights. This religious organization had a hierarchy based on the grading of priests from the lowly novice to the highest rank of arch Druid. Second, the Druids played an important judicial role in Gaulish society, both in religious and secular affairs, and non-compliance to their judgment led to a form of excommunication. Judgments were also directed to cases concerning political issues such as territorial disputes and problems concerning succession.

The involvement of Druids in affairs relating to succession is perhaps indicative of their ceremonial role in selecting heirs during the rites of sacral kingship. The fact that Caesar does not mention any more details to corroborate any of the rituals known from the insular sources merely suggests that he was unaware of them, having only a vague knowledge of the connection between the judicial authority of the Druids and the selection of a king. It is also interesting that Caesar refers to the annual meeting of the Druids at a sacred spot in the territory of the Carnutes, considered to be the geographical centre of Gaul: a Gaulish equivalent to Uisneach in Ireland where the Druids (and later the filidh) held annual assemblies.

## The Vate

Unfortunately, Caesar omits the distinction made between the Druids and the other types of Celtic priest recorded by later writers, namely the vates and the bards, to complete the triadic nature of the hierarchy. The vates appear to have shared some of the sacrificial duties of the Druids but were particularly skilled in the interpretation of portents through various mediums of divination.

The word 'vate' stems from the Gaulish vatis, etymologically descended from the Indo-European bha, 'to speak'. Thus a vate was literally 'the speaker' in allusion to his ability to speak the will of the gods. In Ireland his equivalent was 'the faith', also known by the generic name filidh.

The writer Diodorus Siculus gives us the following account, distinguishing the role of the vate from the Druid:

> *They have philosophers and theologians who are held in much honour and are called druids; they have soothsayers too of great renown who tell the future by watching the flight of birds and by the observation of the entrails of victims; and everyone waits upon their word. When they attempt divination upon important matters they practice a strange and incredible custom, for they kill a man by a knife stab in the region above the midriff, and after his fall they foretell the future by the convulsions of his limbs and the pouring of his blood, a form of divination in which they have full confidence, as it is of old tradition. It is a custom that no one performs a sacrifice without the assistance of a philosopher, for they say that offerings to the gods ought only be made through the mediation of these men, who are learned in the divine nature and, so to speak, familiar with it, and it is through their agency that the blessings of the gods should properly be sought.*
>
> *Histories V, 33, 2-5*

Strabo calls the vates 'diviners and natural philosophers' while describing the Druids as both natural and moral philosophers. This implies that only the Druids were qualified to make judgments concerning what was considered virtuous.

The 4th-century Greek historian Ammianus Marcellinus refers to the vates with the singular title of 'euhages', who 'strove to explain the higher mysteries of nature'. The title 'euphage' means literally 'those who cut well' in reference to their skill at divining through sacrifice. Strabo then goes on to describe the procedure of the sacrifice in similar terms to the above account of Siculus:

> *They used to strike a human being, whom they had devoted to death, in the back with a sword, and then divine from his death struggle.*
>
> *Strabo, Geographica IV. c.198, 5*

## The Bard

The third category of religious official was the bard, a title etymologically linked with the Indo-Aryan 'brhati' or 'sacred verse'. So the Gaulish form of bardos probably means 'the one of the verses', alluding to his primary function of reciting the verses he had committed to memory. Diodorus Siculus supplies the following comments regarding bards:

> *And there are among them composers of verses whom they call bards; they sing to instruments similar to a lyre, applaud some, while they vituperate others and the incantations of the bards have effect on friends and foes alike.*
>
> *Histories 31, 2-5*

This account conforms to the description of bards given in the Irish sources, where we hear of them possessing the power to praise, by which they increased the reputation of their patrons, or conversely the power to satirize, whereby the niggardliness of a thrifty lord would be exposed. As the bards appeared to have been itinerant, travelling from one noble household to another, their upkeep would have been dependent on the congeniality of their host. The system of praise and satire would then assure the bard of a good reception wherever he sought shelter. The bard would also have been an important source of news between the separate communities, bringing a form of social cohesion between them:

> *It was the custom of the bards to celebrate the brave deeds of their famous men in epic verse accompanied by the sweet strain of the lyre.*
>
> *Ammianus Marcellinus, XV, 9, 8*

# Druidic Training

In Ireland the power and authority of both the Druid and the bard was absorbed by the filidh, the only ones of the three grades to survive the religious changes wrought by the arrival of Christianity and the transition from a pagan heritage. The filidh continued as an order until the British encroachment into Ireland during the 17th century AD.

Fortunately details of the training of the filidh have survived the systematic persecution of the order, allowing us a glimpse at a curriculum of instruction that would have remained relatively unchanged since the time of Caesar.

The training of the filidh could take up to 12 years to complete, a period similar to the 20 years Caesar described for the tutorage of novice Druids. The student of the filidh school had to pass through three houses and seven grades of initiation before graduation. The first six years were spent in the 'house of mindfulness', where the adept had the right to carry the bronze branch, a sceptre of office that had bells hanging from it to announce the arrival of the filidh. In his first year the student was known as an ollair or 'beginner', learning the rudiments of grammar and 20 stories. In the second year he became a tamhan or 'attendant' when he was introduced to the ogham alphabet and learned a further 10 stories. From the third to the fifth year he rose to the grade of a drisac or 'apprentice', learning the principles of satire, the law of privilege, 100 ogham combinations and 10 more stories every year. In his sixth year the student became a cli or 'pillar', learning another 20 stories, 48 poems and an introduction to the secret language of poets. The next three years were spent in 'the house of learning', where between the seventh and ninth years the student became an anruth or 'noble stream'. In this course of instruction the student earned the right of carrying the silver branch, learning a further 95 poems and becoming familiar with the Dinnsenchas (the collection of the place names of Ireland and the folklore behind them). He was then taught the three forms of poetic inspiration:

### TEINM LAEGHDA 'THE FIRE OF RECITATION'

By analysing the phraseology of a poem, the poet would recognize and solve a hidden riddle through intuition and an understanding of Ogham metaphors i.e. the secret language of poets.

### IMBAS FOROSNA 'INSPIRATION FROM THE ELEMENTS'

This form of divination consisted of the consumption of the flesh of a totemic animal, the recitation of invocations to the gods followed by a visionary sleep. This was the method employed in the ritual of the Tarbhfess and is remarkably similar to the Greek system of incubation that appears to have been practiced in the spring sanctuaries of Gaul. Cormac's Glossary mentions how practitioners of this form of divination would lie on their backs in a darkened cubicle and cover the eyes with the palms of the hands.

**DICHETAL DO CHENNAIB, KNOWLEDGE BY SPEAKING**

A technique of inspiration based on a system of evocation, whereby the diviner could make a prognosis by reciting prayers addressed directly to the gods.

The final three years were spent in 'the house of the critic'. Here the adept student was qualified to carry the golden branch as he progressed through the final three grades of eces or 'reciter', fili or 'philosopher', and ollamh, 'the beholding hand'. The student learned a further 120 orations, 100 more poems and another 175 stories.

Caesar's description of Druidic training is markedly similar to that of the Irish filidh some 1,500 years earlier:

> *The druids hold aloof from war, and do not pay taxes with the rest; they are excused from military service and exempt from all liabilities. Tempted by these great rewards, many young men assemble of their own motion to receive their training; many are sent by parents and relatives. Reports say that in the schools of the druids they learn by heart a great number of verses, and therefore some persons remain twenty years under training. And they do not think it proper to commit these utterances to writing, although in almost all other matters, and in their public and private accounts, they make use of Greek letters. I believe that they have adopted the practice for two reasons: that they do not wish 'the rule' to become common property; nor those who learn 'the rule' to rely on writing and so neglect the cultivation of the memory, and, in fact, it does usually happen that the assistance of writing tends to relax the diligence of the student and the action of the memory.*
>
> *De Bello Gallico VI, 14*

It is of little surprise that the Druids made use of Greek letters, as cultural links with the Greek trading settlements of southern Gaul existed from around the middle of the 4th century BC, a contact that stimulated a kind of interpretatio Graeco in the religious expressionism of the Druids. This theme particularly influenced the cult of the Celtic Apollo, with the adoption of incubatory rites at the numerous spring sanctuaries in Gaul, some probably dating nearly 200 years before the cultural penetration of Rome had even crossed the Alps.

## Divination

The Irish ogham script was a mystical alphabet based on tree names that developed from an earlier form of notation – that is, a preliterate quantitative system of counts. The construction of the alphabet is clearly not Celtic in origin as several letters employed in the script are not phonetically used in the Celtic tongue. This suggests that the alphabet relied on a non-Celtic prototype, later developed and used to adapt the existing notational system into a script. It is revealing that Caesar refers to the use of Greek letters by the Druids when recording their accounts, indicating that both the use of the Greek alphabet and the notational system of the ogham were born out of the need to quantify through trade between the two cultures. This would suggest that the origins of ogham developed from the Greek alphabet, and more particularly Chalcidic Greek, from the trading centres in southern Gaul circa 2nd century BC.

This is an apparent anomaly, since the earliest ogham inscriptions date from the 4th century AD in insular contexts only. However, this evidence is based on surviving inscriptions in stone. The use of ogham may have originally been restricted to the medium of wood, perhaps due to religious constraint. Indeed, in both Gaelic and Brythonic the word for tree and wood, fid and gwydd, also mean 'letter' and 'alphabet'. This is also reflected in the use of tree names to designate the different characters of the script. If the ogham system was based on a Greek prototype, we would expect to find some evidence of phonetic similarity between the two, the one being dependent on the other. Almost by way of confirmation, we find that six of the 20 letter names of the ogham script are phonetically identical to their counterparts in the Greek alphabet:

| **Letter** | **Greek** | **Ogham** |
|---|---|---|
| A | Alpha | Ailim 'alev' |
| B | Beta | Beith |
| E | Eta | Eadha 'eatha' |
| I | Iota | Idho |
| M | Mu | Muin |
| R | Rho | Ruis |

The ogham alphabet was employed in Ireland as a mystical cipher used and understood by the Druids alone, an exclusiveness that is described in the Book of Ballymote:

> *Now Ogma, a man well skilled in speech and poetry, invented the Ogham. The cause of its invention was that he wanted to prove his ingenuity, and that he thought this language should belong to the learned themselves, to the exclusion of farmers and herdsmen.*

The Irish sources recount how the ogham was employed as a method of divination. In the tale The Wooing of Etain we are told of how staves of yew were inscribed in ogham to reveal the eochra ecsi or the 'keys of divination'. In the Seanchus Mor we further hear of how the casting of lots was employed to decide the outcome of murder trials. This system was known as crannchur or 'the casting of the woods', and involved three possible outcomes: innocence, guilt or the trinity. The trinity was an indecisive outcome requiring the woods to be thrown again until one of the other two results came up. On the 1st-century Gaulish Coligny calendar a similar system is implied in the terms prinni laget ('the laying of the woods') and prinni louden ('the throwing of the woods'), an act that was restricted to the period between the new and first quarter phases of the moon.

In the classical record, it is possible the 3rd-century AD writer Hippolytus was referring to the use of ogham when he described how the Druids used a numerical system of ciphers to predict the future, similar to that employed in the Pythagorean academies. This may allude to the author's vague awareness of the notched numbered characters of the ogham script.

Other forms of divination were shared between the various cultures derived from a common Indo-European origin. We have seen how Siculus described the divinatory practices of the Gaulish soothsayers, which consisted of prediction by use of the flight of birds and the observation of entrails. Both methods were commonly employed in the empire within the cult of the emperor himself, namely in the colleges of the auspices and the haruspices.

In Ireland we learn how birds represented the presence of certain deities – for example, the raven was associated with the Morrigan and the crow with Badbh. Also the direction from which they flew and the noises they uttered allowed the Druid to make a prognosis on what type of person was approaching and from which direction. The ritual practice of bird divination is recorded on the Coligny calendar with the term peti ux, 'from wings above', during the third quarter of the moon in the months of Dumanos ('silence') and Simivisonna ('likened with bird song').

The Coligny calendar was an itinerary designating the auspicious nature of days based on the phases of the moon, with reference to what particular form of divination could be employed by a Druid on a specific day. The Irish sources reveal many instances of when a Druid was able to discern the most favourable time for a certain event to take place. For example, the Druid Cathbadh was able to forecast the best days for the conception of the future king Connor and the birth of Deidre, and when Cu Chulainn should take up arms. Two of the three forms of poetic inspiration are also recorded on the calendar with the expressions ivos ('an evocation') for Dichetal do Chennaib and amb(os) ('inspiration') for Imbas Forosna.

The Irish sources also disclose other forms of divination practiced by the Druids, like neldoracht ('direction from clouds') and cetnad ('repeating verses'), but sadly there are no details as to how they were performed.

## The Doctrine of Rebirth

The classical authors described the Druidic doctrine of rebirth in two different ways: first, that after death the soul transmigrates to a new mortal body; second, that the soul passes to the otherworld, a place that mirrors the world of the living where earthly transactions are continued. Caesar makes a point of emphasizing that the doctrine of rebirth was a fundamental belief of the Druids:

> *The cardinal doctrine which they (the druids) seek to teach is that souls do not die, but after death pass from one body to another; and this belief, as the fear of death is thereby cast aside, they hold to be the greatest incentive to valour.*
>
> *De Bello Gallico VI, 14*

Although Caesar does not specify whether this new life is situated on earth or in the underworld, he later records the Druidic teaching that man was descended from Dis. This is a significant point as Dis was the Roman god of the bountiful underworld, implying the belief that when man is born into this world, his soul had previously existed in the realm of Dis.

Lucan, on the other hand, appears to dismiss the existence of a Druidic belief in an underworld:

> *And it is you who say that the shades of the dead seek not the silent land of Erebus and the pale hills of Pluto; rather you tell us that the same spirit has a body elsewhere, and that death, if what you sing is true, is but a mid point of long life.*
>
> *Pharsalia I, 450-8*

Lucan's account seems clear in defining the Druidic conception of rebirth in terms of a form of reincarnation. Some classical writers appear to support this view by directly associating this belief with the Pythagorean principle of metempsychosis – that the soul of a human or an animal transmigrates after death into a new mundane body, either of the same or different species. Siculus makes the recording:

> *The Pythagorean doctrine prevails among them, teaching that the souls of men are immortal and live again for a fixed number of years inhabited in another body.*
>
> *Histories V, 28, 6*

The 4th-century AD writer Ammianus Marcellinus also recounts a similar tradition, this time quoting from the lost work of Timagenes, who wrote a description of Gaul during the

1st century BC. After describing the vates and the bards he states that:

> *Between them came the druids, men of greater talent, members of the Pythagorean faith; they were uplifted by searchings into the secret and sublime things, and with grand contempt for mortal lot, they professed the immortality of the soul.*
>
> *Ammianus Marcellinus, XV, 9, 8*

It has been argued that the Pythagorean doctrine of the transmigration of the soul is comparable to the Druidic perception of the afterlife. In the former system the soul could jump between species and was dependant on the moral evolution accomplished in each life. Lucan's account supports the tradition that the Druids had a doctrine of rebirth based on the transmigration of the soul, and as we know, Lucan's poetry was repudiated for historical detail.

We also find supporting evidence from other classical writers such as the 2nd-century Greek biographer Diogenes Laertius, who not only reports that Pythagorus himself studied among the Druids but that the said order did have a moral code that a doctrine akin to metempsychosis would require. It involved three precepts: to worship the gods, to refrain from evil acts and to practice bravery. Both Caesar and Mela allude to the connection between the afterlife and the encouragement to commit acts of bravery. So it would seem that bravery itself was considered to be a moral virtue, the practice of which affecting the status of the soul in the next life.

The theory that moral conduct affects the inheritance of the soul in a new incarnation is also found in the Indo-Aryan Rig Veda, the oldest Indo-European composition dating back to the middle of the second millennium BC:

> *Join with Yama and your fathers in the highest heaven, an offering of devotion and sacrifice. Return home unblemished, united with a pure body.*
>
> *Rig Veda 10, 14, v8*

Yama was both the god of the underworld and the ancestor deity of mankind, sharing the attributes of the Celtic Dis mentioned by Caesar. It is also significant that two of the Druidical moral teachings described by Diogenes are mentioned in the Vedic hymn, namely the veneration of the gods and the practice of good deeds.

However, unlike the Pythagorean teaching, the Druidic rule also embraced the existence of an otherworld, a place that not only served as the temporary repository of the soul but also coexisted with the mundane. The following account comes from the 1st-century geographer Pomponius Mela:

*One of their dogmas has come to common knowledge, namely, that souls are eternal and that there is another life in the infernal regions, and this has been permitted manifestly because it makes the multitude readier for war. And it is for this reason too that they burn or bury with their dead, things appropriate to them in life, and that in times past they even used to defer the completion of business and the payment of debts until their arrival in another world. Indeed, there were some of them who flung themselves willingly on the funeral piles of their relatives in order to share the new life with them.*

*Pomponius Mela, De Situ Orbis III, 2, 18-19*

In the insular sources, the otherworld is variously described as a place located across the western ocean in the region of the setting sun, beneath the sea or within the burial mounds (sidhe) of Ireland. The sidhe were believed to be the hostels (bruiden) of the underworld, where the individual deities of the Tuatha Dé Danann retired after their defeat by the Milesians. There, perpetual feasting was observed with food supplied from a cauldron of plenty or from an enchanted beast, which appeared whole again in time for the next session.

In Wales, the underworld was known as Annwn ('the deep') and was ruled by Arawn who likewise possessed a magical cauldron. A common theme suggests that the otherworld was believed to be a place where mortals could enter and leave at two particular times of year: Samhain, the beginning of winter, and Beltene, the beginning of summer. This perhaps reflects the pagan belief that the otherworld was a place where the soul of man could be ferried both ways, spending time in repose before returning to the land of the living in a new incarnation.

A similar perception of the underworld was held by the Greek Orphic sect, which originated in the late 7th century BC. Like the Pythagoreans, they believed in the transmigration of the soul but, like the Druids, they also believed that the underworld served as a temporary place for souls to rest in between various incarnations. The soul would make three incarnations on earth with intervening periods in the underworld before achieving perfection and entering Elysium for all eternity. It is tempting to hypothesize that the Druids held a similar belief.

In the Irish tale The Wooing of Etain we come across the tradition that the soul of the dead is reborn through a person's descendants. In the story, Etain passes through three different incarnations. In the first she is the immortal wife of the god Midhir, when she is transformed through the envious attentions of the god's first wife into the successive states of a pool of water, a worm, then finally a fly. As a fly, Etain falls into the drink of the wife of Etar, a hero of Ulster, thus passing into her womb and being born anew. In this incarnation she marries Eochaidh, the high king of Ireland. She later bears a daughter, also called Etain, her final and third incarnation, in which form she marries Cormac, King of Ulster.

There are two important themes addressed in the story. First, that the soul of Etain passes into her descendants. Second, that Etain represents the goddess of sovereignty, who marries through her sequence of rebirths consorts of descending importance: Midhir the god king, Eochaidh the high king and Cormac the provincial king.

The idea of the soul passing from one incarnation to another through the bodies of a person's descendants has parallels in the religious teachings of the Rig Veda:

> *O Agni, release him to the fathers, when he becomes the oblation of the sacrifice. Give him a new life in his descendants. O lord of creatures let him merge with a new body.*
>
> *Rig Veda 10, 16, v5*

## Transformation and the Ancestor of Mankind

Caesar not only recorded the Druidic belief of the transmigration of the soul but also informs us of the ancestral status attributed to the god of the underworld:

> *The Gauls affirm that they are all descended from a common father, Dis, and say that this is the tradition of the druids.*
>
> *De Bello Gallico VI, 18, 1*

The Irish sources introduce us to a mythological character whose ancestral status is inferred from the great age he achieved through a series of incarnations in both animal and human form. This individual lived through the history of Ireland from its earliest settlement and was able to recount from memory the events that had befallen the land in the intervening periods. The story relates to one Tuan Mac Carell, who described his life history to St. Finnen in the 6th century AD. He explained that he arrived in Ireland with the first race to inhabit the shores, the people of Partholon, all of whom eventually perished so that he alone survived. He wandered around the land for 22 years, when old age finally overcame him with the arrival of Nemed and the second mythological invasion:

> *I was long-haired, clawed, decrepit, grey, naked, wretched, miserable. Then one evening I fell asleep, and when I awoke again on the morrow I was changed into a stag. I was young again and glad of heart.*

Tuan became king of the deer of Ireland until old age once again caught up with him. This time he was born into the shape of a wild black boar:

*I went the rounds of my abode, when I went to the lands of Ulster, at the time old age and wretchedness came upon me. For it was always there that my transformation took place, and that is why I went back thither to await the renewal of my body.*

If Ulster represented the place of his birth, we may interpret this passage as meaning that a person is reborn in the land of his or her birth, or that rebirth occurs within the clan or family. Tuan underwent two more incarnations in a similar fashion, as an eagle and then a salmon. His incarnation as a salmon also seems significant in that this fish always returns to the place of its birth to spawn the next generation. As a salmon, Tuan was caught by a fisherman and consumed whole by the wife of Carell, King of Ulster. Thus he was conceived in her womb and born once again into human form in the same manner as Etain and Taliesin.

The story of Tuan Mac Carell may then describe the rudimentary fragments of the myth surrounding the Celtic Dis as the ancestor of mankind. The name Tuan Mac Carell means 'earthly son of the flesh', a title indicative of the regeneration of the dead prior to their terrestrial rebirth.

In the 9th-century AD Irish text Cormac's Glossary, the concept of the soul being born anew from the earth is given the term Tuirgin or 'an earthly birth'. This is described as 'a birth that passes from every nature into another' – that is, the transformation of the soul from one body or animal into another:

*He gives a transitory birth which has traversed all nature from Adam and goes through every wonderful time down to the world's doom.*

Although Christian symbolism is used to describe the parameters within which Tuirgin is manifested – namely that it exists as long as the universe exists – we have no problem accepting Tuirgin as representing a distinctly Druidic doctrine. Strabo records the idea that (like the Christian author of the glossary) the druids also held a belief in an apocalyptic end of the universe when the immortal souls of men would be destroyed by fire and water.

In the Irish Book of Lismore, dating from the 15th century AD, the tradition associating the delineation of time with the lifespan of animals is also preserved:

*Three life spans of the stag for a black bird;*
*three life spans of the black bird for the eagle;*
*three life spans of the eagle for a salmon;*
*three life spans of the salmon for a yew.*

The same analogy appears in the Welsh tale of Culwych and Olwen, where a series of the oldest known animals are listed. Although the sequence differs given from that above, all four animals are described in an identical context, suggesting a common mythological source:

*The black bird of Kilgowry*
*The stag of Rhedenure*
*The owl of Cwm Cawlwyd*
*The eagle of Gwernabwy*
*The Salmon of Llyn Llyw*

The Welsh poet Gruffud Llwyd, writing in the 13th century AD, described the three animals associated with the power of rejuvenation as: the stag; the eagle; and the salmon. The repeated correspondence made between these three animals and time, and the periodic transformation of the Celtic ancestor god, is indicative of a seasonal myth describing his living and dying in terms of a god of vegetation.

The identification of Cernunnos with Tuan may be implied by their joint association with the stag. The antlers allude to his seasonal nature as a god of vegetation, living and dying in timely rendition to the rising and setting of the stars of the ecliptic. The rising of the full moon in a particular constellation heralding the performance of the sacrifice, offered as a ritual re-enactment of one of his three seasonal deaths.

The timing of the three sacrifices described by Lucan was based on when the Celtic Dis/Cernunnos was envisaged as being seasonally killed by the elemental gods Taranis, Esus and Teutates. Using evidence from the Coligny calendar, I would propose the following correspondences between the triple sacrifice of sacral kingship and the seasonal death of the ancestor god Cernunnos:

| | |
|---|---|
| Riuros, 'The Royal Burning' | Fire sacrifice to Taranis |
| December/January | The winter solstice |
| | |
| Giamonos, 'Sprouting' | Hanging sacrifice to Esus |
| April/May | Beltene |
| | |
| Equos, 'Moisturising' | Immersion sacrifice to Teutates |
| June/July | The summer solstice |

The seasonal re-enactment of the death of the ancestral god was symbolic of the changing weather patterns throughout the yearly cycle. The weather was perceived in the form of the three elements and the gods who ruled over them: Taranis/Lightening, Esus/Wind and Teutates/Rain. All had their seasonal effect on Cernunnos/Earth, allowing the sun to transform from his mythological captivity in the underworld during the winter solstice as Mabon to his ascent as Belenos at Beltene and the summer solstice.

Thus the soul of Cernunnos is transformed into an eagle when he is burned by the fires of Taranis in allusion to smoke rising from its source. When hanged by Esus at Beltene he is transformed into the stag, his antlers associating him with the renewed growth of foliage to trees. Finally he is immersed in the vat of Teutates and transformed into a salmon, the creature that each year returns to its birthplace so that it can spawn anew and be reborn once again into the soul of its descendants.

The transformation of the ancestor god into his animal forms reflects the dispersal of the soul into the three elemental realms after death:

> *Your eyes will become the sun and your breath the wind. In your turn you will go to the sky and the earth and the waters. Your limbs will become the roots of plants.*
>
> *Rig Veda 10, 16, v3*

CHAPTER FOUR

# CELTIC GODS WITH ROMAN NAMES

The question as to whether the Celts possessed a universally accepted pantheon of gods is a complex issue. With more than 400 names of various deities preserved in the surviving epigraphy, the most obvious conclusion to make would be that the gods were venerated primarily at a tribal level. This is confirmed by the fact that only a quarter of these names occur more than once, and when they do so, they appear in distinct regional groupings.

There are exceptions to this rule, however, indicating at the very least that a number of deities were recognized throughout the Celtic world. Perhaps this was the result of religious uniformity impressed by the Druids, the single most cohesive political power in the Celtic culture of the late La Tène period. These gods who transcended the status of the apparently local genii are quite significantly the very deities who were assimilated to the cults of Mercury, Apollo, Mars, Jupiter, Minerva and Hercules after the imposition of the interpretatio Romana (the assimilation of native and Roman deities).

It is to Caesar that the best evidence for the existence of a pan-Celtic pantheon can be ascribed, with the gods named in his list of deities venerated by the Gauls corresponding with the later equations made in the epigraphy of the imperial phases of the province.

It has been claimed that Caesar's description of a Gaulish pantheon was merely a mechanical attempt to describe the gods he encountered in Gaul in terms of their function, equating them with their closest Roman counterpart for the sake of his readership. If this allegation is true (and it probably is), it does not diminish the possibility that a Celtic pantheon existed in a similar form to all the other cultural groups derived from the Indo-European language family. Since over a third of the gods named in the epigraphy are equated with one or other of the deities listed by Caesar, a process of assimilation by function had become endemic to the point of not necessarily being explained by the imposition of the interpretatio alone.

The problem of discerning a Celtic pantheon is further compounded by the nature of the evidence, particularly when more than one Gaulish name is used to address a single Roman god and conversely more than one Roman deity equated to a single Celtic epithet. This principally occurs with the descriptive titles applied to the Celtic Mercury and Mars, where their indigenous functions appear to have overlapped. This does not mean that the same Gaulish god is equated with different Roman gods, but rather enforces the varied abilities of the Celtic Mercury as the many-skilled god whose functions transgress those of other deities. Hence we find the two gods sharing the descriptive Gaulish epithets Visucius ('the powerful') and Iovantucarus ('carer of the young') in their joint capacity as guardians.

The fact that one particular god equated with a single Roman deity shares a number of various Gaulish appellations merely suggests that the god's preferred name varied between regions, depending on the specific function of the god that was to be invoked. For instance, in the territory of the Treveri, Mars was worshipped variously as Entarabus, Smertrius and Lenus, with the adopted name of the god varying between the sanctuaries where he was venerated.

The multiplicity of divine names is therefore not necessarily indicative of an ad hoc system of numerous gods separately defined by each individual tribe. The problem of defining the existence of a pantheon is confused by the veneration of a plethora of local genii apparently invoked as guardian spirits of springs, rivers, trees and even towns.

To determine whether a Celtic pantheon existed prior and subsequent to the interpretatio romana we must look closely at the surviving evidence from the religious inscriptions and interpret the adopted formulae, which can be divided into four categories:

(i) The name of the indigenous deity appears alone – Belisama.
(ii) The name of the indigenous deity precedes that of its Roman counterpart – Sulis Minerva.
(iii) The name of the indigenous deity is preceded by its Roman counterpart – Minerva Belisama.
(iv) The name of the Roman deity appears alone – Minerva.

The first two categories imply that the indigenous deity surpasses the Roman equation both in date and importance, whereas the last two reflect the pre-eminent influence of the Mediterranean import.

In either instance, an established Gallic pantheon coexisted alongside the evident changes brought about by the interpretatio Romana, appearing to specifically target the assimilation of the six gods described by Caesar. The primary objective of interpretatio Romana was to interpret native gods of conquered peoples in terms of their closest Roman counterpart, emphasizing the importance surrounding the cult of the emperor and the worship of the Capitoline triad. The native identity of a god tended to be respected within the corpus of cosmopolitan gods tolerated as long as the cult attached to it was not considered subversive to the imperial authorities.

For example, the Celtic sky god, (equated with Jupiter), preserved elements of Celtic symbolism, where he is most often depicted as a horseman carrying his distinctive motif of the celestial wheel. Symbols that have no parallels in the iconography attached to the Roman Jupiter, so must be seen as evidence of a purely Celtic myth accepted within the interpretatio.

The Celtic goddess, on the other hand, is remarkable in her detached independence from assimilation (except in a very few instances). It was only in her role as consort to her divine partner that she becomes associated with interpretatio Romana and even then she retains her indigenous identity. Hence in the iconography of the Celtic Apollo and Mercury we see her extensive veneration as the native Sirona and Rosmerta. The widespread worship of Epona is also testament to the acceptance and even popularity of a purely Celtic deity within the empire.

In the few examples where the Celtic goddess was associated with a Roman counterpart, that goddess was one of the two goddesses of the Capitoline triad (Juno or Minerva), embodying the principles of the protective mother and the patroness of the arts and invention.

Two of the Celtic gods whose identities appeared to have been totally absorbed into their respective Roman equations were the Celtic Apollo and Mercury. In the iconography of the post-Roman period the Celtic Apollo is often portrayed in the classical tradition as a beardless, semi-clad youth with muscular build, carrying his distinctive lyre. The pre-Roman image of the same deity (as we shall later discuss) was the anthropomorphic snake-limbed god and the enigmatic hybrid animal, the ram-horned serpent. Both of these images persisted into the Roman period but only in the context of describing a purely Celtic myth with other gods – when accompanying the Celtic Mars, Mercury and the antlered god Cernunnos/Dis. When the Celtic Apollo is invoked alone, he appears in his classical guise, although his consorts Sirona and Damona are often depicted carrying a serpent.

The Celtic Mercury seems to have undertaken a similar transformation under the interpretatio Romana. As the principle god of the Celts he was known as Lug, a title adopted in reference to his distinctive tail or lock of hair. In the post-Roman period the Celtic Mercury only retained elements of his native appearance as the bearded god Esus in relation to the myth surrounding the bull Tarvos Trigaranus (Paris column and Trier relief). At Beauvais, the Celtic Mercury is depicted in native style, bearded and accompanied by two ram-horned serpents, but also donning the apparel of his classical associate, wearing the distinctive winged hat (petasus) and carrying the duel serpentine wand (caduceus). It would appear, therefore, that certain aspects of the veneration of the Celtic Mercury were considered intolerable under the interpretatio Romana and that the image of the war-like deity with the lock of hair was replaced with an emphasis on his attributes as a god skilled in crafts and commerce.

## The Influence of Greece and the Spring Sanctuaries

A further clue to the existence of a Celtic pantheon prior to the advent of Rome comes from the historical processes involved in the evolution of religious ideas in Gaul prior to the imposition of imperial conformity.

From the end of the 4th century BC the Druids probably first encountered the influence of Greek culture through trade with their colonial settlements along the southern coast of Gaul and their commercial penetration along the Rhone valley into the interior of the country.

As we have already noted, Caesar mentioned that the Druids adopted the use of Greek letters when recording their public and private accounts. The mystical ogham script also contains elements that suggest a Greek influence in the formation of a system based on quantification. This was probably as a result of the need to record commercial transactions between the two cultures from an early period. If Greek trade had a profound effect on the Celtic economy to the extent of adopting their alphabet and devising a system of notational counting, it is perhaps with the Greeks that we can find evidence of a fusion of religious ideas contributing to the development of a Celtic pantheon.

The adoption and use of spring sanctuaries in Gaul has often been ascribed to the influence of the Greek worship of Apollo. These complexes appear to be evolved from the rectilinear temples of the native late La Tène, and the Hellenistic cult precincts of Apollo – a supposition supported by the fact that many of the spring sanctuaries situated in Provence and Burgundy tended to be presided over by the Celtic Apollo.

To accommodate the needs of both the ceremonial functions of the sites and the visiting pilgrims, a number of auxiliary buildings developed around the ritual shrines, including baths, hostels and dormitories. The spring sanctuaries were Druidic ritual centres, where the beneficial aspects of the gods later equated with Mars, Mercury and Apollo were sought through the curative properties of the springs over which they presided, alongside the administration of prophetic healing.

The ritual involving prophetic healing was known as the incubare, when the patient or pilgrim was induced into a visionary sleep while occupying one of the cubicles of the dormitory. A common practice in Greece was to initiate this rite with the sacrifice of an animal, which the pilgrim would consume before sleeping within its hide. This corresponds to the Druidic practice of Imbas Forosna described in the Irish sources and which we know was also performed in Gaul (termed Ambos on the Coligny calendar). In Greece Ikelos was a god frequently invoked during the process of incubation, a god of dreams who appeared in both animal and human form to his devotees. This god may in fact be addressed in three inscriptions from Britain under the name of an otherwise obscure god Ocelus.

Other types of ritual activity practised at the spring sanctuaries involved the more direct use of the water source to either cure the sick, cleanse the unworthy or curse the wretched. The waters could be used in five various ways:

(i) Internally as a drink.
(ii) By immersion of the body or bathing.
(iii) By ablution or the washing of the face and hands.
(iv) Local application using compresses or poultices.
(v) The deposition of objects as votive offerings in an act of reciprocal sacrifice – that is, the offering of a model limb to cure a limb, a sword for victory, or a lead 'diffixion' for a curse.

## Assimilation or Suppression under Rome

After the initial conquest of Gaul in the middle of the 1st century BC the Roman policy towards the Druidic order and their religious doctrines was ultimately one of assimilation or suppression. Where the veneration of a god and the ritual practices involved in his worship were tolerable, there was little reason why his cult could not be amicably accepted into the swollen ranks of cosmopolitan gods already invoked throughout the length and breadth of the empire. The Roman pantheon itself was an ad hoc amalgam of Greek, Etruscan and Latin gods, so with a mongrel tradition of its own, the state's policy towards the deities of conquered peoples tended to be one of tolerance. The exceptions to this rule occurred when the rites propitiated to the gods were considered to be abhorrent to the people of Rome, like the practice of human sacrifice. A good example of this intolerance was the complete suppression of the bloodthirsty worship of Baal after the fall of Carthage.

In Tacitus' Germania (43, 3) he describes the state policy of equating the gods that the Romans encountered in Germany with their nearest counterpart from among their own pantheon. This process he terms interpretatio Romana.

It is at this point that we reach the fundamental problem concerning our analysis of the existence of a Celtic pantheon. Where a Gaulish title accompanies the name of a Roman god, are we looking at an indigenous god equated with his Roman counterpart or is it simply an instance of a Roman god described with a Gaulish adjective? This problem is further confounded with the realization that there also existed a counter system of interpretatio Gallico. With the implications of Roman conformity, the Druids were left with the inevitable problem of how to express Gallic mythological narratives while conforming to the constraints imposed on them. The only option open to them would have been to adopt an undercurrent repertoire, using Roman imagery to express principles of their own native traditions.

Roman policy towards the Druids was two-fold: to destroy the cohesive political power they had enjoyed previously and to put an end to the ritual observances that were considered to be barbaric and potentially subversive. The imperial successors to Caesar adopted a series of measures to ensure that the religious order was kept within the constraints of the Pax Romana. Under Augustus, the policy towards the Druids was one of the passive isolation of the group from social position and the political administration of the province. Suetonius recorded that the Druid religion:

> *... in the time of Augustus had merely been forbidden to Roman citizens.*
>
> *Suetonius, Claudius, 25*

The loss of citizenship and all its social and political benefits was a great incentive to deprive the Druids of their traditional support from the Gaulish nobility, from whose number they also relied on for new pupils.

The second aim of the Augustan policy was to replace the centralized power of the Druids, embodied in the annual assembly convened in the forest of the Carnutes (in the proximity of Orleans). As this was the political sounding post for the arch Druid, Augustus set out to replace it with an official alternative within the provincial administration that the Druids were excluded from. This measure was accomplished by first decreasing the importance of the assembly as it existed. After the revolt of Vercingetorix the assembly was moved from the territory of the Carnutes (who had instigated the revolt under the arch Druid) to Bibracte, the hilltop oppidum of the pro-Roman tribe of the Aedui. Thereafter Tacitus records that the Druidic collegium was moved again, this time from Bibracte to Autun, the newly named provincial town of Augustodunum (also within the control of the Aedui). At approximately the same time in 12 BC, Augustus established an annual religious festival at Lugdunum (Lyon), which was to be celebrated every year on the 1 August.

This was the traditional date for the Celtic celebration of Lugnesad in honour of the god Lug/Esus after whom the city had been named. The motive for this action was unmistakable. An indigenous religious festival honouring their principal god, Lug, was replaced with the cult of the divine emperor. Here the Augustales (the priests of the imperial cult) celebrated the genus of the living emperor before the altar of Roma, the sacred personification of Rome. The power of the most important god of the Druids was made subordinate to the emperor, and his veneration was absorbed into the identity of his equation under the interpretatio Romana. The new festival was dedicated to Mercury and Maia and was presided over by a chief priest recruited from among the Aedui.

The imperial policy under the next emperor, Tiberius, focused on modifying the macabre aspects of Druidic worship – now that their political authority had subsided, it was time to reform their religious practices. Thus the practice of human sacrifice was forbidden by senatorial decree, an action that must have had some impact as the Druids appear to have replaced it with a more modified form of blood-letting:

> *There still remain traces of atrocious customs no longer practiced, and although they now refrain from outright slaughter, yet they still draw blood from the victims led to the altar.*
>
> *Pomponius Mela, De Situ Orbis III, 2, 18*

Some tolerance was also shown towards the milder aspects of Druidic teaching, for it was during the reign of Tiberius that the significant Gaulish monument, the Paris column, was erected in Lutetia, the chief oppidum of the Parisi. This monument is remarkable in that alongside the depictions of Roman deities we find an ostentatious display of Gaulish gods, showing an indigenous mythological narrative alongside their closest Roman parallels. Significantly, the Gaulish gods are inscribed with just their Celtic names, so in order to comply with the interpretatio Romana we must presume that the myths portrayed among the Celtic deities reflect similar myths among the adjoining Roman gods. This fact is important in that it is a prime example of the working of interpretatio Gallico. This monument is a crucial piece of comparative evidence to use when interpreting the mythological narrative of the Gundstrup cauldron.

The next emperor, Claudius, took a more intolerant stance:

> *He very thoroughly suppressed the barbarous and inhuman religion of the druids in Gaul…*
>
> *Suetonius, Claudius, 25*

Whatever form the Claudian persecution of the Druids took, it appears to have been successful in further isolating their religious practices from the mainstream of Gaulish society, especially from urban areas. Their plight is alluded to during the reign of Nero by two writers, who agree upon their apparent exile to wooded locations on the periphery of society:

> *They teach many things to the nobles of Gaul in a course of instruction lasting as long as twenty years, meeting in secret either in cave or in secluded dales.*
>
> *Pomponius Mela, De Situ Orbis, III, 2*

Lucan adds:

> *And you, O druids, now that the clash of battle is stilled, once more have you returned to your barbarous ceremonies and to the savage usage of your holy rites. The innermost groves of far off forests are your abodes.*
>
> *Pharsalia I*

Lucan's reference to the clash of battle describes the Boudiccan revolt in Britain during AD 60/61. An event sparked by the despoiling of the royal house of the Iceni. It has been hypothesized that the Druids were instrumental in stirring the revolt of the Iceni and the neighbouring tribes as a counter offensive to the Roman incursions into North Wales – a military campaign instigated to eradicate the Druidic renegade stronghold behind the mountains of Snowdonia. Tacitus adequately describes the siege of the island of Mona (Anglesey), where the Druids had been pushed to make a desperate last stand with their backs to the sea:

> *The enemy lined the shore in a dense armed mass. Among them were black robed women with dishevelled hair like furies, brandishing torches. Close by stood druids, raising their hands to heaven and screaming dreadful curses. This weird spectacle awed the Roman soldiers into a sort of paralysis. They stood still and presented themselves as a target. But then they urged each other on, and were urged by the general, not to fear a horde of fanatical women. Onward pressed their standards and they bore down on their opponents, enveloping them in the flames of their own torches. Suetonius garrisoned the island. The groves devoted to Mona's barbarous superstitions he demolished. For it was their religion to drench their altars in the blood of prisoners and consult their gods by means of human entrails.*
>
> *Tacitus, Annals XIV, 30-31*

Nine years later, Tacitus describes what could possibly be the last stand of the Druids as a political force. In AD 69 a certain Druid called Mariccus stirred the Boii into a doomed insurrection in north-east Italy, hoping that Rome's troubles over the imperial succession would divert the attentions of the army. The revolt was crushed and the problem of succession was resolved with the elevation of the able general Vespasian. Tacitus records how in AD 70 the burning of the Temple of Jupiter on the Capitoline Hill was interpreted by the Druids as an omen for the collapse of Rome and the shift of power back to the nations across the Alps, a prophecy that was never to materialize.

It is not until the 3rd century that references to Druids are mentioned again in the classical sources, suggesting the political importance of the Druids had waned to a mere religious curiosity. The Scriptores Historia Augustae only mentions the activities of three Druidesses, recorded as making predictions on behalf of the emperors Aurelian, Diocletian and Alexander Severus.

In the 4th century AD the Gaulish poet Ausonius describes a dynasty of famous rhetorics, descended from the Druids of Armorica. They were distinguished in the art of oratory in the rhetoric school of Bordeaux. There Phoebicius officiated as priest in the temple of Belenus and also taught in the school, as did his son Attius Patera and grandson Delphidius. During this period the skill of Gaulish rhetorics was such that their tutorage was in great demand by the noblest families of Rome.

Although the Druids did not survive the process of assimilation in Gaul as a political force, as a religious movement they endured. Those members who did not adapt their ceremonial practices were pushed to the periphery of their own society and eventually faded into obscurity. As vates and bards they continued to function as soothsayers and rhetorics, and as the sacrificial rituals of the nemeton (grove) gave way to the prophetic healing rites of the spring sanctuaries, their bloodthirsty gods became healers. At the spring sanctuaries a modified form of Druidism not only survived but became a popular focus for Roman pilgrims, with even emperors making sojourns to the sites. Caracalla visited the springs at Baden Baden, and both Diocletian and Maximian made pilgrimages to the sanctuary of Apollo Belenus at Aquileia. The priests of these sites gradually abandoned their Gaulish titles for the new Roman terms of antistes, flamen, ocelus, curator or sacerdos. Although the names of their gods and their priests had changed, the Druids' doctrines and mythology remained, for all intents and purposes, Gaulish.

## The Celtic Pantheon

Unfortunately only two separate lists describing the gods of the Celtic pantheon have been left to us by the classical sources. One is presented by Caesar and the other is supplied by Tacitus' account of the two Viromanduans (serving in the praetorian guard), who described the gods they venerated back home in Gaul. The two accounts are independent testimonies that significantly agree on the fact that the pantheon consisted of six deities, four of which are identical with their Roman equations. Caesar relates to the Gallic pantheon thus:

> *Among the gods they worship is Mercury. There are numerous images of him, they declare him the inventor of all arts, the guide for any road or journey, and they deem him to have the greatest influence for all money making and traffic. After him they set Apollo, Mars, Jupiter and Minerva. Of these deities they have almost the same idea as all other*

*nations. Apollo drives away diseases, Minerva supplies the first principles of arts and crafts, Jupiter holds the empire of the skies, Mars controls wars. To Mars, when they have determined on a decisive battle, they dedicate as a rule whatever spoil they may take. After a victory they sacrifice such living things as they have taken, and all other effects they gather into one place. In many states heaps of such objects are to be seen piled up in hallow spots, and it has not often happened that a man, in defiance of religious scruple, has dared to conceal such spoils in his house or to remove them from their place, and the most grievous punishment, with torture, is ordained for such an offence. The Gauls affirm that they are all descended from Dis, a common father, and say that this is the tradition of the druids.*

*De Bello Gallico, VI, 21, 1*

## MERCURY

Archaeological evidence stands testimony to Caesar's comment on the popularity of the Celtic Mercury, with his images and inscriptions appearing to be far more numerous than any other deity. Caesar's description of the three functions attributed to Mercury are also endorsed from the many epithets (almost 50) found in the epigraphic record.

From Isere we find a dedication to Mercury Artaios, 'of various skills', in direct allusion to Caesar's 'inventor of all arts'. It is this very quality that provides a clear comparison to the pan-Celtic god Lug. In the Irish story of The Second Battle of Mag Tured, Lugh is given the title Samildenach, 'equal in all the crafts'. Lugh is also called Lamfhada, 'of the long arm', equating him with his Brythonic namesake Lleu Llaw Gyffes, 'of the skilful hand'. This confirms the universal recognition of one god by the same name and attribute by different Celtic peoples. This is corroborated by the fact that no fewer than 18 oppida, from as far apart as northern Britain, southern Gaul and the Rhineland, were named after Lug. The widespread veneration of the god is not confirmed in the epigraphy, indicating that his cult was not popularly accepted under the interpretatio Romana.

So far, only three inscriptions have been found – in Switzerland, Gaul and Spain – all describing the god in the plural both in the nominative, the Lugoves, and the dative, the Lugovibus. In the inscription from Switzerland the Lugoves were invoked as the domesticis, 'the escorts', presumably reflecting his attribute of 'protector of travellers'. The inscription from Spain was dedicated by a local guild of shoemakers, an interesting association since in the Welsh Tale of Lleu, both he and Gwydion disguised themselves as enchanted shoemakers who could make shoes from seaweed and sedges 'with the appearance of Cordovan leather'. The Welsh Triads describe Lleu as one of the three golden shoemakers of Britain, the golden element perhaps indicative of a solar affiliation.

In chapter two we discussed the solar symbolism of Lugh in the Second Battle of Mag Tured, concluding that the sun was perceived as the golden slingshot shot forth by Lugh's sling – a religious metaphor describing how the god influenced the path of the sun. We know that the Romans equated Lug with Mercury, and that the planet Mercury makes its synodic movements around the sun more swiftly than any other satellite. Does this mean that the Celtic Mercury was associated with travelling because of his celestial attribute of guider of the sun? Lugh's title, 'of the long arm', is reminiscent of a similar title given to the Vedic god Savitr ('the impeller'), also known as 'of the broad hand', who guided the passage of the sun from dawn until dusk:

> *The broad handed god raised his two arms and all offered obedience, the wind and the water stopped in their motions upon his command.*
>
> *Rig Veda 2, 38, 2*

In the Rig Veda the sun was described as being borne upon a chariot fastened together with golden pins and Savitr was its driver. The maxim of the myth was that the course of the sun was guided by a vehicle drawn by Savitr – whether this vehicle was a chariot, a golden shoe or a sling depended on the religious metaphor adopted.

Caesar's description of the Celtic Mercury as the guide for journeys is also substantiated by a number of other epithets found in the epigraphy: Nundinator, 'of marches'; Veatori, 'the guide'; Cimbrianus/Cimiacinus, 'of wayfarers'; and Andescox, ' who steers before'. The god's association with money-making and trade is also verified by the inscriptions, where he is described as: Mercalis, 'of trade'; Negotiatori, 'of commerce'; Admerius /Atsmerius, 'the distributor'; and Cissonius, 'of success'.

Mercury was also venerated in the Gaulish tongue under the name of Esus, 'he that raises', to whom Lucan ascribes the sacrifice by hanging. One of the two medieval commentators to Lucan adds the following information: 'The Gauls believe that Esus is Mercury, or at least so he is worshipped by the traders.' The evidence for Esus in Gaulish iconography is scanty, with three possible examples. The first and best example comes from the Tiberian Paris column, where the god is not only depicted hacking at the foliage of a tree in which the bull Tarvos Trigaranus is concealed, but is also named. The second example comes from a stone relief from Trier where the same mythological imagery is repeated but the god is not named, although on the reverse side of the stone the god is identified as the Celtic Mercury, accompanied by his native consort Rosmerta. The final piece of evidence comes from Lezoux, where a large stone image of Mercury is inscribed with the term 'Apronius made this Esus' – Apronius perhaps being the Gaulish sculptor of the statue, inscribing his work to the god with whom he was most familiar.

## APOLLO

The classical Apollo was originally the god of light in all its beneficial aspects, not just the disc of the sun, which was the function of Helios. As the god of light, all things dark were his enemy. Consequently he was believed to retreat to Hyperborea during the winter months, the land of perpetual light in the extreme north. From this seasonal exile he returned every spring with the increasing power of the sun. He was principally envisaged as the protector of cattle and crops, and the regulator of the extreme heat of summer.

Apollo was also seen as the god of music, prophecy and healing, and it is this latter attribute that Caesar refers to in his equation of the Celtic Apollo with his Roman counterpart. This corresponds to the original function of the god as first perceived by the Greeks, when he was originally called Paieon 'the healer'. The Druids associated the practice of prophetic healing at the spring sanctuaries most especially with Apollo than any other god. Hence we find native epithets emphasizing this particular aspect of the god: Amarcolitanus, 'adored with good omens'; Bassoledulitanus, 'leads support with good omens'; Cobledulitavus, 'directs good omens from above'; and Matuicus, 'of fortune'.

The benevolent and fruitful aspects of the god as the power of the sun was invoked with the descriptions: Atepomarus, 'returns with fruit'; Virotutis, 'source of strength'; Demiuncus, 'bestower of growth'; and Grannus, 'of the grains'.

Associations were also made between the Celtic Apollo and the sea, perhaps reminiscent of the sun's descent into the sea on the western horizon every dusk. This event had profound significance for the Druids, as sunset initiated a new day and signalled the beginning of a ritual celebration. We later learn from the bardic tradition in Wales that the Beltene ritual commenced with 'the song of the western cudd', alternately referred to as 'the death song'. In this regard the Gauls venerated Apollo with the names: Anextiomarus, 'who joins the house of the sea'; Moritasgus, 'ruler of the sea' and Antenociticus, 'withdraws before the night'.

The Beltene celebration was the most important religious feast of the Celtic Apollo. Commemorating the first day of summer, it fell during the full moon of the Gaulish month of Giamonos. The name Beltene is believed to mean 'the fires of Beli' – that is, the time when bonfires were lit to honour the victory of the summer aspect of the sun. In this regard, Apollo was invoked on the Continent as Apollo Belenus, his most common epithet. Inscriptions to Belenus appear in clusters in Noricum (northern Italy) Provence and Burgundy, and the importance attached to his cult was such that no fewer than three emperors visited his shrines.

In Gaulish religious symbolism, the dualistic nature of the Celtic Apollo was expressed in terms of the two ram-horned serpents (as Belenus the victorious summer sun and Maponus the imprisoned sun of winter). This tradition survived in the later Welsh story of Lludd and Llevelys, the two serpents which fought every May Eve (Beltene). An analysis of two of the most popular names of the Celtic Apollo confirms his identification with the ram-horned serpent.

The title Belenus and its variant forms Bellinus, Bellenus, Belinus and Beleinos all emphasize the double-syllable pronunciation found in the insular form of the name Bile and Beli. The name Bele is the etymological antecedent to the old French belier or 'ram' and the Latin belua or 'beast', suggesting the god's fertility-giving attributes as the summer sun expressed in terms of the sexual vigour of the ram. Hence Belenos was 'the ram-like one'.

The solar aspects of the ram-horned serpent is implied by several depictions of the beast with the tail and fins of a fish. This possibly symbolizing the ability of the sun to swim through the realm of the sea after setting in the West, emerging the following morning in the East. The hot waters that fed the spring sanctuaries would then have been conceived as emanating from the subterranean ocean, warmed by the ram-horned serpent during his nightly journey and thus acquiring its healing qualities.

The next most popular name for the Celtic Apollo was Borvo and its derivatives Bormo and Bormanus, etymologically descended from the Indo-European stem wrmo or 'snake'. Thus we find the two most popular names for the Celtic Apollo are nouns rather than adjectives, describing him in terms of the religious hybrid creature, the ram-horned serpent.

The two consorts most frequently found accompanying the Celtic Apollo were Sirona ('of the evening') and Damona ('of sleep'). Both suggest a link with the visionary sleep associated with the cult practice of incubation. Indeed an inscription from Bourbonne-Lancy refers to Damona in the context of the incubare. It is worth noting that both Sirona and Damona share the same attribute of carrying a snake, invoking the goddess as the nurturing mother of Maponus, 'the young son', not yet old enough to have grown his ram horns.

## MINERVA

Caesar recognized just one goddess in the Celtic pantheon, whom he identified by function with Minerva, the patron of arts and crafts. In Rome she was more specifically associated with the crafts traditionally performed by women, such as sewing, weaving and dying, but this role was later incorporated into the arts of music, painting, cobbling, acting, sculpture and the schooling of children. By the time Minerva had become assimilated with the Greek Athena, she acquired both her war-like attributes and her moisture-giving qualities, enriching crops with light, warmth and dew.

If Caesar's description was correct in recounting the Celtic conception of a single goddess, her multifaceted ability must be seen to represent the primordial earth goddess as the embodiment of the female principle of creation. The earliest cosmological concept shared between the Indo-European cultures was the recognition that the universe was divided into two constituent parts, the sky and the earth. In the Rig Veda the sky god was Dyaus ('the sky'), who was perceived as the heavenly bull, while his female associate was Prsni ('the earth'), envisaged as the dappled cow – a tradition shared with the early Greek conception of Zeus and Persephone.

The fundamental problem with accepting Caesar's allusion to a single goddess is that it does not conform to the evidence of the numerous goddesses inherent in both the insular sources and the epigraphic record. This problem is amplified by the fact that the list given by the Viromanduans also mentions only one goddess but she is equated with Diana.

A clue to understanding the Celtic view of a single goddess, who was also many, may be found in the concept of the triple mothers. In the Celtic world the cult of the triple mothers (Matres or Matronae in the Celtic form) is more prevalent than that of any other deity. As the name suggests, the distinctive feature of the cult was that the goddess was depicted in threes (though very occasionally in pairs and quadruples). The number three was of profound importance to the Druids, who taught in triadic riddles, practised the triple sacrifice to a triumvirate of elemental gods, and applied the exaggeration of tripling to emphasize the sacred in their iconography. In this regard, then, the triple mothers concept was the symbolic representation of a single deity, triplicated like the Celtic Mercury to denote her all embracing attributes.

In Ireland and Wales Minerva's creative nature was recognized in the character of the goddess Danu/Donn, the progenitor of the entire pantheon of gods. The singular aspect of her as the divine mother is also remembered in Wales and Gaul as Madron/Matrona, 'the mother' of Mabon/Maponus, 'the divine son'. In Ireland the divine mother corresponds with Boann ('white cow') who was the mother of Oenghus Mac Ind Oc ('the young son') – the Gaelic Mac Ind corresponding to the Brythonic Mab On.

Caesar's connection of the Celtic goddess with Minerva stems from her many facets regarding arts and crafts. In this persona we find her identified as the Irish goddess Brighid, the triplicated daughter of the Dagdha and patroness of smith craft, healing and poetry. The 'Brig' element means 'exalted' and is found in her British and Gaulish equivalents of Brigantia and Brigindo. In Ireland the importance of the goddess was such that her popularity survived the religious changes that came with the arrival of Christianity, her status being relegated from goddess to saint. The feast day of the saint fell on the same date as the festival of the goddess, 1 February, the first day of spring heralded by the lactation of ewes (Oimlec) at a time of purification (Imbolc). The traditions surrounding the saint embrace many of the attributes of her pagan predecessor, especially in her capacity as nurturing mother, with her symbolic association with milk. When the saint was born, she was suckled on the milk of a white red-eared cow and later possessed cows that could be milked three times a day, producing an abundant lake. And like Athena, Brighid was associated with the appearance of dew in the otherwise dry months of summer, when she was said to hang her wet cloak on the rays of the sun. This quality of the goddess is also represented in Gaul by the name of the divine consort of the Celtic Mercury, Rosmerta, 'she that immerses in dew'.

A consistent theme emerges associating the goddess as nurturing mother with the providence of water, whether it be the source of sacred rivers (Boann), the dew (Rosmerta) or the life-giving properties of water explained in terms of milk (Brighid). Over a dozen goddesses whose names were given to rivers could be recited, suffice it to say that each region had its own mythological rendering for the origin of a specific river. When equated with Juno, she was invoked in the triple form as the Iunones, representing the attribute of the mother of all creation and the guardian genus of womankind. Juno was especially worshipped among women during childbirth and the period of breastfeeding that followed. In the same manner, the triple mothers were most usually depicted nursing babies, bearing cornucopia or paterae, all symbols of nourishment. In Bath (England), Minerva was equated with the native goddess Sulis, who presided over the spring healing sanctuary prior to its redevelopment after the Boudiccan revolt. The name Sulis is derived from the term salis meaning 'close to water'. Sulis was venerated in Gaul as Sulevia Idennica Minerva and elsewhere in Britain in the triple form, the Suleviae.

Another common epithet for Minerva was Belisama, 'likened to Beli', appearing in two inscriptions from the Pyrenees and evident in the French place names Belleme, Balesme, Blismes and Blesmes. The name strongly associates her with the Celtic Apollo as Bele 'the ram like', possibly indicative of her fertility as the ewe producing the first milk of spring. In one Gaulish epithet for Minerva, the goddess is called Cabardiacensis, 'the heron that conveys wealth', a title that we shall later see refers to the legend describing the transformation of the goddess into a wading bird (usually a crane) after her inundation by the sacred river.

## JUPITER

Caesar equated the Celtic sky god with Jupiter essentially because they shared the attributes of ruling the heavens, from the movement of all celestial bodies to the course of the weather.

As the god of weather Jupiter was invoked by the Romans as: Fulgurator/Fulminator, 'the flasher of lightening'; as Tonans, 'the thunder'; and as Pluvius, 'of the rain'. The most frequent Celtic epithet applied to Jupiter also referred to his elemental attribute as wielder of the thunderbolt. On seven altars he is invoked as Taranus, 'thunder', and Taranucnus, 'the thunderer', with a widespread distribution from Britain to Dalmatia. We also have the account of Lucan, who also names the sky god as Taranis, propitiated (the commentators add) by the burning of victims inside a hollow log. This perhaps re-enacts the sacred significance of the oak being struck by lightening far more frequently than any other tree. Maximus of Tyre informs us that: 'The Celts devote a cult to Zeus, but the Celtic image of Zeus is a lofty oak.'

The ritual use of the oak by Druids is recorded by Pliny, alluding to the importance attached to mistletoe that grows on its branches and the fact that the Druids always carry a sprig of the tree when performing religious duties. The link between the Celtic sky god and the oak is exemplified in the imagery of the votive pillars called 'Jupiter giant columns' distributed in eastern Gaul and the Rhineland. These monuments are often adorned with foliage and bark designs suggestive of an oak tree. Surmounting the columns is the Celtic sky god, usually depicted as a horseman riding down a snake-limbed man of gigantic proportions – the anthropomorphic Celtic Apollo as Borvo. The imagery reflects a purely Celtic myth with no apparent classical precedent – another example of interpretatio Gallico.

The Celtic Jupiter had no more than a dozen native surnames, most of which identify him as the presiding god of a local mountain, much akin to the conception of Zeus on Mount Olympus. Hence at Brescia in Cisalpine, Gaul, he is called Brixianus; at Mount Ladicus in Spain he is Ladicus; in the great St Bernard Pass in the Alps he was invoked as Poeninus; and in Austria he was called Uxellinus, 'of the highest'. He was also invoked as the 'protector of the tribe' – as Beisiriassas by the Bigerriones of the Pyrenees, and as Parthinus by the Parthini of Pannonia.

Other, more abstract, names were also used to address the Celtic sky god, such as Bussomarus, 'the bushy mouthed' (in reference to his beard) and Ambisagrus, 'of the surrounding cloak'. The latter is perhaps an allusion to him galloping through the night sky on his steed, his cloak trailing behind him, as he is sometimes portrayed on the Jupiter giant columns. In one instance Jupiter is also invoked as Cernenus (not to be confused with Cernunnos), meaning 'of the head' – an allusion to the head of the heavenly bull, a religious motif we will encounter in a later chapter.

Outside the military zones of the Rhineland, eastern Gaul and northern Britain, the beneficial nature of the sky god was invoked in the form of the hammer god sometimes named as Sucellus, 'of nourishing juice'. The imagery surrounding the hammer god shows him as the benevolent bringer of the regenerative rains, nourishing the parched soils of the fields and vineyards during the summer months – in which capacity he was prominently venerated in the grape-growing regions of Burgundy and the Rhone valley. His cult was very popular with more than 200 images of him surviving in the form of stone reliefs and bronze statuettes. The images follow a regular religious formula, often depicting the hammer god as a mature bearded man wearing a short tunic and the distinctive thick gallic cloak known as a sagum. The tools specifically associated with him are a long shafted hammer, which he strikes to herald the arrival of the rains, and a cup or drinking jar, displaying his moisture-giving role. On a few of the effigies he is endearingly named as Sucellus or Succelus, describing his connection with the cultivation of the vine.

Although no inscriptions have emerged identifying the hammer god with Jupiter, there are a number of reasons to regard his cult as a native variant of the more fruitful aspects of the sky god. Such a relationship was not embraced within the repertoire of the interpretatio Romana because it was too alien a concept and its following was too dispersed among the vine-growing rural communities.

From Vienne in the lower Rhone valley comes a bronze statuette of the god, whose long-shafted hammer terminates with a large, barrel-shaped head from which radiates a series of smaller heads, forming the shape of a wheel (the motif of the Celtic sky god). On another statue from Premeaux (France), the god is depicted with star symbols etched onto his tunic, similar to the circles he adorns on a statuette from the Rhineland. These appear to be celestial symbols identifying the Gaulish hammer with the Celtic sky god.

At Sarrebourg near Metz, Sucellus is accompanied by a consort named Nantosuelta ('she that was covered by the river'). This name equates her closely with the Irish goddess Boann, who also was consumed by a river in a mythological tale that appears to relate to a point of fundamental religious lore. If Boann and Nantosuelta are synonymous, then Sucellus should logically correspond to the former's consort deity in Ireland, namely the Dagdha, 'the good god'. The Dagdha was also known as Eochaid Ollathair, 'the horseman all father', a name that conjures up a possible connection with Phoulonivos Stellos ('the starry one who evokes the foal'), the father of Epona by a mare. This title evokes the image of the sky god as a horseman, corresponding with the constellation of Sagittarius. Another name for the Dagdha describes the prominent motif of the Celtic sky god in Ruadh Rofhessa, 'of the red chariot wheel'. As we shall later discuss, with the evidence contained within the iconography of the Gundstrup cauldron, this refers to the Celtic sky god as Auriga, 'the charioteer', who holds the broken wheel of Gemini.

The Dagdha's possessions also closely match those associated with the iconography of Sucellus. The Dagdha was said to have possessed an inexhaustible cauldron called the Undry, which, like the classical cornucopia, could supply a limitless amount of food. A magical vessel probably identical to the cup of the hammer god. The Dagdha was accredited with a weapon variously described as a club, an iron staff and an eight-pronged fork attached to a wheel. In the Irish tale The Intoxication of the Ulstermen we are informed that the weapon had a rough end, which could kill nine men in a stroke, and a smooth end that could reanimate them:

> *Under the club the bones of his enemies were like hailstones under horses hooves.*

This is an interesting allusion to the awesome power of the club, using language relating to stormy weather and the mount of the sky god as a horseman. The club was therefore symbolic of the thunderbolt similar to the bludgeoning power of Sucellus' long-shafted hammer. The fact that the hammer had such a long shaft implies that the tool was possibly regarded as a fencing mallet, suggesting a mythological connection between lightening and boundaries. A comparative association is also made in the Second Battle of Mag Tured with the Dagdha's wheeled fork:

> *A wheeled fork, to carry which requires the effort of eight men, so that its track after him was enough for the boundary ditch of a province. Wherefore it is called the 'the track of the Dagdha'.*

The bronze sheet covering of a religious sceptre from Farley Heath in Surrey (England), shows an identical wheeled fork to that of the Dagdha's, the wheel and the fork denoting the symbolic origin of lightening originating from the sun.

In the insular sources we find a similar reference to the birth of the Celtic Apollo from the sky god, just as the Vedic god Agni was born of the waters. In the Welsh tradition Mabon was the son of Madron ('mother') and Mellt ('lightening'). As previously mentioned, Mabon corresponds to the Irish god Mac Ind Oc, who was the son of the Dagdha and Boann: in Vedic terms, the birth of Agni as the sun born between Dyaus the sky and Prsni the earth, or the heavenly bull and the dappled white cow.

## MARS AND DIANA

The Gaulish god whom Caesar equated with Mars was not only invoked as a god of war but, like his classical counterpart, was envisaged as a god of protection.

The Roman Mars was worshipped in a number of festivals as a god of fertility, such as the Dea Dia and the Ambarvalia during May, when he was invoked to protect the fields, cattle and the family, and to ward off illness, disease and bad weather. The Celtic Mars was also primarily a tribal protector, a function inferred by his common native name Teutates/Toutates, 'the protecting father', found in inscriptions in both Britain and Gaul. As a god of protection, he too was associated with war-like attributes and the ability to ward off sickness.

The marshal aspects of the Celtic Mars are attested by the multitude of indigenous surnames recorded on inscriptions: Vicinnus, 'the combatant'; Beladonnis, 'the destructor'; Belatucadrus, 'pleasing in slaughter'; Segomo, 'of victories'; Cicolluis, 'giver of scars'; Caturix, 'king of battle'; Cnabetius, 'the vigorous'; Arixio, 'of fury'; Vorocius, 'the destroyer'; Vesontius, 'the fierce'; Entarabus, 'the perisher'; and Sutugius, 'of the fearful limb'. Caesar's reference to the Gaulish religious practice of offering spoils to the god in heaps is testified by his epithets: Camulos, 'of the heap'; and Camulorigi, 'the king of the heap'. A custom performed not only on the Continent but in Britain and Ireland – the Irish sources remembering him as Cumhail the father of Fion.

The healing attributes of the Celtic Mars are also alluded to by his surnames and by the number of spring sanctuaries over which he presided in Britain and Gaul. The Treveri invoked him as Smertrius, 'the immerser', and Lenus, 'of the vat', often alongside the goddess Ancamna, 'the river maiden'. Significantly these names describe a function of the god that is also recorded by Lucan and his commentators regarding the human sacrifice propitiated to Teutates (where the victims were immersed headfirst into a vat). We must therefore assume that a healing ritual practised at the spring sanctuaries was performed in a similar fashion to the seasonal sacrifice that was practised in the rites of sacral kingship, the two sharing the same goal of appealing to the god to heal by reciprocal sacrifice.

At the healing sanctuary in Lydney, Gloucestershire, Mars was invoked as Nodens, 'of the waves', a title associating him with water (also inferred by the depictions of the sea on the mosaic pavement of his shrine). In the Welsh sources Nodens was remembered as Nudd or Lludd Llaw Ereint, 'of the silver hand', a name that links him directly with the Irish god Nuada Argatlamh, 'of the silver arm'. Thus both his name and epithet strongly tie him in tradition with the curative power of water, 'the wave with the silver arm' perhaps denotes the crest of a breaking wave.

In the tale of Boann we are told of how the river Boyne was formed when the waters rose from the well of Nechtan in three waves and drowned the goddess. Boann was the wife of Nechtan ('clear water'), a god synonymous with Nuada, which thus equates her with Ancamna of the Treveri. What we appear to have here is a regional variant of the mythological story relating to the Celtic Mars as a healer god whose vat or spring overflows, drowning the maiden aspect of the goddess, who is subsequently transformed into a crane.

The Celtic Mars was also strongly associated with the sacred grove known by the Celts as nemeton. These ritual sites were distributed throughout the Celtic world, reflecting the widespread influence of Druidism on the entire culture during the late La Tène, from Fidnemed in Ireland, Medionemeton in Scotland, Vernemeton in England to Drunemeton in Anatolia and Nemetobriga in Spain.

Inscriptions from Britain and Gaul associate both the Celtic Mars and his consort with the function of the grove. In Lincolnshire he appears as Rigonemetis, 'the king of the grove' and in Bath he is invoked as Loucetius, 'of the twilight', in the company of the goddess Nemetona (both also appearing together at Mainz). In Altripp, in the territory of the Nemetes, Nemetona appears with Mars, while elsewhere Loucetius is accompanied by Bellona, the Roman personification of war. The nemeton was literally 'the place of fury', where the more macabre rite of the immersion sacrifice was performed alongside those propitiated to Esus and Taranis.

At the spring sanctuaries, however, his worship was more benign. It was in the grove that the warlike qualities of the Celtic Mars had to be satisfied alongside the goddess as the personification of the battle fury, known in Ireland as the goddess Nemhain and invoked at Grenoble as the triple Nemetiales.

The Viromanduans had equated the goddess of their homeland not with the many-skilled and warlike Minerva but with Diana. Diana was primarily the goddess of the moon and of hunting. A distinctive feature of her worship was that she was venerated in sacred groves (nemii) for which reason she was known as Nemorensis. It was probably this aspect of Diana which the Viromanduans found to be familiar with the goddess they worshipped in their homeland.

## Dis or Hercules

The last god in the Celtic pantheon described by Caesar is compared with the Roman god of the underworld, Dis. This equation is interesting because Dis was a relatively minor deity in the Roman pantheon, being only invoked in conjunction with the cthonic goddess Proserpina. The minor status of Dis does not initially correspond with the important role attached to his Gaulish counterpart, whom Caesar informs us was considered by the Druids to be the ancestral deity of their nation. The concept that the god of the underworld was also the ancestor of mankind is not without precedent in the Indo-European tradition.

According to the Rig Veda, the god of the underworld was Yama, the first mortal man born of the sun god Vivasvan, fated to be the first to experience death and hence to find the path between the realms of the living and the dead. He was thus seen as the ancestor of mankind and the king of the underworld, the guide of souls to the land of the immortals in the highest heaven.

It would appear that Caesar chose Dis to describe the Celtic god of the underworld to emphasize his benevolent aspects. The name Dis was derived from his original title Dives Pater, 'the father of riches', for he was not only a god of the underworld but also the bestower of all the wealth and fertility that could be attained from the earth for the benefit of mankind.

The implied importance of the Celtic Dis is not evident from the epigraphic record surviving in Britain and Gaul, with no inscriptions equating the god under the interpretatio Romana with a native surname. In fact, the only dedications made to Dis – or Dives – Pater date from the 2nd century AD, distributed on the fringes of the Celtic world in southern Germany and Dacia (modern Rumania). Here, Dis is usually depicted holding a scroll (the list of the dead), sometimes in the company of a consort, Aericura, whose imagery is reminiscent of that attached to the cult of the triple mothers.

Within a purely Celtic context, it must be presumed that the correspondence between Dis and his native equivalent was not wholeheartedly embraced under the interpretatio Romana, suggesting that an alternative identification was adopted instead. A clue to an alternative appellation for Dis comes from the list of the Gaulish pantheon given by the two Viromanduans, who in place of Caesar's Minerva and Dis name Diana and Hercules. If Hercules was the god used to assimilate the functions of the Celtic god of the underworld, there should exist a mythological resemblance between the two that served for the later interpolation.

Hercules was the mortal son of Zeus who became immortal by completing a series of 12 tasks that were prescribed for him through the Delphic oracle. The 12 tasks of Hercules are usually recognized as representing a Greek variant to the story of the Phoenician god Melkart, who had to defeat the 12 hostile beasts of the zodiac. Caesar provides a crucial clue to the association between Hercules and a myth describing the seasonal movement of the signs of the zodiac, with the Celtic Dis. After describing Dis, Caesar relates that his importance was such that they measured their days by nights – that is to say, Dis was strongly associated with the night sky. We may therefore assume that the Druids had the same perception of Dis as the Greeks had of Hercules: that a myth concerning the god explained the seasonal movement of the constellations along the ecliptic.

Only a few dedications of Hercules are known from the epigraphy but all suggest a peculiarly cthonic association described by his native surnames. In north-east Gaul, in the territory of the Belgic tribes, he is invoked 11 times as Magusanus, 'of the plain'. In the Irish sources the term magh or 'plain' is often used as a generic name for the underworld. The wealth-giving attributes of the god are also suggested at Narbonne and Gers where he was invoked variously as Illunnus Andoses, 'endower of the soil', and Toleandossus, 'the bearer of endowment'.

An interesting correlation between Hercules and the Celtic Dis is described in the eyewitness account of the 2nd-century AD writer Lucian of Samosata. When staying in Gallia Narbonenis, Lucian encountered a picture of the Gaulish god Ogmios, described as an old man, bald with a sun-darkened face. He led a retinue of willing followers with a delicate chain of gold and amber connecting his mouth with their ears (see page 65). The imagery corresponds with the name of the god, 'keenly mouthed'. A Gaulish bystander explained to Lucian that the god was depicted carrying a club and wearing a lion skin because they believed that eloquence was more potent than strength and was attained in old age. Hence Hercules was called Ogmios in the Gaulish tongue.

In Ireland the same god was known as Oghma and was similarly accredited with the gift of eloquence, being the inventor of the mystical ogham script and bearing the title Cermait, 'the honey mouthed'. The sun-scorched face of the Gaulish Ogmios is also alluded to in another of Oghma's surnames, Grianainech, 'the sun faced'. The psycho-pomp function of the god appears to be suggested by the fact that he leads a procession of compliant followers, the souls of the dead, to the underworld.

In the Veda his counterpart's name is Yama, a word phonetically identical to Oghma, who is likewise described as 'the gatherer of men'. The symbolism of the dead being led by a chain is repeated as the motif on a number of coin issues from Armorica, which depicts a large head connected to a number of smaller heads by a chain (see *Figure 9*).

**FIG. 9.** *Coin portraits of Ogmios from Aremorica in Gaul.*

In the Welsh sources the god of the underworld is described in two variant forms. In the first branch of the Mabinogi he is Arawn, 'the silver tongued', a name linking him with the gift of eloquence similar to Oghma/Ogmios. Later, in the tale of Culhwch and Olwen, he appears as Gwynn Ap Nudd, (corresponding to the Irish god Fion Mac Cumhail). Welsh folklore describes Gwynn as a gigantic huntsman who leads the nightly hunt across the sky, summoning and binding the souls of the dead along his path.

In France a similar folklore surrounds the enigmatic origins of the famous Italian commedia dell'arte character, Harlequin. Hellequin is first recorded during the 12th century AD, and was perceived as a wild giant huntsman who wielded a club. He too led a party of huntsmen across the sky and guided a retinue of doomed souls to the underworld. The name Hellequin may well be a later corruption of the Latin eloquens, and 'eloquence', as Lucian informs us, was the name for Hercules in the Gallic tongue. So like Gwynn, Hellequin was a surviving folk memory of the Celtic Dis.

In Gaulish iconography Ogmios/Dis is most frequently portrayed as the stag-antlered god Cernunnos. The image of the god follows a distinct formula throughout his monumental repertoire. He is antlered and often holds a torc and/or one or two ram-horned serpents, which are sometimes fed from a vessel of fruit in his lap. The two ram-horned serpents represent the dualistic nature of the Celtic Apollo. The imagery would therefore describe the cthonic role of Cernunnos as the winter host of the sun, nourishing it before it is reborn anew during the celebration of Beltene.

Despite his numerous depictions, the stag-antlered god is only named once on the Paris column, where he appears in a similar fashion to Ogmios, elderly and bald but this time with a beard. The emphasis on the old age of the deity alludes to his ancestral role. The name of the god Cernunnos literally means 'the headfirst one' and possibly relates to three religious meanings (in typical Druidic fashion):

(i) That from his head the souls of the dead are bound with eloquence.
(ii) How the victims who represent him in the seasonal sacrifice are plunged.
(iii) The attribute of antlers denotes the renewed growth of vegetation.

The cthonic nature of Cernunnos is demonstrated on the Rheims altar (see *Figure 10*). Flanked on each side by Mercury and Apollo, Cernunnos adopts his typical crossed-legged posture. From a purse on his lap he pours a stream of gold coins, from which a stag and a bull take nourishment. Above his head is a rat, an animal associated with the underworld from its ability to burrow through the earth. Besides being a creature of plague and pestilence, its presence was also considered a portent of rich harvests and hence wealth. The dark complexion of Ogmios/Oghma is ascribed to the scorching heat of the sun.

If the Celtic Dis was a god of vegetation, the metaphor may allude to the flagging of plants during the height of summer (July/August), a period known to the Greeks as the dog days and in the Gaelic tradition as the month of Iuchar, 'of the serpent'. This is an allusion to the ascent of the sun as the ram-horned serpent. If this correlation is correct, the immersion sacrifice would be an appeal to the god Teutates to bring rains by the ceremonial re-enactment of a mythological event: Teutates immersing Cernunnos into a vat to relieve his scorching. This event took place in the Gaulish month of Equos, 'the moisturising', and appears to have been depicted on plate V of the Gundstrup cauldron.

**FIG. 10.** *The Rheims altar.*

CHAPTER FIVE

# THE RITUAL YEAR

Before looking at the mythological narrative depicted on the Gundstrup cauldron in more depth, we shall now turn to the textual evidence provided in the Coligny calendar. This is the only other example of a recognized Druidic work, which offers us a glimpse into the ritual year as it was observed by the Gauls in the late La Tène period.

## A Druid's Almanac

The Coligny calendar was discovered in 1897 at Coligny near Bourge-en-Besse, Ain (France) and remains to this day the only example of a Celtic calendar surviving from the Late Iron Age. Although fragmentary, the original artefact was once a single bronze plaque measuring 1.5 by 1 metres and despite the fact that only half of the tableau remains, it still constitutes the largest surviving Gaulish text. Its survival is even more astonishing when we consider that, like the Gundstrup cauldron, the calendar was deliberately dismantled prior to its final deposition. This suggests the co-ordinated destruction of a nearby Druidic sanctuary during the persecution under Claudius (see *Figure 11*).

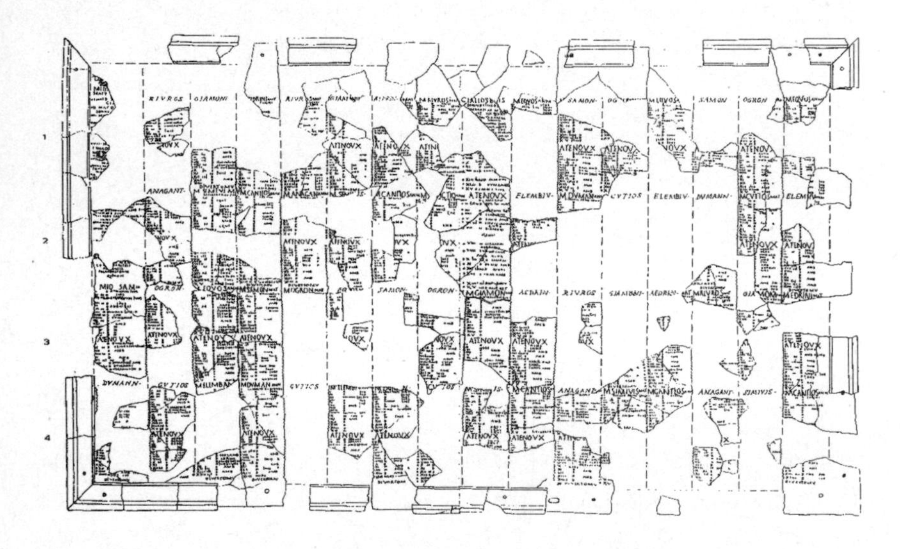


**FIG. 11.** *The Coligny calendar.*

Although the language inscribed on the tableau is Gaulish, both the script and the numerals employed are of a Roman character, indicating that the calendar was drafted during a period of conformity – between the conquest of Caesar and the Claudian Persecution (50 BC and AD 50). The most likely date would have been c. 10 BC during the implementation of political and religious reforms under the emperor Augustus, with the reorganization of the Gaulish province centred on the cult of the emperor at Lugdunum (Lyon). This was also the time when the Julian calendar was introduced into Gaul, an event that probably initiated the need for the Druids to preserve their ritual agenda (based on lunar months) while conforming to the official requirements of the newly imposed solar calendar.

The Coligny calendar regulated five lunar and solar years together by inserting two intercalary months every two and a half years to a regular sequence of 12 months. The authors of the calendar appear to have been aware of the Metonic cycle, whereby every 19 years lunar and solar time fell short with each other by five days. To address this problem, the Druids employed a system using six full months of 30 days termed Matu ('fortunate') and six hollow months of 29 days called Anmatu ('unfortunate'). The intercalary months were given the status of full months. To accommodate the shortfall of five days in every Metonic cycle, the Druids adjusted the month Equos by one day so that despite being a hollow month, every fourth year it contained 30 days.

This system intimates that the Druids not only had knowledge of the Metonic cycle, which required 110 hollow months and 125 full months, but also had an understanding of the Callippic cycle, whereby the full moon would fall on the same solar date at the beginning of each 19-year period. The calendrical computations on the tableau worked out a system whereby the full moon would always fall on 18 November at the beginning of every 19-year cycle in the Julian system of reckoning (or day 15 of Samonos in the Gaulish). In the present era these cycles would begin in the years 1918, 1937, 1956, 1975, 1994 and 2013. This conforms to the view that Samonos is identical with the Irish Samhain as the first month of the Celtic new year falling in the autumn.

The calendar was based on a ritual lunar itinerary that was apparently devised some time before the conquest of Gaul and was probably influenced by a similar Greek system, encountered during contact with their settlements in southern Gaul. Indeed, the insertion of two intercalary months every first and third year closely resembles the system employed in Athens at that time.

Before discussing the names of the months and their seasonal significance, it would be logical to first look at the construction of the calendar in terms of the layout of the month and the various rituals named in the text. The calendar shows that certain rituals are often associated with a specific phase of the moon, confirming Pliny's statement that the Druids attached religious importance to the sixth day of the moon.

## The Months

Each month was divided into two fortnights, centred on the full moon, each with its own numerical sequence. The first half of each month were numbered days 1 to 15, commencing from the new moon up to the full moon, with day 8 representing the first quarter. The second fortnight varied between 14 and 15 days, depending on whether it was a full or a hollow month. The full moon fell after day 15 of the first fortnight, called Atenoux, 'returning nights', in reference to the transition to the waning half of the month when the nights grow increasingly darker towards the new moon. Similarly, at the end of each month the term Divertomu, 'the turning is with us', was used to denote the visual disappearance of the waning crescent and its subsequent reappearance as a waxing crescent.

## The Days

Each line designating a day followed a uniform pattern, containing up to six parts to its construction:

### (I) THE PEG HOLE

The first part of each day line is introduced with a peg hole, which allowed for the use of a marker to keep a record of time as a daily ritual.

### (II) THE NUMBER OF THE DAY

Then follows the number of each day in the two fortnightly sequences.

### (III) THE TRIPLE SIGN

The next space on each line occasionally included the cryptic triple sign, commonly believed to describe the portion of the day when a specific ritual activity was to take place. As the name suggests, the triple sign consists of three vertical strokes, one or two being intersected by a horizontal notch. The intersections can appear on either side of each stroke or through the middle of it. The use of three notches indicates that each day was divided into three parts, similar to the system employed in Rome when recording which third portion of the day would be disrupted by solemn rituals of purification. In Rome the day was divided thus:

Manes – from sunrise until nine.
Ad Meridiem – from nine until three.
Suprema – from three until sunset.
A great majority of the days were not disrupted by rituals at all, and courts could be held in session at any hour. These days were known as Fasti ('working') and comprised of 244 days of

the year. Days where courts were disrupted for one portion of the day only were called Nefasti ('not working'), incorporating a further 109 days. The remaining eight days of the year were set aside for the Dies Intercisi when two portions of the day's hearings were cancelled.

Evidence that the Celts also possessed a system of dividing the day into thirds is recorded in the Irish sources, where we are informed that Connor MacNessa spent the first part of each day participating in outdoor activities, the second portion playing board games and the final part drinking ale and feasting.

On the calendar, the days without the triple sign out-number those with by approximately three to one, a similar ratio that existed between Fasti and Nefasti days. Therefore days equivalent to working Fasti days would not require the use of the triple sign. Where the triple sign has only one notch intersected with a stroke, we may assume represents Nefasti days (occurring some 185 times), while those with two notches were Dies Intercisi (occurring seven times).

## (IV) THE DAILY DESIGNATION

After the triple sign, the next formulaic description of the day refers to the auspicious nature of the day and the importance of twilight or nightly activities. Hence we find the following five terms:

MD: Matu Diies – 'Fortunate day', inferring that days generally were not so unless specifically stated;

D: Diies – 'Day' without auspicious nature.

N: Nocts – 'Night', usually occurring alongside Innis R (see below).

NSDS: NoctsDiies – 'Night to day' or dawn.

DSNS: DiiesNocts– 'Day to night' or dusk.

## (V) TYPES OF RITUAL

After the auspicious nature of the day, seven different types of ritual activity are then named according to the various phases of the moon:

AMB

Amb(os), relates to the Irish Imbas and the Vedic Amba, meaning a warning gained through 'inspiration'. It is the Gaulish equivalent of the practice of Imbas Forosna in Ireland, a ritual that was performed in the rites of prophetic healing inside the spring sanctuaries and during the seasonal re-enactment of the Tarbhfess. This ritual occurs more than 200 times on the calendar, on odd-numbered days only. In the first fortnight, its practice was restricted to days 5 and 11, the three days before or after the first quarter phase of the moon. In the second fortnight, Amb occurs on every odd-numbered day except day 1, which was the first day of the full moon. Outside this formula, we find that an Amb is cancelled when it overlaps with an unexpected Innis R, suggesting the seniority placed on the latter ritual.

The most complete reference to this term is given on day 5 of Samonos with the expression AMB RIX RI, or 'inspiration directed to the king'. This alludes to the seasonal sacrifice of the bull at Samhain, a re-enactment of the Tarbhfess that corresponds with the mistletoe ceremony described by Pliny. He states that this ritual occurred on the sixth day of the moon and involved the sacrifice of two white bulls. Samonos means 'seeding', a name referring to the mistletoe berry that first comes into fruit during this month.

IVOS

Ivos means to 'call out' or 'evoke', its general meaning being to vocally invoke the gods. This ceremony of evocation was primarily confined to the week around either side of the new moon – that is, between the third-quarter and first-quarter phases of the moon. These evocations do not occur every month but are spaced between 115 and 118 days apart and, as we shall soon see, refer to the planet Mercury during its synodic movements around the sun.

Outside this recognized pattern, Ivos also occurs as a special event called SINDUI IVOS, 'in this day an evocation'. This occurs twice a year, once on day 9 of Giamonos or Simivisonna and on day 10 during Elembivos or Edrinos in alternating years. These evocations appear to demarcate a period of four full moons between the festivals of Beltene and Lugnesad. The term Ivos is also present in the name of the month Elembivos, in which Lugnesad always fell, meaning 'the evocation of the stag'. The connection between the feast of Lugnesad, 'the bounty of Lug', and the stag describes the seasonal myth of Lug consuming Cernunnos as an offering of first fruits.

Ivos also occurs on day 3 of Samonos – that is, two days before the Amb Rix Ri ritual described above. The two longest-surviving terms for this Ivos are Exo Ivos, 'herein an evocation', and Exin Gidum Ivos, 'herein a hidden evocation'. Both statements allude to the special nature of this Ivos compared with the expected ones, and the event was probably related to the mistletoe ritual on day 5 of the same month.

Finally we find that Ivos appears in one more isolated instance in the year, falling on day 13 of Riuros. It is introduced by one of the most provocative statements in the entire text: DEVORTOM LUG RIVRI IVOS, 'the turning is with us, to Lug an evocation of the royal burning'. In this instance, 'the turning' refers to the winter solstice, which falls in the month of Rivros (December/January). This suggests a myth relating to Lug/Esus retrieving the sun from its most southerly position in the sky; it is also apparently linked to the Celtic sky god Taranis, whose victims were offered by fire, an act described by the name of the month itself. When we look closer at the iconography of the Gundstrup cauldron, we may discern the same myth depicted on plate III, with the sky god holding his motif of the chariot wheel (grasped on the other side by Lug).

INNIS R

This ritual appears 62 times on the calendar and always occurs at night. The most complete form of the ritual term is INNIS ROG(A) TIT(ULA) or 'denials and proposals observed', and appears to intimate a form of judicial assembly. The name relates to a bardic ceremony recorded by the Welsh poet Taliesin, which involved the use of 'the trees of purposes, solutions and doubts'. If these two ceremonies are the same, we would expect the use of staves of wood to resolve issues, as a divinatory tool similar to the use of the ogham characters in Ireland. All of these events were held within four days of the first and third quarter phases of the moon.

TIOCOBREXTIO

This term literally means 'the house with direction'. The latter part of the word is cognate with the Gaelic term Cymrieth ('with authority'), the generic term for 'law'. The Tiocobrextio would then be the name of a Druidic law court. From the calendar we can deduce that these law courts were only held four times a year (or five when the year has a 13th intercalary month). These courts were of a higher authority than those designated by the term Innis Roga Titula, which were far more frequent events. The latter would have dealt with public disputes, while the Tiocobrextio settled issues concerning points of law. The Tiocobrextio is actually named in the text as being instrumental in the drawing up of the calendar. It was convened on the first quarter of Giamonos and Elembivos, or Simivisonna and Edrinos in alternating years. There was, however, a fixed session held on day 14 of Cantlos, the last full moon of the year. The court session held during Elembivos/Edrinos lasted for two days, conforming to the evidence described in the Irish sources of the importance attached to legal settlements during the festival of Lugnesad.

PETI UX

Peti Ux means 'from wings above', a term denoting the times when augury or divination by the flight of birds could be practised. This ritual was confined to the third quarter of the moon in the months of Simivisonna ('likened with bird song') and Dumanos ('of silence'), names emphasizing the religious significance attached to the ritual of Peti Ux. Diodorus Siculus alludes to the Druidic practice of divination by the flight of birds:

> *... they have soothsayers too of great renown who tell the future by watching the flight of birds.*
>
> *Histories V, 28*

This testimony is further confirmed by Cicero in his description of the Aeduan king and Druid Divitiacus:

> *He claimed to have the knowledge of nature which the Greeks call physiologia, and he used to make predictions, sometimes by means of augury and sometimes by means of conjecture.*
>
> *De Divinatione I, 90*

A stone-carved stelae from Corgoloin (Cote d'Or) depicts a god accompanied by a dog with two birds perched on his shoulders. Their beaks are pointed towards his ears illustrating the oracular power of bird song (see *Figure 12*).

**FIG. 12.** *Stelae of god with singing birds from Corgoloin.*

PRINNI LAGET

The last two rituals named on the calendar are intimately related forms of divination using wooden sticks, probably not dissimilar to the use of ogham staves in Ireland.

Prinni Laget means 'the laying of the woods'. As the name suggests, this describes the practice of a system of prediction based on the drawing of lots akin to the sortilege of Rome.

The ritual observance of Prinni Laget was confined to days 1 to 9 in the first fortnight of the month.

## PRINNI LOUDEN

The term Prinni Louden, 'the casting of the woods', implies a variant system using the same wooden sticks but this time by means of throwing them to the ground and making random prognoses from the patterns formed between them. A clue to how such patterns were deciphered may be found in the alphabetical characters of the ogham, where each letter is constructed of a stem line intersected by strokes – that is, the manner in which they fall on either side of the stemline or across it. Like the practice of drawing woods, these castings were confined to between the new moon and the first quarter.

A recent discovery in Stanway, Essex, may actually represent the equipment necessary for the performance of Prinni Louden. From the excavated grave of an individual classed as a ritual specialist, a number of curious objects were unearthed, including surgical instruments, a supposed gaming board and some mysterious metal rods.

The gaming board is unusual in that it is divided into squares (eight vertical and 12 horizontal) but has 26 counters (13 for each side). This leaves an extra piece for each side without a starting position along the 12 horizontal squares. However, the location of the pieces as they were placed on the board in situ offers us an alternative explanation for the function of the board (see *Figure 13*).

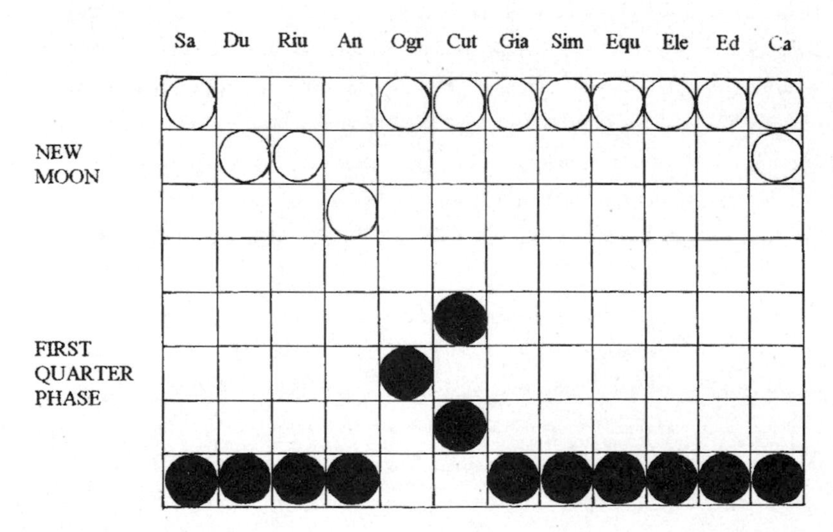


**FIG. 13.** *The Stanway divination board.*

If we were to suppose that each of the 12 horizontal squares represents one of the regular months of the Druidic year, the placing of the extra 13th piece on the board might be expected to indicate the location of the two extra intercalary months. Indeed, on examination we find that the extra pieces are placed in the first and seventh columns corresponding to the placing of the two intercalary months before Samonos and Giamonos respectively. This seems to suggest that the apparatus was not for gaming but rather for recording calendrical observations, with the two sets of pieces representing fortunate and unfortunate outcomes to readings made during each month.

The next question to answer is: readings of what? Alongside the board were found eight rods, four made of iron and four made of a copper alloy, each terminating with a distinctive triangular flight. It has been surmised that these rods were possibly used for casting, like the procedure described in Prinni Louden. It is worth noting that the triangular ends of the rods are reminiscent of the feather (flesc) signs used to introduce the direction of reading on the stem lines of ogham. If the rods were cast for divination then readings could subsequently be made from the positions in which they had fallen in relation to an adopted stem line.

In this instance the board would have been used to record the results of readings covering the period of the next year ahead. The eight vertical squares would then represent the eight days between the new moon and first quarter phase in which, as the Coligny calendar informs us, the practice was confined to.

## (VI) FORECASTING

The next daily designation used on the calendar represents a system of forecasting, whereby the names of months were included as day headings in other months. Previously this system had been interpreted as a form of weather prediction, with the proposed formula: 'during the month of X we have the weather of months Y and Z'. This would be hardly likely, in my opinion, since the science of meteorology, even by today's standards, is a pretty hit-and-miss affair. It is therefore doubtful that the Druids employed a system of weather prediction based on a fixed prognosis; if they did, their profession as diviners would have been unnecessarily open to scrutiny.

It would be more feasible to regard these terms as following events that could be predicted with a degree of certainty, such as the cyclical movement of celestial bodies. For such a system to work the months on the calendar would be named after the constellations the full moon was in at that particular time. We should therefore expect the naming of months in other months to describe the different celestial positions the moon traverses as it changes phase.

After the sun, the moon is the fastest-moving celestial body, taking between two to three days to travel through each constellation. This hypothesis seems more credible when we consider that the purpose of the calendar was to intercalate a lunar ritual itinerary with solar time reckoning, and that these rituals were closely observed at particular phases of the moon. The calendar emphasizes the ritual importance placed on the moon during its quarter phases so that the moon's expected position in the sky during a particular phase was duly recorded.

These forecasts of the moon's quarterly movement across the sky show that the months were named after the constellations of the ecliptic and describe a seasonal myth that is depicted in detail on the Gundstrup cauldron.

## Names of the Months

The next step in our brief analysis of the Coligny calendar is to investigate the names of the months and hence attempt an interpretation of their religious significance in the seasonal myth.

The two intercalary months were termed Ciallos B(u)is, 'the gathering together', in allusion to the time of year that the Druids held their triennial assembly. In Ireland we know that the great assembly of Tara was convened every three years and that it was held variously at Samhain and Beltene. This suggests that Ciallos Buis was the Continental parallel to Tara, being held alternately during the intercalary months placed before Samonos and Giamonos every three years. Thus, unlike the 12 regular months of the calendar, Ciallos Buis was not named after a constellation but after the assembly that was held during this specially allocated period (when time between the sun and moon was synchronized). The out-of-time nature of these intercalary months is emphasized by every day within them being named after all the regular months in sequence.

The following introduction accompanies the second intercalary month:

| | |
|---|---|
| Ciallos Buis | The gathering together |
| Sonnocingos | The procession of song |
| Amman m m xiii | A duration of 13 fortunate months |
| Lat ccclxxxv | 385 days |
| Amb an Taran m | Inspired from the fortunate Taranis |

Similarly the following conclusion is recorded along with the first intercalary period:

| | |
|---|---|
| Amb Rix Tio | With the king's inspiration, the house |
| cobrextio cariedit | With direction forecasts |
| Oxtantia | For the purpose of establishing |
| Pogedortonin | The fixing of dates |
| Quimon | Of every five years |

From these two fragmentary pieces of information we can deduce that the Druidic body known as the Tiocobrextio convened during Ciallos Buis to make laws and calendrical reckonings with both the authority of the king and the sky god Taranis.

The ritual term for this convention was 'the procession of song', perhaps in allusion to an understanding of planetary harmony similar to the Pythagorean perception of celestial cycles. The names of the 12 regular months on the calendar describe a fundamental belief in the dualistic nature of the cosmos, a system based on the two-fold division of the year into a light and a dark half.

The months were named after the constellations of the ecliptic in which the full moon was expected to enter at that time, directly opposite to the celestial position of the sun. With this in mind it comes as no surprise to find that the translations of the months' names reveal a deliberate use of meanings that stood in antithesis to each other, so that a seasonal myth was outlined in terms of paired opposites. This was the seasonal rising-and-setting relationship shared between the constellations of the ecliptic, and was used to describe a cosmological narrative that, to the Druids, was depicted in the stars. The paired opposites are as follows:

| | | | | |
|---|---|---|---|---|
| I | Samonos<br>'Seeding'<br>October/November<br>Full moon in Taurus<br>Feast of Samhain | GROWTH | VII | Giamonos<br>'Sprouting'<br>April/May<br>Scorpio/Ophiucus<br>Feast of Beltene |
| II | Dumanos<br>'Silence'<br>November/December<br>Gemini | SOUND | VIII | Simivisonna<br>'Bird-like song'<br>May/June<br>Sagittarius |
| III | Riuros<br>'Royal burning'<br>December/January<br>Cancer<br>Sacrifice to Taranis<br><br>Winter solstice | ELEMENTS | IX | Equos<br>'Moisturizing'<br>June/July<br>Capricorn<br>Sacrifice to<br>Teutates<br>Summer solstice |

| | | | | |
|---|---|---|---|---|
| IV | Anagantios<br>'House of the eaten up one'<br>January/February<br>Feast of Imbolc (Oimlec)<br>Leo | MISTLETOE | X | Elembivos<br>'Evocation of the stag'<br>July/August<br>Feast of Lugnesad<br>Aquarius |
| V | Ogronos<br>'Keenly runs'<br>February/March<br>Virgo | FLOWING | XI | Edrinos<br>'Causes to run'<br>August/September<br>Pisces |
| VI | Cutios<br>'House of the hound'<br>March/April<br>Vernal Equinox<br>Libra | CANINES | XII | Cantlos<br>'Tail of the dog'<br>September/October<br>Autumn Equinox<br>Aries/Cetus |

From the list of paired months above, the following opposing qualities can be recognized.

The first pair divides the year into winter and summer. The year commenced in Samonos (Samhain) when the mistletoe ceremony was performed in conjunction with the re-enactment of the Tarbhfess in the rites of sacral kingship. The decapitation of the bull represented the death of Apollo Belenus and the seeding was the conception of the Celtic Dis in the form of the first production of mistletoe berries. This should correspond with the full moon in the constellations of Taurus and Orion. At the opposite time of the year, the month Giamonos, 'sprouting' celebrated the first arrival of summer when Apollo Maponus is released from his winter captivity and ascends as the victorious sun Belenus. The term 'sprouting' refers to the mistletoe coming into flower at this time, personified as the antlered deity Cernunnos, who should be recognized in the constellations Scorpio/Ophiucus.

The second pair relates to the presence of bird song at opposing times of the year. During Dumanos, the month of silence, few birds would be heard, while in Simivisonna all birds are in full song. In both months the divinatory rite of Peti Ux was performed.

The third pair corresponds to the practice of seasonal sacrifice by means of the elemental forces of fire and water in direct relationship to the two extreme positions of the sun during the solstices. Hence we find that in the month of Riuros ('the royal burning') victims were offered to Taranis through the element of fire to regenerate the power of the sun at the winter solstice. Then, at the adjacent time of the year when the power of the sun had began to scorch the vegetation on the summer solstice, victims were offered to Teutates by drowning during the month of Equos ('moisturizing'). This sacrifice re-enacted the mythological event of 'the protecting father' dowsing the sun-scorched Ogmios, otherwise known as Cernunnos ('the headfirst one') after his seasonal motif of being immersed in a vat. On the Coligny calendar this sacrifice is mentioned on day 15 of Equos with the term Ganor, 'the consummation'.

The fourth pair of months alludes to the anthropomorphic transformation of Cernunnos as the god of vegetation, personified in the mistletoe plant. In Anagantios, he is described as being in 'the house of the eaten up one', a seasonal metaphor for the disappearance of mistletoe berries at this time of year. Then, during the month of Elembivos, 'the evocation of the stag', Cernunnos is referred to as the antlered god, representing the time when the mistletoe stops flowering. Both months thus suggest a link between the consumption of the mistletoe plant and the sacred mead of the goddess. During the month of Anagantios the Irish feast of Oimlec fell on 1 February. This was the feast day of the Christianized Saint Brighid, whose folklore associated her with an abundance of milk. Similarly, during Elembivos the festival of Lugnesad ('the produce of Lug') was held commemorating the marriage of the goddess of sovereignty with the consumption of her sacred mead. It would be tantalizing to speculate that here we have a reference to two types of sacred libation prepared from the mistletoe plant; one extracted from the berries and known as the milk of the goddess at Oimlec, and the other infused from the flowers and prepared into a mead

The two months that make up the fifth pair are both associated with a metaphor for flowing or running, perhaps indicative of a myth concerning the initiation of rains as a consequence to the consumption of the mistletoe. Ogronos, 'the keenly running', succeeds Anagantios just as Edrinos, 'causes to run', follows Elembivos.

The sixth and final pair of months alludes to two dogs, which coincidentally represent the time of the two equinoxes in the year. This seems to describe a myth whereby the sun was envisaged as passing out of and into the realm of the underworld in seasonal allegory, with the two dogs being the two guardian hounds standing sentinel at the entrance to the land of the dead.

## The Planet Mercury

The calendar employed a system of recording the astronomical movements of the moon during its quarter phases; and the months were named after the constellation in which the full moon passed at a particular time of year.

The creators of the calendar were aware of the discrepancy between the periods of a solar and lunar year, and applied a system of adding intercalary months every two and a half years to make up the differential. Not only did they have an understanding of the Metonic cycle, they were also aware of the Callippic system of adding an extra five days every 19 years to keep the two calendars synchronized. With such a profound knowledge of the cycles and movements of the sun and moon, the next line of enquiry must surely be to discuss the possibility that the calendar also observed and recorded the cycles of other celestial satellites.

After the sun and moon, the next brightest object in the sky is Venus but unfortunately I cannot determine any reference to the cycles of this planet on the calendar. However, there is a possibility that the Druids turned their gaze to the more mysterious and elusive movements of the planet Mercury. Although the Druids would have been aware of the synodic movements of Venus (the time it takes for a planet to orbit the sky before reaching the same place again), the characteristics of Mercury appear to have afforded it a more reverential status.

As an inner planet Mercury shared the same cyclical events as Venus, rising and setting as a morning star in the east before disappearing into the glare of the sun, only to re-emerge as an evening star to the west. Unlike Venus, Mercury was considered to be far more mysterious and threatening, being the fastest-moving planet that never wandered more than one zodiac sign away from the inhibiting glare of the sun. It was the close proximity of Mercury to the sun that came to associate the planet with primitive solar mythologies, materializing in the Graeco-Roman world as the swift-moving, wing-heeled messenger of the gods, Hermes/Mercury.

The possible importance of this planet to Druidic ritual observance may be inferred by Caesar when he described the principal god of the Celts to be Mercury. He also stated that their perception of the god to be the same as all other peoples – that is, sharing the same function and astronomical attributes. This tradition is confirmed in the solar myth described in the Irish story the Second Battle of Mag Tured. Here Lugh controls the malign power of the sun, conveyed by the metaphor of him blinding the poisonous eye of Balor with a magical slingshot. The next problem to address is to discern whether there is any evidence of recording the synodic movements of Mercury within the text of the Coligny calendar. The synodic period of Mercury takes 116 days to complete (the Mercurial month) or approximately four lunar months. As a morning star Mercury appears for 48 days to the east of the sun before disappearing for 20 days behind it (the superior conjunction). Mercury then re-emerges to the west of the sun as an evening star for a period of 28 days, after which it disappears for a further 20 days as it passes in front of it (inferior conjunction). (See Figure 14, overleaf.)

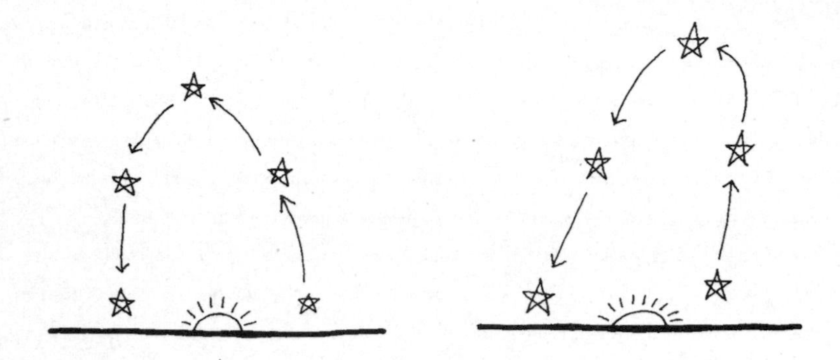

**FIG. 14.** *The Synoptic movements of the planet Mercury.*

Our first clue comes from the placing of the two intercalary months at two-and-a-half-year intervals, which divides the lustre of five years (termed 'the procession of song') into two counts of eight Mercurial months. If Mercurial months were individually observed and recorded on the calendar, we should expect to find some evidence of ritual activity celebrating these events at regular intervals. The term Ivos, or 'evocation', occurs almost exclusively in the week surrounding the new moon, lasting between four and nine consecutive days. This is significant in that the new phase of the moon allows for the best possible conditions to observe Mercury before the twilight of sunrise or sunset.

Ivos is not placed in the first or last week of every month but is distributed between alternative months (occasionally two) with an average period of between 115 and 118 days covering three consecutive occurrences of Ivos. This suggests a system whereby an Ivos heralded the Mercurial month as it appeared as an evening star with a second Ivos announcing Mercury's reappearance as a morning star. That is to say, an Ivos was held to celebrate the re-emergence of Mercury as either a morning or evening star after its disappearance into (or conjunction) with the sun.

I would like to close this chapter by drawing attention to a silver coin of the Taurisci, which dates from the 1st century BC and summarizes the cosmological doctrines of the Druids into three parts (see *Figure 15*).

**FIG. 15.** *The Taurisci coin summarising druidic cosmological lore.*

At the top of the coin, seven wings are depicted, representing the seven planets recognized throughout the ancient world. The wing emphasized the wandering nature of these stars in relation to the multitude of fixed stars. Across the middle portion of the coin are 29 pellets arranged in three rows, with the crescent moon depicted to the right. This refers to the number of days in a lunar month, which begins at the new moon. Towards the bottom is a portrait of the Celtic Mercury with a pair of wings emanating from his neck, a composition that appears on Celtic coin issues inscribed with Ulatos Ateula, 'the flying one who returns in flight'. This title refers to the rising and setting motions of the planet Mercury between its periodic disappearance into the sun. The head is surrounded by four evenly placed pellets. This represents the four lunar months it takes for one Mercurial month to elapse.

We have now analysed the mathematical and cosmological implications of the Coligny calendar, which has given us insight into the main ritual events celebrated during the year. Our next task is to relate this evidence to the mythological tradition preserved in other examples of religious iconography in Gaul – particularly, the Gundstrup cauldron and the Paris column. Mythology is the dramatic interpretation of the laws of the cosmos, its cycles and rhythms often expressed in numerical symbolism. To the Druids, this number was three; the number of their teaching tool, the triad and their perception of the virtues of the earth goddess. It was also the number associated with their principal god Mercury, whose planet followed a three-petalled star around the fires of the sun.

CHAPTER SIX

# THE COSMIC CAULDRON

Mythology is the collection of popular and cultural ideas formulated into a religious narrative, devised to explain the movements of celestial bodies with the procession of the seasons. Mythological narratives comprise two parts. The first relates to the description of Creation, of the universe and mankind, and is known as cosmogony. The second addresses the need to explain the cycles and rhythms recognized in the movements of heavenly bodies and how they delineate periodic time with the effects manifested on earth in the form of seasonal change and the power of the elements. This is known as cosmology.

## A Secret Cosmology

We have learned how the Coligny calendar testifies to the astronomical knowledge of the Druids in understanding the relationship between the movements of the sun, the moon and the planet Mercury. If the Druids recognized and recorded the synoptic movements of the wandering stars, they would certainly have understood the seasonal rising and setting motions of the fixed stars of the ecliptic. Such knowledge is also endorsed by the Coligny calendar, with its system of predicting which constellation the moon would rise in during its quarterly phases.

Many ancient societies used mythological characters and creatures to describe the constellations of the ecliptic and their seasonal movement, and the consequential changes these brought on nature. Hence we find the origins and development of the zodiac in such civilizations as Babylon, Assyria, Egypt and Greece, where the ability to use the stars to predict the movements of satellites progressed to the later divinatory 'science' of astrology.

It would not be entirely hypothetical to suggest that the Druids also possessed their own traditions relating to a zodiac and a consequent mythological cycle explaining seasonal change. The classical sources are not entirely silent on the matter. Caesar relates of the Druids:

> *They have some discussions as touching the stars and their movement, the size of the universe and the earth, the order of nature, the strength and the powers of the immortal gods, and hand down their lore to the young men.*
>
> *De Bello Gallico, VI, 14*

It is interesting Caesar refers to the immortal gods in the same passage that he describes the Druids' practice of teaching cosmological lore to their students; a lore that was taught in secrecy. Caesar informs us in a previous passage:

> *... they do not think it proper to commit these utterances to writing...*
> *that they do not wish the rule to become common property.*
>
> *De Bello Gallico, VI, 14*

Ammianus Marcellinus also alludes to the secrecy the Druids attached to their teachings:

> *... they were uplifted by searchings into secret and sublime things...*

The question is: what was the lore concerning the movement of the stars that the Druids held in such secrecy? A secret that Lucan conveniently expands on:

> *To you it is given to know the truth about the gods and*
> *deities of the sky, or else you alone are ignorant of the truth.*
>
> *Pharsalia I, 450*

If by the term 'gods and deities of the sky' Lucan is repeating Caesar's allusion to 'the strength and powers of the immortal gods', it would suggest a vague understanding that the Druids conceived their gods as being represented in the stars. We may now have our first clue to the composition of the Druidic zodiac. Lucan adds that the Druids' 'truth' in understanding the 'deities of the sky' was entirely different to that perceived in the classical tradition.

The question of what this peculiarly Druidic interpretation of the night sky comprised of to make it so profoundly different to that of their neighbours would appear to be a hapless task, since this star lore was kept secret, even apparently from the Romans. However, I believe that the chance discovery of the Gundstrup cauldron is the key to unlocking this age-old mystery. With the cosmological evidence contained within both the Coligny calendar and the iconography of the Paris column, the five inner plates of the cauldron can now be put back together in their original order. An order that will describe an astronomical chart in the form of a schematic mythological map of the night sky.

## A Lunar Zodiac

Both Caesar and Pliny remarked on the fact that the Druids measured the passage of days and months, by nights and the phases of the moon respectively.

Pliny further adds that they quantified years in terms of 'ages' consisting of 30-year periods. A period also recorded by Plutarch in his description of the otherworldly island of Ogygia. Here, every 30 years when the 'night watchman' entered the constellation of Taurus, a party of novices would journey to the said island to receive instruction in the sacred arts. If the term 'night watchman' applies to the moon, we can interpret this as meaning that Druidic 'ages' (and the year) commenced when the full moon entered Taurus.

If the Gundstrup cauldron does represent a pictorial narrative of the night sky then the evidence from the Coligny calendar would confirm that the procession of the zodiac was measured by the seasonal passage of the full moon rather than the sun. Since the full moon is always in the opposite star sign to the sun, Lucan's comment that the Druids stood alone in their interpretation of the 'gods and deities of the sky' would seem justified.

To prove that the Druids did indeed gauge the zodiac by the progression of the full moon through the constellations of the ecliptic, we must look at the case of Samhain/Samonos. The Irish sources inform us that the Celtic New Year commenced at Samhain falling on the solar cross-quarter day of 31 October. The evidence from the Coligny calendar supports this tradition, with the placing of Samonos as the first of the 12 regular months of the year (Samonos and Samhain being cognate Celtic names). The calendar further informs us, by way of the term Trinux Samoni Sindiu, 'herein the three nights of Samon', that Samhain was originally held during the three nights of the full moon of the lunar month of October/November. If the position of the sun was used to designate the appropriate time for the celebration, we should expect to find a symbolic correspondence with the zodiac sign of Scorpio. But if the position of the moon was used, we should expect to find an association with Taurus the bull.

In Ireland, Samhain was particularly associated with the slaughtering of excess cattle before winter quartering, an act that I would suggest reflects the seasonal re-enactment of the Tarbhfess in the rites of sacral kingship. The bull sacrifice is also referred to on day 5 of Samonos as Amb Rix Ri, 'inspiration directed to the king'. This is the same ritual described by Pliny in his account of the slaying of two white bulls during the mistletoe ceremony. The name of the month means 'Seeding', a term describing the religious significance of the cutting of the mistletoe when it first begins to come into fruit when the full moon enters Taurus. This tradition is also exemplified by Plutarch's description of the initiation of Druidic training, when the 'night watchman' entered Taurus and both the year and the 'age' were thought to begin.

## The Paris Column

Having looked at the evidence contained within the Coligny calendar, let us now explore the evidence presented in other examples of Celtic religious iconography so that we can approach the task of interpreting the cauldron's narrative by comparative analysis.

The evidence contained on the Tiberian Paris column is to my mind of crucial significance, as it describes a purely Celtic myth using its closest classical parallels: the only complete example of the practice of interpretatio Gallico.

During construction work on the site of Notre-Dame cathedral, in 1711, four relief-carved stone blocks were discovered. These blocks once formed a column erected by the sailors of Paris during the reign of Tiberius. The importance of this monument lies in the fact that the Gaulish deities were depicted and named alongside their Roman counterparts and not assimilated with them. This suggests that, for a brief period under Tiberius, indigenous religious expressionism maintained a homogeneity of its own despite the implementation of interpretatio Romana.

## THE FIRST STONE

The first stone, which lay at the top of the column, depicts Jupiter and Vulcan in juxtaposition to the native gods Esus and Tarvos Trigaranus, 'the bull with three cranes' (see *Figure 16*). The correspondence between these two pairs of deities becomes clearer if we identify Jupiter with Tarvos Trigaranus. Jupiter represents the archetypal Indo-European sky god, known to the Aryans as Dyaus 'sky' and to the Greeks as Zeus, 'sky', recognized in both cultures in the form of the heavenly bull. Esus would then be equated with Vulcan, the artificer of the gods of Olympus. Such an equation would not be entirely out of keeping as Esus was a pseudonym for the Celtic Mercury, who Caesar informs us was 'master of all the arts' and who is easily recognized in the Irish Lugh Samildenach.

**FIG. 16.** *Stone 1 of the Paris column, depicting Esus/Vulcanus and Tarvos Trigaranus/Jovis.*

The mythological meaning shared between Jupiter and Vulcan in Roman terms would be difficult to interpret if it were not for the respective equations to Esus and Tarvos Trigaranus. On the column, Esus is depicted hacking at the foliage of a tree, usually identified as a willow, behind which the muscular bull stands with three cranes on his back. The composition of this myth is repeated in the iconography of a stone relief from Trier, where Esus chops at the trunk of a tree, in the branches of which are nestled the three cranes and the head of the bull (see *Figure 17*). Although Esus is not named on the relief, on the reverse side there is an image of the Celtic Mercury alongside his native consort, Rosmerta. The Trier stone would then suggest a link between Esus/Mercury, Rosmerta/three cranes and Tarvos Trigaranus.

**FIG. 17.** *The Trier Relief.*

If we are to consider that the Paris column relates to a specific Celtic myth in terms of its closest classical parallel, we must first recognize which one is intended, the supposition being that the component parts of both myths rendered the same religious meaning. Therefore, if the myth is broken down into a simple formula, the classical myth should become apparent:

(i) Esus/Vulcan hacks with his axe;

(ii) Towards the bull/sky god;

(iii) To release the three cranes/Rosmerta.

Now to interpret the same formula into Greek terms:

(i) Hephaestus hacks with an axe;

(ii) Towards Zeus;

(iii) To release the goddess.

Anyone familiar with Greek mythology would instantly recognize that this formula describes the events surrounding the birth of the goddess Athena, who interestingly was equated by the Romans with Minerva, the goddess of the Celtic pantheon identified by Caesar. In the Greek variant of the myth, Hephaestus hacked at the head of Zeus, from which Athena emerged fully armed. An ancient epithet of Athena was Tritogeneia, 'born of the flood', in allusion to her birth from the torrent of blood that subsequently flowed from the head of the sky god. This was a symbolic metaphor for her association with the life-giving properties of water.

In the depiction on the Paris column, the goddess is represented by the three cranes, similar to her portrayal in the cult of the triple mothers elsewhere in the Celtic world. The attributes of a mother goddess and her association with a flood is remembered in the Irish tale of Boann and the formation of the river Boyne (Bovinda). When Boann approached the well of her husband Nechtan (which was forbidden her) the waters of the well rose up in three waves and consumed her so that she lost a leg, an arm and an eye:

> *Along the elf mound of Nechtan's wife,*
> *along the forearm of Nuada's wife,*
> *along the land of the sun,*
> *along the dwelling of the moon,*
> *along the young one's naval string.*
> *The Colloquy of the Two Sages*

This event makes two interesting points. The first relates to a myth whereby the goddess is drowned in a cosmic stream, related in terms of 'the land of the sun' and 'the dwelling of the moon' – that is, the ecliptic. If this cosmic stream was the Milky Way then we have another clue to one of the cosmological doctrines of the Druids. The second point is that as a consequence of being drowned, the goddess is transformed into a crane.

In Ireland, the so-called Druids' posture emanated from the disfigurement of the goddess in the form of a sleeping crane with one eye open, standing on one leg with one arm outstretched. This posture was called the Corguinecht or 'the tricky crane' and was assumed by Druids when they recited the glam dicinn ('poets execration'). The image of the crane emphasizes the attributes of the goddess in relation to the source of not only the celestial river, but all rivers.

In Greece, Athena was worshipped under the pseudonyms of her first three priestesses, Agraulos 'the bright air', Paridorus 'the dew', and Herse 'the rain'. All three names were invoked when the aid of Athena was sought in times of draught. The water-giving virtues of the goddess in the corresponding Gallic myth is suggested by her name on the Trier stone, where she is invoked as Rosmerta, 'immerses in dew', the function of the goddess as the transformed crane.

The imagery of Tarvos Trigaranus is repeated in the form of a votive bronze statuette found at Maiden Castle in Dorset, where he is represented by a three-horned bull carrying the busts of three female figures on his back. Although their heads are distinctly human, their bodies take on a bird-like appearance, confirming the interchangeable symbolism of the goddess and the crane, perhaps in allegory to a seasonal transformation. One of the outer plates of the Gundstrup cauldron also depicts the transformation of the goddess in the form of a crane.

The scenario of the myth surrounding Esus, Tarvos Trigaranus and the transformation of the goddess into cranes describes a cosmogonical event; an act of creation that involved the birth of the Celtic Athena.

In the Rig Veda, two hymns relate to the act of creation that closely resemble aspects of the myth presented on the first stone of the Paris column. The first hymn relates that all things were created in the primordial sacrifice of a being known as Purusa:

> *From thunder the heroine was born and from the heroine came forth life. At his birth he encompassed the earth on all sides.*
>
> *Rig Veda. 10, 90, v 5*

Viraj, 'the heroine', was the creative female principle who when paired with a god became manifest as his shakti ('power'). That is to say, the god gained his attributes as consort of the goddess, in a similar way to how the king had to symbolically marry the goddess of sovereignty in the rites of sacral kingship. This helps us to understand how the Celtic goddess was perceived as both a singular entity and the consort of the Celtic Mercury, Apollo, Mars and Jupiter.

In the second Vedic hymn, the creator is named Visvakarmen, 'the All Maker', who is described as a multi-faceted god similar to the Celtic Mercury, being a master craftsman in the skills of carpentry, sculpture and smithery:

> *... from the earth the one god formed the sky, his arms spanned between them, from the wood of the tree he carved the sky from the earth.*
>
> *Rig Veda. 10, 81, v 3-4*

It would be tempting to think that the iconography surrounding Esus, Tarvos Trigaranus and the tree explains an identical Creation myth.

## THE SECOND STONE

The second stone on the Paris column reveals another element of the same myth. This stone depicts the Gaulish deities Smertrius and Cernunnos alongside the classical divine twins Castor and Pollux, presumably because under the interpretatio they shared the same attributes.

The first problem we encounter in interpreting the relationship between this stone and the first stone is that there is no classical correspondence shared between Vulcan, Jupiter and the divine twins (see *Figure 18*). We must therefore assume that the intent is to equate Smertrius and Cernunnos as divine twins in respect of them being the sons of the sky god. The two twins were collectively known as the Dioscuri, 'the guardians of the sky'. Castor 'the horse tamer' was born mortal while his brother Pollux (Polydeuces) 'the wrestler' was immortal. When Castor was killed, Pollux appealed to Zeus to allow him to join his brother in the underworld. Zeus eventually took pity on his plight, granting him the right to spend alternate periods in the infernal regions with his brother and among the gods in the heavens. Other tradition also relate to how Zeus conferred celestial status on the twins, usually identified as the constellation Gemini, or as the morning and evening star aspects of the planet Venus.

**FIG. 18.** *Stone 2 of the Paris column depicting the divine twins Smertrius/Pollux and Cernunnos/Castor accompanied by similar portraits on Gaulish coins.*

From this legend three aspects can be discerned that were shared between Smertrius, Cernunnos and the Dioscuri:

(i) That the myth relates to two twin sons of the sky god;

(ii) Who lived and died in alternate periods;

(iii) Who were placed among the stars.

The living and dying aspects of the Dioscuri alludes to the rising and setting cycles of a particular celestial event. To the Greeks, this was recognized in the movements of Venus, with its transition from morning to evening star. The Gaulish twins, however, may have represented a different astronomical event.

The living and dying nature of the Gaulish twins is inferred by their indigenous titles on the column, describing their respective roles in a seasonal myth commemorated in the immersion sacrifice propitiated to Teutates. Hence we find that the Celtic Mars is addressed as Smertrius, 'the immerser'. Other inscriptions in Gaul invoking Mars Smertrius confirm this equation. Smertrius would therefore be the immortal twin, who periodically immerses his brother Cernunnos, 'the headfirst one'. The antlers of Cernunnos emphasize his status as the mortal twin who has to undergo a seasonal cycle of living and dying as the god of vegetation and the keeper of the underworld.

The identification of Smertrius as the immortal twin and Cernunnos as his mortal brother is supported by an inscription from Bezier (France) dedicated to Mars Divannos, 'the divine', and Dinomogetimarus, 'one whose strength is seized by the sea'. The latter title alludes to Cernunnos being plunged into the vat of the Celtic Mars in a religious metaphor for a celestial representation of the god descending into the sea.

A second clue that helps us to understand the cosmological function of the Gaulish twins comes from the iconography surrounding the Indo-Iranian cult of Mithras, which, outside its hard-core following in the army, gained unprecedented popularity in Gaul during the 2nd century AD. Its popularity may have stemmed from the fact that the cult of Mithras shared an almost identical religious meaning with the mythological narrative depicted on the Paris column (see Figure 19).

Central to the mythology of Mithraism was the sacrifice of the heavenly bull by the god Mithras, an act that brought about the creation of life. When Mithras plunged his knife into the neck of the bull, a stream of blood poured out and from it grew the plant of the sacred beverage hoama (the Vedic Soma). Wheat grew from the bull's spinal column and from its seed all beneficial species were born. This myth is reminiscent of the mistletoe ritual described by Pliny where, in return for the acquisition of the mistletoe berry from the oak (the tree of the sky god), two bulls were sacrificed.

**FIG. 19.** *Depiction of the Triple Mirthas.*

A similar ritual act is portrayed on inner plate II of the Gundstrup cauldron, where a helmeted figure (the Celtic Mars) is depicted in triplicate slaying a bull, from the neck of which a stream of foliage pours out. This bull has the distinctive feature of a single horn protruding from the forehead. The earliest symbol for the constellation of Taurus comes from Assyria, where it is depicted on clay tablets in the form of a one-horned bull. If the single-horned bull also represents Taurus, the Celtic Mars must be represented by the neighbouring constellation of Orion. The appearance of these two constellations on the cauldron was deliberately disguised, not only by reversing their respective positions, but by depicting them in triplicate.

This explains why Samonos/Samhain was the first month of the year when the full moon entered the constellation of the bull and the seeding of the bull was re-enacted with the bull sacrifice and the cutting of the mistletoe.

The association between the bull and the Celtic Mars is found in other contexts too. From Bouhy near Entrains (Nieves) there is a dedication to Mars Bolvinnus, 'of the white bull', a title linked with Pliny's reference to the two white bulls. From Marienthal, Alsace, there is a relief dedicated to Mars Medru depicting the god helmeted, carrying a spear and accompanied by a bull (see *Figure 20*). The name Medru is based on the stem Med, denoting mead. In Rome a votive plaque was inscribed to Mars Toutati Medurinis ('protecting father of the flowing mead') by 'the knights of the emperor'. In this respect, he is also invoked in Britain as Mars Meduris, 'of the boiling mead'. The basis of the myth would seem to be that the Celtic Mars was involved in the sacrifice of a bull, which procured the seed of the bull in the form of a sacred mead. The name Medru is ultimately linked with the archaic rendering of the Irish god Midhir (Medros) who also possessed a magic cauldron, enchanted cattle, and whose bruidhe was guarded by three cranes. The name may also prove to be etymologically associated with the god Mithras himself.

**FIG. 20.** *Relief of Mars Medru from Marianthal.*

The cosmological implications of the Mithraic bull sacrifice is described in the iconography of the triple Mithras – Mithras and the two Dadophori or 'torch bearers' (see *Figure 10*). One of the Dadophori is called Cautes who holds his torch upwards, signifying the waxing power of the sun in Taurus. Counterwise, his associate Cautopates holds his torch downwards, symbolizing the waning power of the sun in Scorpio.

If the Celtic Mars is to be identified with Orion/Taurus, similar to Cautes, we would expect his twin to be associated with the constellation of Scorpio – presuming an almost identical cosmological myth is intended. Above Scorpio is the constellation of Ophiucus, 'the snake bearer', which covers more of the ecliptic than does Scorpio. Does Ophiucus therefore represent Cernunnos in the same manner as Orion does Smertrius?

In Gaulish iconography, Cernunnos is most frequently portrayed holding aloft a ram-horned serpent (sometimes two), a motif readily recognizable in the name of Ophiucus. On inner plate IV of the Gundstrup cauldron, Cernunnos appears holding up the serpent, mimicking the act described in the name of the constellation we would expect to find him in, if the theory so far is correct. The living and dying nature of the Gaulish twins would thus have represented the cosmological myth explaining the rising and setting relationship shared between the constellations of Orion/Taurus and Scorpio/Ophiucus.

The rising and setting twins is a cosmological tradition shared among many of the derivative cultures of the Indo-European language family. The myth describes how cosmic order is maintained against the forces of chaos after the initial act of Creation. Among the Greeks the twins were remembered as the Dioscuri, while in the Rig Veda they were collectively known as the Asvins, 'the horsemen' (on the Paris column the Dioscuri are accompanied by horses). The Asvins were rarely named individually and always performed their beneficial acts together. They are most frequently described as accompanying Usas, the goddess of the dawn, indicative of their celestial role of proceeding the sunrise. In the Vedic hymn The Riddle of the Sacrifice, the opposing movements of the Asvins are alternatively applied to Indra (the principal god of war and consumer of the Soma) and Soma (the personification of the sacred beverage).

> *The one in the future is said to have passed and the one who has passed is said to be in the future.*
> *O Soma, your deeds with Indra are joined as you turn the axle pole of the sky.*
>
> *Rig Veda I, 164, v 19*

> *The one god vanishes and returns according to his nature: The same womb bore the immortal one and the mortal one. The pair constantly revolve in opposite turns; when one is seen the other disappears.*
>
> *Rig Veda I, 164, v 38*

Hence, the immortal Indra/Smertrius and the mortal Soma/Cernunnos rotate across the sky in opposition. When one rises above the horizon to the east, the other has set to the west so that when one is seen, the other has disappeared. This is an exact description of the rising and setting nature of Taurus/Orion and Scorpio/Ophiucus, delineating the dark and light halves of the year. Thus, taking into account the evidence from the Coligny calendar, the position of the full moon was gauged to interpret the seasonal significance of the two opposing constellations. When the full moon entered Taurus in the month of Samonos ('seeding'), the Tarbhfess was re-enacted with the sacrifice of the white bull and the acquisition of the mistletoe berry instigating the new year in October/ November. When the full moon entered Ophiucus/Scorpio in the month of Giamonos ('sprouting'), Cernunnos ascended the sky, releasing the captive power of the sun in the form of the ram-horned serpent, his antlers symbolic of the renewed growth of vegetation as he emerges from the underworld. As the Celtic equivalent of Soma, he is recognized as the flowering mistletoe during the feast of Beltene, the first day of summer.

In the Vedic hymn The Marriage of Surya, the cosmological significance of the divine twins is expressed in terms of the wedding procession of the goddess Surya, a metaphor for the progression of the moon along the ecliptic. Savitr (Esus) gives Surya to Soma (Cernunnos), while Agni, the Apollonian light that precedes the sun, leads the entourage. Both Indra (Smertrius) and Soma (Cernunnos) were rival suitors, described as the two luminaries who symbolized the wheels of Surya's chariot. These luminaries are described as the constellations: Agha when 'they kill the cattle' – Smertrius slays the bull of Taurus; and Arjuni when the goddess returns home and is wed to Soma. Soma being the personification of the sacred mead like his Celtic counterpart Cernunnos. The cyclical nature of the two constellations as the luminaries that drive the seasons is thus summed up in the following two verses:

*The two exchange positions to and fro their movements create an illusion.*
*The two are like youths dancing a circuit.*

*One looks over creation whilst the other is constantly reborn with the seasons.*
*He is borne aloft like a banner before the dawn of a new day. He gives the gods their portion as he divides the sky amongst them.*
*With the moon he marks the cycles of life.*

*Rig Veda 10, 85, v 18-19*

Indra was the warrior god, the greatest consumer of the Soma juice and the equivalent of the Celtic Mars, Teutates, 'the protecting father' of the tribe. This was the god whom the king had to mimic in the rites of sacral kingship by preparing and drinking the mead of the goddess of sovereignty. A drink the Aryans prepared from the plant Soma, identified by the druids with the mistletoe. This brew was the personification of the Celtic Dis and was believed to impart wisdom and eloquence to the initiates qualified to drink of it. In Wales the god of the underworld was known as 'the silver tongued' (Arawn) and in Ireland and Gaul as 'the keen mouthed' (Ogmios), names alluding to poetic skill. A quality that was shared with the Vedic god Soma, who was 'the tongue of the gods', and the giver of 'perfected speech in the heart of the poet'.

CHAPTER SEVEN

# THE SEED OF THE HEAVENLY BULL

In chapter six we discussed the idea that the narrative of the Gaulish divine twins Smertrius and Cernunnos on stone two of the Paris column described the seasonal rising and setting relationship shared by Orion/Taurus and Ophiucus/Scorpio. These constellations divided the winter and summer halves of the year and were initiated by the festivals of Samonos (Samhain) and Giamonos (Beltene). We also saw the same myth referred to on plates II and IV of the Gundstrup cauldron, with Smertrius slaying the white bull of Taurus and Cernunnos holding the ram-horned serpent. If these scenes represent constellations of the ecliptic, the other three inner plates should depict the star groups placed between them, completing the exposition of the cosmological myth.

## The Head of the Bull

The theory could be tested by using a hypothetical model that both the base plate of the cauldron and the first stone of the Paris column relate to the same myth concerning Esus and the bull Tarvos Trigaranus. The deduction that the human figure represented on both compositions can be identified with Esus, is supported by the portrayal of his posture and his distinctive lock of hair. The same figure is depicted five times on four of the cauldron's plates, always in the same posture, with both legs bent and toes pointed as if he were raised from the ground – in allusion to his name 'the raised one'. In four of the five depictions the figure has a curly lock of hair (in the fifth image he wears a bull-horned helmet that covers the feature). The lock of hair is referred to in the Celtic Mercury's other title, Lug, 'lock' (of hair). Evidence that Esus/Lug had such a lock of hair is found in the Irish story of the Tain Bo in which Lugh is described in the following terms:

> *A great well-favoured man, then, broad, close shorn hair upon him, and yellow and curly his back hair. A green cloak wrapped round him. A brooch of white silver in the mantle of his breast. A tunic of silk reaching down to his knees.*

(Interestingly, the figure of Esus on the cauldron wears a similar tunic down to the knees.)

How may we discern this mythological scene in the night sky? Our first clue comes from the Rig Veda. In Vedic terms, the universe was envisaged as formed from two bowls, the earth and the sky. The bowl of the sky was an upturned vessel holding the cosmic ocean; the upright bowl represented the earth, which contained physical creation. Between the two bowls was the middle space through which the sun and moon made their passage as they rose and set. If the Gundstrup cauldron depicts the constellations of the ecliptic along the narrative of the inner plates, it may well reflect the Indo-Aryan conception of the sky as an upturned bowl. The position of the plate at the base of the vessel would relate to the highest point on the celestial vault, the circumpolar region. By comparing the imagery of the base plate with the stars of the circumpolar region, we can recognize a number of identical features from the context of their composition. Starting from the constellation of Cepheus, the following comparisons can be made (see *Figure 21*):

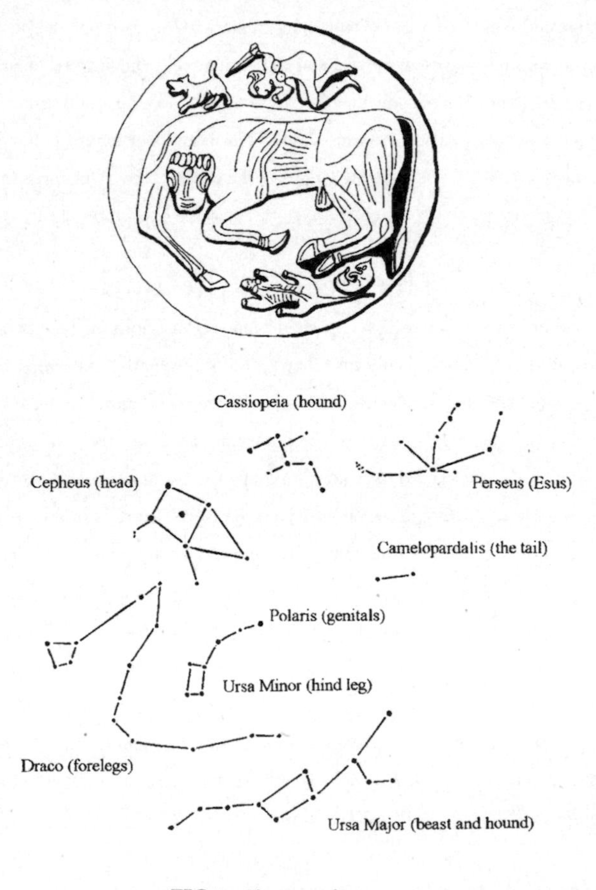


**FIG. 21.** *The circumpolar star.*

### (I) CEPHEUS.

The shape of Cepheus closely matches the head of the bull on the plate. The two eyes, horns and snout are easily recognizable, as well as the star representing the third horn on the bull's forehead (indicated on the plate by a hole). The triple-horned bull is a common motif in Celtic art, with almost 40 examples found in Britain and Gaul (most usually in the form of bronze figurines).

The head of the bull was apparently important in relation to the myth concerning the birth of Athena/Minerva – as described on stone one of the Paris column. The most important cosmological feature of Cepheus is that the Milky Way seems to emanate from it in two directions. In the Rig Veda, the source of Soma was said to have come from the head of the bull.

### (II) DRACO

Spatially, the winding constellation of Draco represents the two forelegs of the bull on the plate.

### (III) URSA MINOR

Ursa Minor would then correspond to the hind leg(s) of the bull, leading up to Polaris, the North Star, which would then represent the genitals of the animal.

### (IV) ANDROMEDA

The position of Andromeda fits the location of the hound that accompanies Esus above the bull.

### (V) PERSEUS

The shape and siting of Perseus then corresponds with Esus. The name Perseus stems from the Greek per, 'very' or 'great', with the latter part Seus perhaps relating to the Celtic Esus.

### (VI) URSA MAJOR

The lizard-like creature beneath the hind leg of the bull would match Ursa Major, representing chaos attacking the genitals of the heavenly bull during the act of creation.

## Soma and the Milky Way

In the Irish sources the importance of the Milky Way and the cause of its flooding is described in the story of Boann, 'the white cow', and the formation of the river Boyne (Bovinda), 'of the white cow (bull)'. It is a mythological tale, connecting the formation of the celestial river with the origins of all the rivers on earth. In Gaelic the Milky Way was known as Bothar na Bofinn, 'the road of the white cow'.

An analogy of the same myth is preserved in the Welsh tale of Culwych and Olwen from the Mabinogi, where the goddess is likewise equated with the Milky Way as Olwen, 'she of the white track'. The hero of the story, Culwych, has to complete a number of impossible tasks, an allusion to the hero's quest and the beasts of the zodiac. The father of Olwen (like the bull in the sacrifice), is destined to die by decapitation before his daughter can marry, similar to Athena being born from the head of the heavenly bull.

In the Rig Veda the source of the Milky Way is directly linked with the head of the bull and the transformation of the goddess into a wading bird:

*The knowing one revealed the secret place of the adored bird.*
*Like a cloak the milk poured from the head of the bull, the two*
*drank from its waters from beneath its feet.*

*Rig Veda I, 164, v 7*

The same hymn also identifies the flowing milk descending to the Asvins. If the Asvins are the divine twins synonymous with Smertrius and Cernunnos, this describes how the Milky Way crosses the ecliptic twice on the constellations of Orion and Ophiucus:

*I evoke the bull of plentiful milk and the hands of its skilful milker. Inspiration gained through the skills of Savitr. I am eager to applaud the vessel of milk placed upon the fire. The mother of plenty is born seeking her calf. This cow gives milk and increase to the Asvins.*

*Rig Veda I, 164, v 26-27*

The overall myth concerning the circumpolar region describes a cosmogonical event, when the heavenly bull was dismembered during the act of creation. From the sacrifice the life giving waters of Soma were released. This regenerative cosmic juice was variously explained in terms of the blood or seed of the bull, or the milk of the cow. The activating god was perceived by the Druids to be Esus/Lug, known in the Rig Veda by numerous appellations – 'the all maker', 'the impeller' or Tvastr, the skilled artisan of the gods. In all these varied forms he actively released the positive female principle into creation from the body of the bull and the milk of the cow. In the Rig Veda the heavenly bull was known as Dyaus, 'the sky', and his consort was Prsni, 'the earth', invoked as 'the dappled cow':

*Strong and endurable, the father and the mother guard the broad expanse of the sky. Like two beautiful maidens the two world halves are formed and adorned in many colours by the father. The skilful charioteer cleanses the sky. He daily milks the seed of*

> *the dappled cow and the bull bursting with seed. He benevolently created the two world halves, measured them and placed them apart with the immortal river.*
>
> *Rig Veda I, 160, v 2-4*

Dyaus was also envisaged as Parjanya, 'the thunderer' (a title linking him with the Celtic Taranis), god of the fructifying rain invoked as the bull bursting with seed and the androgynous cow whose udders swell with milk. Parjanya was the bull of the sky who revealed himself with the three voices of thunder, lightening and rain:

> *Plant your seed and roar with thunder.*
> *Encircle the earth in your flying chariot sprinkling water from your up turned leather bag;*
> *Level the hills into a plain.*
> *Immerse from the great vat and release the flowing rivers.*
> *Soak the earth from the sky.*
>
> *Rig Veda V, 83, v 7-8*

The upturned leather bag alludes to the inverted bowl, the cauldron of the heavens that contained the cosmic ocean. The Vedic Aryans shared this cosmological tradition with their Indo-European cousins – the Druids – who bequeathed to us their perception of the upturned cauldron of the night sky in the beautiful iconography of the vessel found in a peat bog near Gundstrup.

## The Mistletoe

In his Natural History, Pliny recorded a Druidic ceremony that relates directly to the mythology surrounding the seeding of the heavenly bull:

> *Here we must mention the awe felt for this plant (the mistletoe) by the Gauls. The druids, for so their magicians are called, hold nothing more sacred than the mistletoe and the tree that bears it, always supposing that tree to be an oak. But they choose groves formed of oaks for the sake of the tree alone, and they never perform any of their rites except in the presence of a branch of it; so that it seems probable that the priests themselves may derive their name from the Greek word for that tree. In fact, they think that everything that grows on it has been sent from heaven and is proof that the tree was chosen by the god himself. The mistletoe, however, is found but rarely upon the oak; and when found, is gathered with due religious ceremony, if possible on the sixth day of*

> *the moon (for it is by the moon that they measure their months and years, and also their ages of thirty years). They chose this day because the moon, though not yet in the middle of her course, has already considerable influence.*
>
> *They call mistletoe by a name meaning, in their language, all healing. Having made preparation for sacrifice and a banquet beneath the trees, they bring thither two white bulls, whose horns are bound then for the first time. Clad in a white robe, the priest ascends the tree and cuts the mistletoe with a golden sickle, and it is received by others into a white cloak. Then they kill the victims, praying that god will render this gift of his propitious to those to whom he has granted it. They believe that the mistletoe, taken in drink, imparts fecundity to barren animals, and that it is an antidote for all poisons. Such are the religious feelings that are entertained towards trifling things by many peoples.*
>
> *Natural History, xvi, 249*

The mistletoe rite comprised of two parts. The first was the cutting of the mistletoe from the tree, looked on as a gift offered by the god associated with the oak, the sky god. The second consisted of the bull sacrifice, an offering made in reciprocity for the appropriation of the sacred plant. These two acts also appear to be related on two plates of the Gundstrup cauldron and suggest a rite that was re-enacted to commemorate a seasonal myth involving the four Gaulish divinities depicted on the Paris column.

The first part of the ritual mimics the cosmogonical myth of Esus and the release of the goddess in the form of the three cranes.

The cutting of the mistletoe was analogous to the seeding of the bull. As the mistletoe was cut, two white bulls were simultaneously sacrificed beneath the tree, an act that pre-empted the feast. This suggests that the ceremony closed with the consumption of their flesh similar to the Tarbhfess ritual. The sacrifice is depicted on plate II of the cauldron, with Smertrius slaying the bull in a reciprocal act to Esus cutting the mistletoe on the base plate (I). On the Paris column this same scene is depicted in the form of Smertrius holding aloft a headless ram-horned serpent. The connection between the ram-horned serpent and the white bull at first appears obscure unless we assume that they both represent the Celtic Apollo. A reference to a solar attribute attached to a white bull is found in the Irish story of the Tain Bo. Here we encounter two supernatural bulls whose constant rivalry eventually led to conflict between Ulster and Connaught. The dark bull of Ulster was called Donn, 'dark one', corresponding with the heavenly bull as the weather/sky god Taranis:

*Thundering brown bull... who roars, who lets forth the rains of the west and its cloudy night.*

The other bull was called Finnbenach, 'the white breasted', who is then described in terms of a solar deity:

*Red was the bull Finnbenach, Finnbenach the red was the sun of the east, the white horned and white breasted.*

The meaning of the mistletoe ceremony, then, would be something like this:

During the month of Samonos, when the full moon entered Taurus, the cosmic act of Creation was re-enacted to initiate the new year.

The Irish name for the Milky Way was 'the road of the white cow or bull', suggesting the belief that when the white bull of the Celtic Apollo was slain, its soul was perceived to transcend the Milky Way. This coincides with the Greek concept of Apollo visiting the land of the Hyperboreans in the extreme north every winter. The Samonos rite interpreted the mistletoe berry as the seed of the heavenly bull Tarvos Trigaranus. The white bull represented the strong summer aspect of the sun, or Belenus, who is decapitated and consumed prior to his soul ascending the Milky Way into his winter captivity as Maponus the winter sun.

Pliny states that the mistletoe was known as 'all healing' and was taken in a drink as an aphrodisiac and an antidote. The Gaulish name of the plant was Vivisca, 'the water of life', confirming the medicinal properties attributed to it. The mistletoe's association with a heavenly origin must stem from its life cycle of growing high up in the canopy of trees and never touching the ground. It mostly grows on willows, apples and poplars, so when it appears on oaks, which is rare, its sacred importance is enhanced as representing the seed of the god of the oak, namely the sky god. This is emphasized in the various Gaelic names for mistletoe: dour dero, 'oak water', and sugh an darauch, 'sap of the oak'. The mistletoe is evergreen, fruiting during Samonos (October/November) and continuing to ripen until Anagantios (January/February). The plant then remains dormant until the Gaulish month of Giamonos, 'Sprouting', (April/May) when the small trefoil flowers come into bloom during Beltene, heralding another aspect of the myth when Apollo Maponus is transformed back into Belenus.

The relationship between the Celtic Apollo as the fluctuating power of the sun and the Celtic Dis as the mortal twin who lives and dies as the god of vegetation, is intrinsically bound in the seasonal narrative. This same symbiotic relationship is described in the Rig Veda as elements of the sacrifice. Agni is the fire who consumes the sacrifice of Soma, reflecting the Apollonian aspect of the burning heat of summer and the consumption of the ritual oblation:

*Like a newborn child he bellows in the wood, the tawny race horse strained to win the sun.*
*He unites with the sky's seed that grows great with milk. With kind thoughts we pray to him for far reaching shelter.*
*He who is the pillar of the sky, the well-adorned support, the full stalk that encircles all around, he is the one who by tradition sacrifices to the two great world halves.*

*Rig Veda IX, 74, v 1-2*

Thus the Milky Way is the stalk that 'encircles all around', joining the realm of the sky to the earth as it descends below the horizon, the path that connects the land of the immortals with the land of the living.

The only myth surrounding Soma in the Rig Veda refers to his retrieval from the highest heaven by the eagle Vena or alternatively by Indra himself. A parallel story in the Welsh Mabinogion tells of how Lleu transformed into an eagle and flew to the top of an enchanted oak tree. As Lleu was the equivalent of the Celtic Mercury, we may interpret this tale as describing the ascension of Esus along the Milky Way or cosmic tree to acquire the mistletoe either at Samhain or Beltene.

**FIG. 22.** *Gaulish coins depicting Ulatos Ateula.*

On Gaulish coin issues we find the depiction of the bust of a youthful god with wings attached to his neck called Ulatos Ateula, 'the flying one who returns in flight' (see *Figure 22*). The name Ulatos is cognate with the British Bladud, a semi-mythological king recorded by Geoffrey of Monmouth in his History of the Kings of Britain. The father of Bladud was Rhud Hudibras, 'the large stag of the wheel', referring to Cernunnos as the constellation of Ophiucus. The story relates to how Bladud resigned the kingship of Britain after suffering a crippling injury, and became a swineherd. One day he is led by a stray pig to a spring presided over by the goddess Minerva. The blemished king drinks of the waters and is cured. The site of the spring was Bath, where interestingly a large stone relief still survives of a bearded god with long, wavy hair and wings attached to his neck, identical to the Gaulish rendition of Ulatos (see *Figure 23*).

**FIG. 23.** *Stone shield depicting the British god Bladud from Bath.*

The retrieval of the mistletoe by Esus in this instance applies to the blooming of its flower in May and describes the religious lore behind Beltene. Following the hanging of Cernunnos, the summer was initiated with the blossoming of trees and as a result of Esus's actions, the captive power of the winter sun is transformed from Maponus to the victorious summer sun Belenus. As the object of the sacrifice, Cernunnos was consumed by Belenus, the Dionystic god sacrificed to the Apollonian power of the sun in a reverse scenario to that which was perceived to happen during Samhain.

In this regard, the Celtic Dis resembled the Greek god Dionysus as the personification of the sacrificial offering. In Greek tradition Dionysus appeared in his first incarnation as Zagreus, the youngest son of Zeus and heir to Olympus. As the horned child, he was torn to pieces and consumed by the Titans. Athena intervened and saved his heart, from which Zeus created the twice-born Dionysus. The name Zagreus, 'torn to pieces', was also used as a pseudonym for the beneficial aspect of Hades, the god of the underworld later equated with the Latin deity Dis.

Strabo, in his Geographica, mentions the existence of an order of Gaulish priestesses on an island situated beyond the mouth of the river Loire. They were known as the Semnitae and worshipped a god that the author equated with Dionysus.

The identification of this native god with Dionysus appears to have been made on two points of similar religious lore. First, the Celtic god in question resembled the divine attributes of Dionysus as a living and dying god of vegetation and the personification of a sacred libation, namely the Celtic Dis alias Cernunnos. Second, the rituals observed by the Semnitae resembled those practised by the Dionystic worshippers known as the Maenads, 'the frenzied ones'. Strabo informs us that once a year the priestesses ritually dismantled and rebuilt the roof of their temple in one day. If they dropped any roofing thatch a sacrificial victim was selected from among them. They would then be torn to pieces and their body carried through the precinct to the cry 'Evoi', meaning 'we summon' (related to the term Ivos from the Coligny calendar). To Strabo the ritual must have seemed identical to the torch-lit processions of the Maenads on Mount Parnassus, a rite also restricted to women in which, intoxicated, they tore to pieces animals such as deer, goats and oxen. They then ate their flesh to commemorate the death of Zagreus at the hands of the Titans.

The Semnitae are also recorded by Diogenes Laertius but here they are addressed as the Semnothoi, 'speculators of the seed', the seed being in all probability the mistletoe:

> *Some say that the study of philosophy was of barbarian origin. For the Persians had their Magi, the Babylonians and the Assyrians the Chaldeans, the Indians their Gymnosophists, while the Celts and the Galatae had seers called Druids and Semnotheoi.*

Thus we find a class of priests separate from Druids who specialized in the rituals of the divine seed in the role of seers and who were possibly involved in the preparation of the sacred mead imbued from the said plant. Evidence that a sisterhood was associated with the mead of the goddess of sovereignty is found in both the insular and classical sources. In the Welsh poem *The Spoils of the Deep*, attributed to Taliesin, we are told of the cauldron that was warmed by the breath of nine maidens. In Ireland, a sisterhood of 19 nuns attended a perpetual fire at the sanctuary of St. Brighid in Kildare. Gerald of Wales points out that the nuns of Kildare were not allowed to blow the flames with their breath, perhaps suggesting the modification of a previously pagan practice. Pomponius Mela described a Gaulish shrine on the island of Sena, also tended by nine virgin priestesses:

> *By their charms they are able to raise the winds and seas and turn themselves into what animal they will, to cure wounds and diseases incurable by others and predict the future.*

Sena was one of a group of islands that Mela calls the Cassiterides, traditionally located off the west coast of France. Sena may be the small island of Sein off of the Pointe du Raz in Brittany – that is, beyond the mouth of the Loire. In another account, the writer Posidonius recorded the sisterhood of priestesses of the Galliceniae, whose precinct was also closed to men.

The tradition of a sisterhood of nine priestesses also survives in the Vitae Merlini of Geoffrey of Monmouth, where they were said to be located on the Insula Pomorum:

> *That is the place where nine sisters exercise a kindly rule over those who come to them from our land. The one who is first among them has the greater skill in healing, as her beauty surpasses that of her sisters. Her name is Morgen, and she learned the uses of all plants in curing the ills of the body. She knows too, the art of changing her shape, of flying through the air…*

Both Mela and Geoffrey allude to the healing arts of the sisters, perhaps reminiscent of their skill in preparing the sacred libation from mistletoe, which Pliny described as being imparted in a drink and used to cure all poisons. The name of the high priestess, Morgen, is a later corruption of 'Morrigan', 'the great queen', the archetypal personification of the Irish goddess of sovereignty.

## The Mistletoe Head

Further clues to the mythological association between the mistletoe and the Celtic Dis comes from a particular artistic motif represented within the repertoire of decorative styles inherent in La Tène art. This motif follows a uniform formula, comprising of a human head crowned with two lobed or comma-shaped leaves with a trefoil flower engraved on the forehead.

The symbolism appears to describe the growth cycle of the mistletoe, which every year grows into a fork at the end of each stem. The small trefoil flowers appear in the fork, being replaced by fleshy white berries later in the winter. The transition from flower to berry is depicted by the head, representing the berry, with the image of the flower impressed upon the forehead. The opposing lobed leaves that surmount the head reflect the position of the berry (as the head) in the previous year's fork (see *Figure 24*).

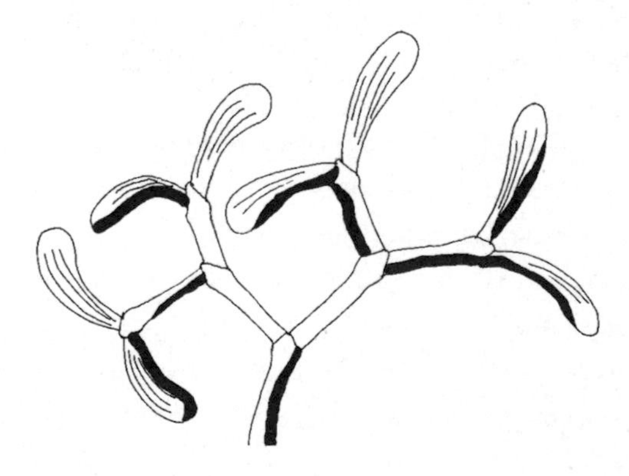

**FIG. 24.** *The growth cycle of the mistletoe plant.*

The best examples of the mistletoe head come from the remains of two stone pillars in Germany, dating from between the 5th and 4th centuries BC. A four-sided pillar from Pflazfeld depicts the repeated imagery of the lobed head with trefoil markings surrounded by 'S' patterned symbols, an inverted triangular point situated above the head and the relief of an acorn at the top. The 'S' markings are used in other La Tène contexts to denote the thunderbolt of the sky god, and the presence of the acorn suggests that the pillar represented an oak tree. The theme of the pillar thus links the mistletoe deity with a mythological narrative associating him with two of the principal attributes of the Celtic sky god, the oak tree and the lightening bolt. Unfortunately the top of the pillar was broken off during the 17th century, but a stone head from Heidelberg is believed to have once stood at the pinnacle of a similar pillar to that found in Pfalzfeld. Again, the head bears the distinctive lobed leaves and the trefoil flower on the forehead (see *Figures 25* and *26*).

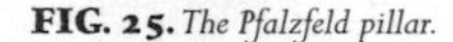

**FIG. 25.** *The Pfalzfeld pillar.*

**FIG. 26.** *The Heidelberg head.*

A bronze horse trapping from Waldalgesheim depicts the upper portion of a deity with arms raised in a similar posture to the gods shown on the outer plates of the Gundstrup cauldron. The lobed leaves are here stylized into an 'S' shape, suggesting a religious connection between the mistletoe plant and its origin from the realm of the thunder god, the seed born from lightning so to speak (see *Figure 27*).

This association is reflected in the rural folklore of France and Switzerland, where the hanging of a bough of mistletoe or 'thunder besom' was said to protect people from lightening and fire. In England the rural custom of burning the bushel (a woven ball of mistletoe and hawthorn withies) occurred at about the time of the winter solstice, a practice that may allude to the close affinity shared between the mistletoe and lightening. In the Coligny calendar, the month in which the winter solstice falls is named Riuros, 'the royal burning'. We know from Lucan that victims were offered to Taranis by the element of fire in a hollowed log, a rite that may have survived into recent times with the burning of the Yule log at Christmas. The victim placed in the log may thus have represented the Celtic god envisaged as the mistletoe, Dis or Cernunnos, in re-enactment of his seasonal death. Diodorus recounts the following tradition of the burning of victims by the Gauls to placate their gods:

> *It is in keeping with their savagery that they practice a unique impiety in their sacrifices; they keep evil doers in custody for five years and then impale them in honour of their gods. They construct enormous pyres and then devote them together with many other first fruits. They also use prisoners of war as sacrificial victims in paying honour to their gods.*

**FIG. 27.** *The Waldalgesheim trapping.*

CHAPTER EIGHT

# THE LOST ZODIAC

Having identified the base plate of the Gundstrup cauldron with the stars of the circumpolar region, we are now left with the seemingly hapless task of recognizing all the constellations of the ecliptic on the remaining inner plates. Previously we discussed the supposition that the depictions of Smertrius and Cernunnos on the Paris column represented the seasonally opposing constellations of Taurus/Orion and Scorpio/Ophiucus, the rising and setting divine twins depicted on inner plates II and V of the cauldron.

## Plate II

Despite attempts to conceal the plate's relationship to its respective celestial model suggests that plate II in particular had a marked significance not recognized among the other plates. The tripling of the image indicates the priority of the plate as the first scene of the narrative and the reverse order of the constellations perhaps points out the direction in which the plates had to be read: in an anti-clockwise direction from right to left. It may be that the two constellations were known to be recognizable even to those uninitiated in Druidic star lore, so that their images had to be camouflaged to maintain the secrecy regarding the other constellations on the plates.

Using the order of the inner plates proposed in chapter one, in relation to the rites of sacral kingship, I will now attempt a step-by-step analysis of the plates' depictions as they are read sequentially in an anti-clockwise direction. This method mimics how the constellations of the ecliptic are read as they rise and set over the horizon. Each recognized constellation will be accompanied by the relevant Gaulish name from the Coligny calendar, exposing the secret meanings behind the cosmological narrative that is the lost zodiac of the Druids.

## Taurus/Samonos

The depiction of the bull sacrifice on plate II corresponds with the constellations of Taurus and Orion (see Figure 28). The lunar month covering the period of October/November when the full moon rises in Taurus is termed Samonos, 'of seeding', in the Coligny calendar.

The image describes the mythological event of Smertrius slaying the single-horned bull of Taurus. Pliny offers us some insight into the background of this myth in his description of the mistletoe ceremony, explaining that two white bulls were sacrificed to the god of the oak in return for the acquisition of the mistletoe berry during that month. The white bull thus represented the Celtic Apollo, who must make his seasonal return to the land of the extreme north at the beginning of winter. This was initiated by the symbolic sacrifice of a white bull that re-enacted the cosmic event depicted in the stars. The soul of the bull/Taurus was then perceived to ascend the Milky Way, 'the track of the white bull', to the circumpolar region of the sky. In return, the sky god, as the heavenly bull, relinquished his seed in the form of the mistletoe berry on his sacred tree, the oak. This seed was the conception of Cernunnos, the Celtic Dis of Caesar.

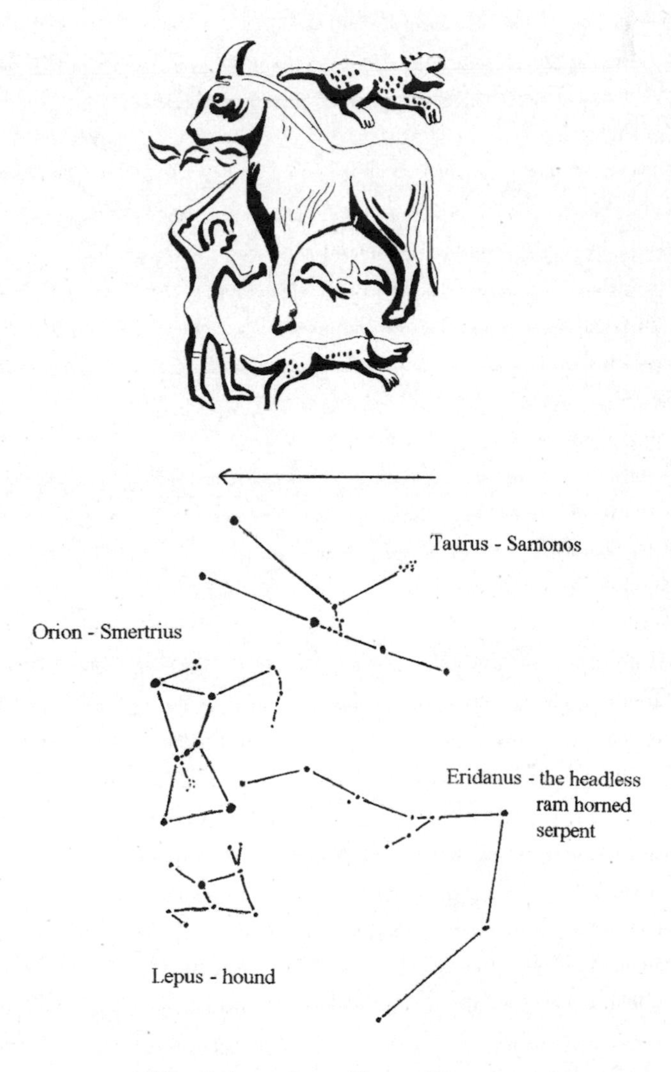


**FIG. 28.** *The constellations of Taurus and Orion.*

The same myth is depicted on the Paris column, with Smertrius holding the headless body of the ram-horned serpent, an alternative rendition of the death and beheading of the Celtic Apollo as Belenus (the summer aspect of the sun). In the Rig Veda a parallel myth survives in the story of Indra and the beheading of the sacrifice, where Indra beheads the sacrifice in anger at its attempt to disrupt the cosmic order, Rta. He then takes the head to the man 'who offered Soma' – that is, the sky god whose seed was the mistletoe. Another hymn identifies the rebellious sacrifice as the son of Indra, who usurped his father's authority by receiving the offerings of Soma and the victims of the bull sacrifice:

> *Standing high above the broad earth the bull with the pointed horn roared. He guards in every combat the presser of Soma which fills his two stomachs.*
>
> *Rig Veda 10, 28, v 2*

Yet another hymn recognizes the son of Indra as Vrsakapi, 'the virile head' and 'destroyer of sleep', who like Apollo, returned periodically to his home in the north.

The ritual act of beheading had a particular significance to the Celts. Among warriors it was regarded as the repository of the soul and power of a vanquished enemy. The head was thus sought as a trophy and was traditionally placed at the entrances to sanctuaries and to individual homes. Strabo records:

> *There is also a custom, barbarous and exotic, which attends most of the northern tribes. When they depart from the battle they hang the heads of their enemies from the necks of their horses, and when they bring them home, they nail the spectacle to the entrance of their homes.*

The placing of heads at entrances might reflect a tradition based on a religious precedent, such as the slaying of a white bull and its subsequent decapitation during Samonos, the beginning of the New Year. Archaeological evidence for such a ritual practice comes from a sanctuary in Gourney, Picardy, that dates back to the 4th century BC. Here the bones of oxen had particular reverential treatment, carried out by specialist officials who were probably Druids. The bulls were sacrificed at the centre of the sanctuary beneath a large post that represented an oak tree. Each ox was killed with a precise blow at the nape of the neck. The heads were then given further ritual treatment with the removal of the lower jaw bone and the hacking off of the muzzle by a sword blow (similar to that depicted on plate II). A sword rather than an axe may have been used to identify the sacrifice with the martial god Smertrius. This appears to be a ritual act symbolic of silencing the spirit of the dead beast, suggesting a belief that the skull could continue to speak after death, similar to accounts of the speaking head from the insular traditions of Wales and Ireland. The skulls were then deposited in both flanking ditches surrounding the entrance of the sanctuary.

The religious importance of silencing the animals may be related to in the story of the screaming serpents in the Welsh tale of Lludd and Llevelys (recognized in Celtic iconography as the ram-horned serpents). The silencing of the ox would then follow a tradition of symbolizing the seasonal death of Belenus and his talismanic concealment at the beginning of the year. The silencing of the bull is a matter addressed in the next month described on the Coligny calendar.

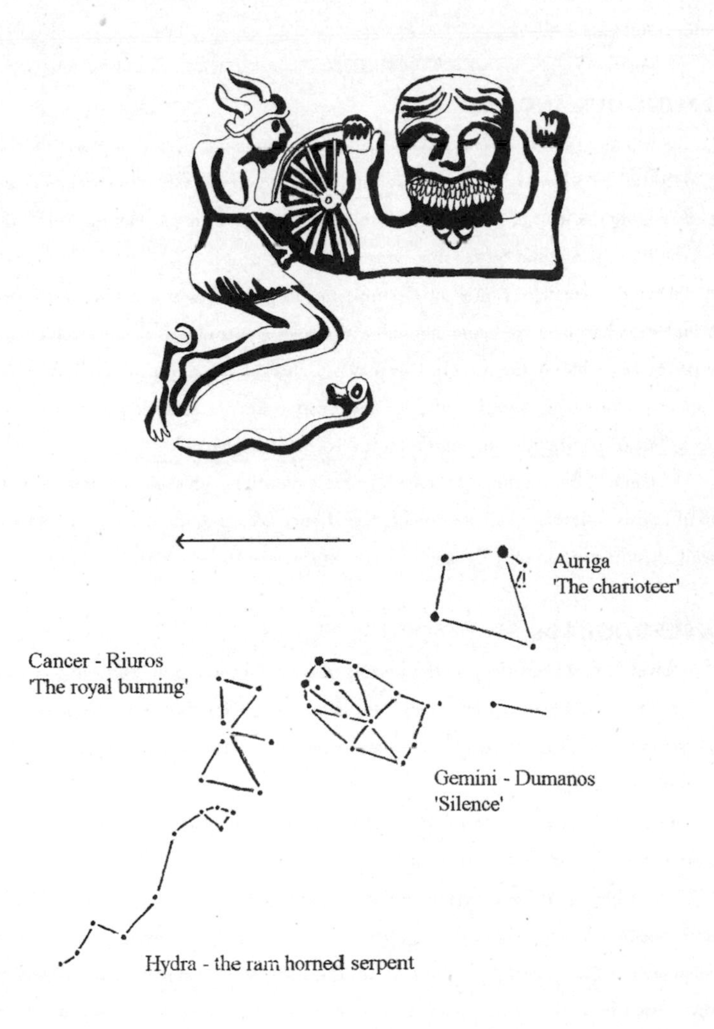


**FIG 29.** *The constellations of Gemini / Cancer.*

# Plate III

Plate III depicts the scene of a large bust figure holding a broken chariot wheel in the company of a smaller, full-length figure, recognized by his posture as Esus. Beneath Esus a ram-horned serpent lies on its back, surrounded by three griffins. The griffin is usually associated with the classical Apollo and is used in this instance to reveal the identity of the serpent as his Celtic counterpart. The larger bust figure holding the wheel presumably represents the Celtic sky god with his distinctive attribute. The imagery of plate III depicts the next section of the ecliptic incorporating the constellations of Gemini, Cancer and the neighbouring systems of Auriga and Hydra (see *Figure 29*).

## GEMINI/DUMANOS

The Gaulish month of Dumanos, 'of silence' covers the lunar period of November/December when the full moon enters the sign of Gemini, depicted on plate III as the broken chariot wheel. By comparing the map of Gemini with the wheel we may discern why the hub is deliberately placed off-centre and the spokes misaligned.

Taking the wheel to represent Gemini, the large bust figure would then correspond to Auriga, 'the charioteer' (a name applied within classical tradition that conveniently describes the sky god as holder of the wheel). This may perhaps indicate a connection between Auriga and the chariot wheel of Gemini, based on an earlier Indo-European myth later reinterpreted by the Greeks but retained within the cosmological lore of the Druids.

The name of this month, 'of silence', reflects the aftermath of the decapitation of the white bull of Taurus and its ritual concealment. The silence describes the subsequent lack of bird song during this time, when only the robin, wren, starling and missel thrush are rarely heard.

## CANCER/RIUROS

The next month of Riuros covers the period of the full moon in the following constellation of Cancer. The position of Cancer above the head of Hydra the snake identifies it with the representation of Esus standing above the ram-horned serpent, reaching out to clutch at the wheel of Gemini.

The name Riuros, 'the royal burning', suggests that it was during this month that the burning sacrifice was offered to Taranis.

The burning sacrifice describes a ritual connected with the mythology surrounding the winter solstice, which occurs during this month. The myth involved Esus/Lug grasping the broken wheel of the sun, itself emblematic of the star's weakened power (also represented as the inverted ram-horned serpent), as he draws it in: an allusion to the sun's annual death and rebirth.

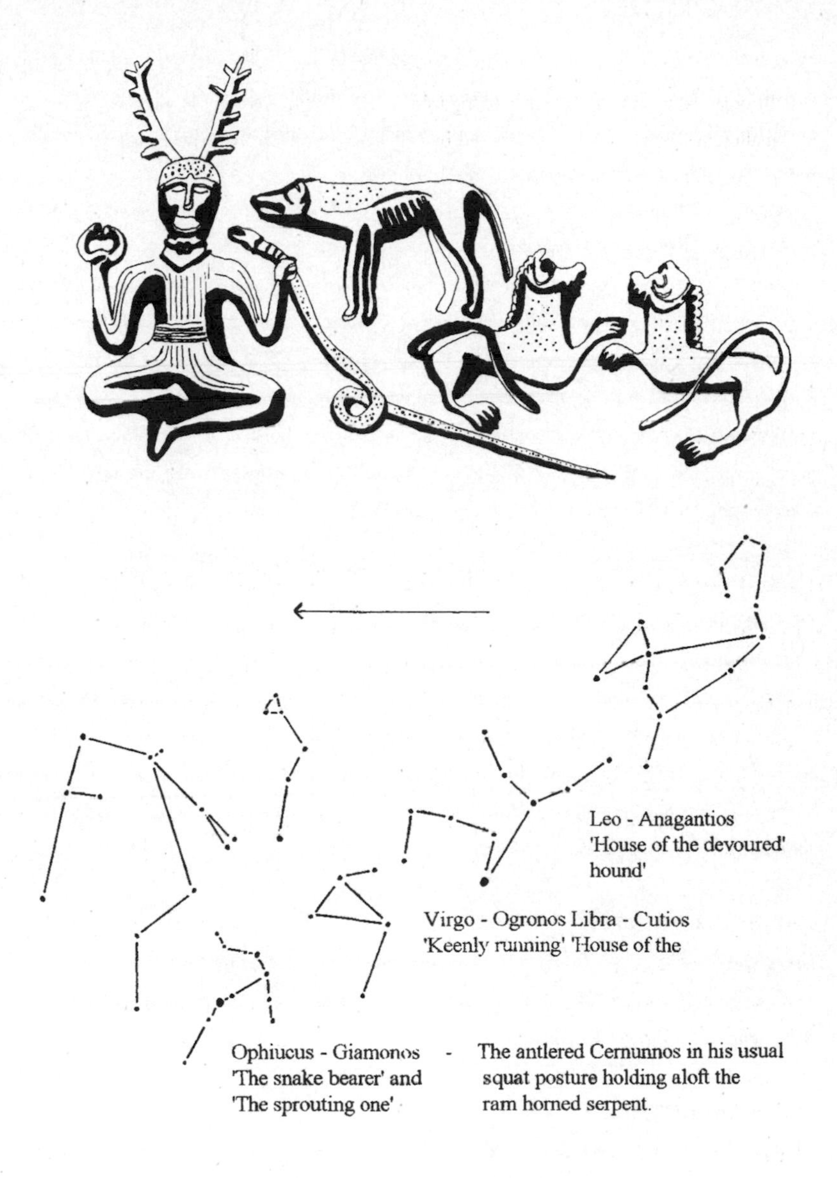


**FIG. 30.** *The constellations from Leo to Scorpio.*

In this aspect the Celtic Apollo was known as Maponus, who was kept in mournful captivity after being stolen when three days old – a metaphor for the solar standstill that lasts for the same period of time. The Acts of St. Vincent records a pagan conception of the solstice event, where a fiery wheel appears to a group of pagans who had gathered outside their temple to observe the spectacle. The wheel, which was engulfed in flames, hurtled down a hill towards a nearby river, but then reversed back up the slope after 'drinking' its waters. The account seems to relate to a pagan ceremony where the participants held a nightly vigil at the winter solstice, starting at sunset and closing at sunrise the next day.

Further clues to the ritual observed at the winter solstice are given in the Coligny calendar. On day four of Riuros, the ceremonies are introduced with the term Brigiomu, 'the exalted one is with us'. Then on day 13 the following sentence describes the role of Esus/Lug in retrieving the disc of the sun when the full moon enters Cancer: 'Devortomu Lug Rivri Ivos' – 'The turning of Lug is with us, an evocation to the royal burning'. That is to say, at the full moon a fire sacrifice is offered to Taranis to release the disc of the sun into the hands of Esus so that he can draw the sun from its most southerly position along the horizon. The result of this cosmic event is referred to on day four of the next month (Anagantios), where the reborn sun is acknowledged with the phrase 'Ociomu' – 'The young one is with us'.

# Plate IV

The next plate in the sequence is plate IV, which ends on the left-hand side with the representation of Cernunnos as the constellation Ophiucus/Scorpio. So we must presume that the narrative described on the rest of the plate relates to the stars lying between Cancer and Scorpio (see Figure 30). The narrative of the plate can be divided into four distinct compositions: two battling lions; the lion pursuing a man on the back of a salmon; Cernunnos holding the ram-horned serpent, accompanied by a stag and an attendant hound; and two bulls placed in the upper corners.

## THE BATTLING LIONS

The next constellation we should expect to encounter on the far right of the plate is that of Leo. As if by sheer chance, we find in this quadrant two opposing lions taking up the spatial positions of Leo and Virgo along the ecliptic:

## LEO/ANAGANTIOS

The fact that the lion representing Leo is facing to the left instead of the classical fashion of facing to the right merely reinforces the variation of cosmological interpretation between the two cultures as impressed by Lucan. The month when the full moon entered Leo is called Anagantios, 'the house of the eaten up one', an obscure name that perhaps refers to the fate of this lion as a result of fighting the opposing lion. This lunar period covers January/February, when the mistletoe stops producing berries – an event in the sacred plant's life cycle possibly referred to in the mythological story surrounding the consumed lion.

**FIG. 31.** *The La Tène sheath.*

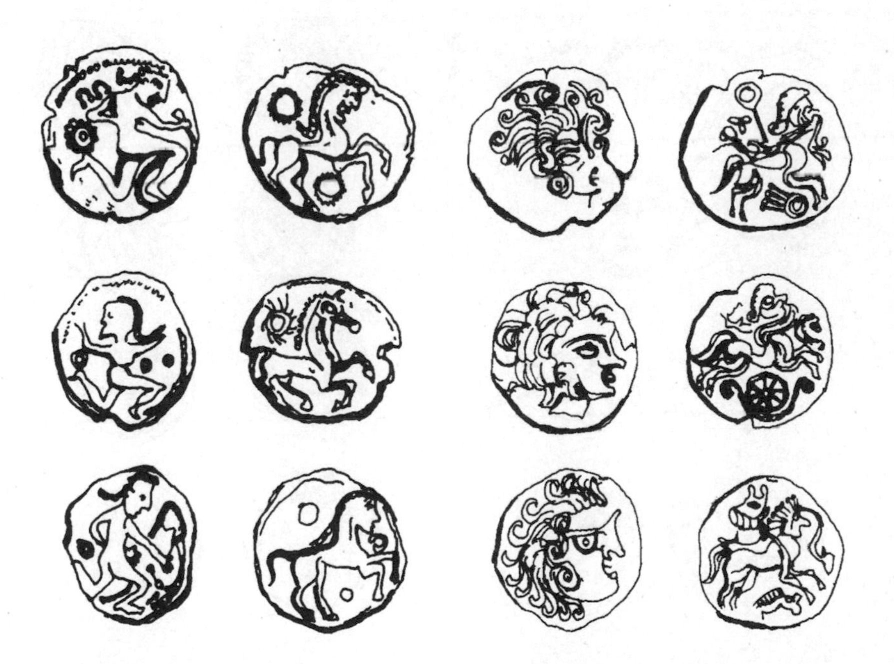

**FIG. 32.** *Gaulish coins depicting the swift-footed Esus as Ogronos.*

**FIG. 33.** *Gaulish coins depicting Esus pulling the chariot of the sun.*

**FIG. 34.** *Detail from the Aylesford Bucket.*

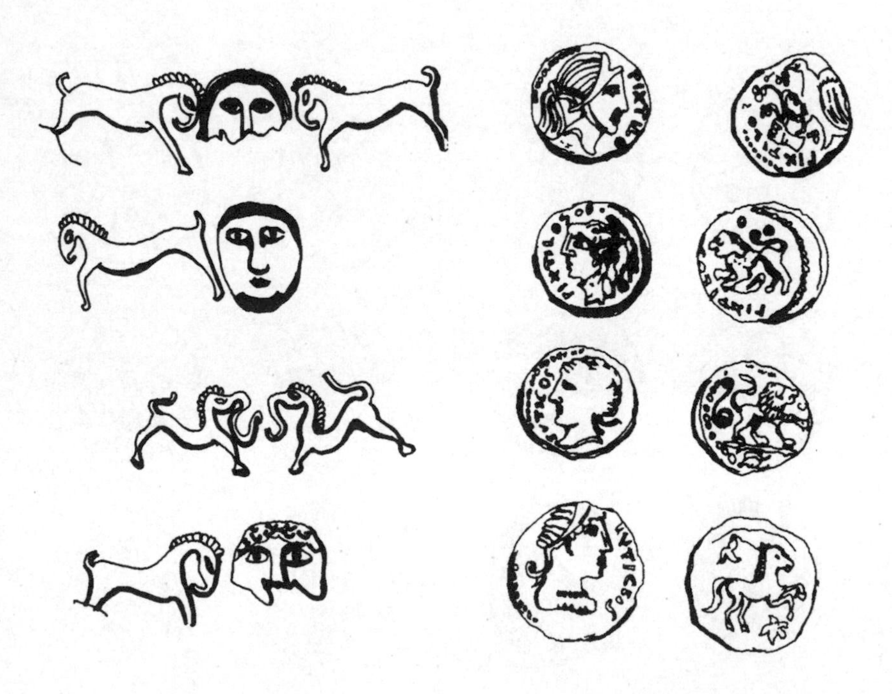

**FIG. 35.** *Details from the Marlborough vat.*

**FIG. 36.** *Gaulish coins of Rixtilos and Suticos.*

## VIRGO/OGRONOS

This month covers February/March and is represented by the full moon passing into Virgo. The right-facing lion is named as Ogronos, 'the keenly running one', describing his eagerness to pursue and consume his adversary, Leo.

The mythological interpretation of the battling lions is difficult to assess without finding further clues to the identities of the pair, presuming that they represent the transformed incarnations of two gods. A clue may be found on one of the outer plates of the Gundstrup cauldron, where the large bust figure of the goddess is flanked on both sides by images of Esus descending a vine (to the underworld?) and wrestling with a lion. This would initially suggest a cosmic battle between the Celtic Mercury and the Celtic Dis over the goddess, who is central to the composition.

The association between these two gods and the form of the lion also appears in the insular sources. In Wales Lleu is generally named as Llew, 'the lion', and in the account of Lucian of Samosata the god Ogmios was said to have been clad in a lion skin similar to the classical Hercules. The identification of Cernunnos with the mistletoe and his seasonal consumption is not only implied by the name of the month Anagantios ('the house of the eaten-up one'), but is also featured on another of the cauldron's outer plates. Here, beneath a god holding aloft two hippocampi, Cernunnos is shown being torn to pieces by a beast as the Dionystic sacrificial god.

Evidence for this supposition may be found in the imagery of a decorated bronze sword sheath from La Tène, dating from the 2nd century BC (see *Figure 31*). Here the same scenario of the battling lions is replaced with a pair of opposing equine creatures, which, like the lions on the cauldron, have protruding tongues. Above these animals a stag is portrayed, representing the presence of Cernunnos in the myth.

In analogy, therefore, the swift-footed Celtic Mercury is represented by the right-facing lion, 'the keenly running' Virgo. On a number of Gaulish coin issues Esus/Lug is depicted running with a circular disc attached to his heel. In the constellation of Virgo the brightest star of the group, Spica, would be similarly attached to the rear heel of his equine/lion celestial image (see *Figure 32*).

The equine association with Esus is further referred to in the imagery of various other coin issues from Gaul, where he appears as a horse with a human head (with his distinctive curly lock of hair) drawing the solar symbol in the form of a chariot (see *Figure 33*). The Aylesford bucket also shows the two opposing equine creatures, this time in the company of Cernunnos as the lobed mistletoe head (see *Figure 34*). On the Marlborough vat we find the same symbolism of the tongue-protruding equines facing each other. Both accompanied by the head of the respective gods they represent. (see *Figure 35*).

Two Gaulish coin issues appear to confirm the proposed identities of the two lions. The right-facing lion of Anagantios is portrayed with the inscription Rixtilos, 'the cultivated king', a title also accompanying the image of the god as a sprig of mistletoe. The left-facing lion Ogronos appears with the inscription Suticos, 'the procurer of juice', this time describing the god Esus acquiring the plant from the oak (see *Figure 36*).

## LIBRA/CUTIOS

The next lunar month named in the Coligny calendar is Cutios, 'the house of the hound', falling during March/April. This corresponds with the hound that accompanies Cernunnos and represents the constellation of Libra. The hound was traditionally associated with healing, hunting and protection. In Greek mythology the three-headed hound Cerebus guarded the entrance to the underworld, and it is in this regard that the beast stands sentinel beside Cernunnos. In the Rig Veda the infernal god Yama possessed two hounds:

> *Go to the right and avoid the sons of Sarama, the two brindled four eyed dogs, and join with your fathers at the feast of Yama. Yama offers him to the guardians of the path, the two brindled four eyed dogs, watchers of men. O king offer him a better life. The two black heralds of Yama consume the souls of the living, as they hunt for men with widened nostrils. They return us to a new life illuminated by the sun.*
>
> *Rig Veda 10, 14, v 10-12*

The conception of two hounds guarding the entrance to the land of the dead was also apparently envisaged by the Druids, the hounds being represented by the two constellations in which the full moon passes during the autumn and the vernal equinoxes. This was a metaphor for the sun increasing and decreasing in strength as it passes between the realms of the living and the dead, an event marked by the nocturnal passage of the moon through Cutios (Libra) in the spring and Cantlos, 'the tail of the dog' (Cetus) during autumn.

The location of the hound Cutios as Libra for the lunar period March/April coincides with the Greek festival of Elaphebolion, 'the deer shooting'. This was also known as the Artemision, when the goddess Artemis/Diana was worshipped as the goddess of hunting, the deer being her favourite prey. In the 1st century AD, the Greek writer Arrian wrote that the Gauls celebrated the following custom to the goddess Artemis:

> *Some of the Celts are obliged to make annual sacrifice to Artemis. Others offer the goddess a hoard of treasure which is made up of this: For a hare that they have caught they place two obols on the heap; for a fox a drachma, for the fox is a craftier creature, always lying in ambush and is the scourge of hares – this is why more is put down for it;*

> *For a wild goat four drachmas because it is a much bigger animal and more valuable game. The next year, when Artemis' birthday comes around again, they open the hoard and with the sum collected they buy a victim, a sheep, goat or a calf if there is enough money. Once sacrifice has been made and the first fruits offered to the huntress, according to their respective customs, they regale themselves and their dogs. On that day the dogs are even crowned with flowers to emphasize that the festival is given in their honour.*

Artemis was equated by the Romans to Diana, whom the Viromanduans described as corresponding with their native goddess. It is also significant that Cutios falls during the Greek celebration of Elaphebolion, since on the plate Cernunnos is depicted with antlers. This leaves one to ponder whether the birthday of the Gaulish Diana was honoured during this month, when the hounds were crowned with flowers.

## OPHIUCUS(SCORPIO)/GIAMONOS

The next lunar month on the calendar is Giamonos, 'the sprouting', alluding to the configuration of Ophiucus as representing the antlered god Cernunnos. This falls during the lunar period of April/May when the full moon passes through Ophiucus and Scorpio. In fact Ophiucus covers more of the ecliptic passage of the sun than Scorpio, the two groups being considered by the Druids as representing the same constellation, with Scorpio forming the tail end of the ram-horned serpent held by the god.

During this month the feast of Beltene was celebrated to welcome in the summer when the Celtic Apollo was transformed from the winter sun Maponus to his summer aspect as Belenus. An alternative name for the festival was given in Ireland as Cetsamhain, 'the other seeding', implying a ritual similar to that which was performed during Samhain/Samonos proper. The month of Giamonos coincides with the brief blossoming of the mistletoe flower, suggesting that a rite involving the plant was also practiced during this time.

The image of Cernunnos with his sprouting antlers and holding up the Apollonian ram-horned serpent indicates a mythological story connecting the flowering of the mistletoe with the release of Maponus from his winter captivity; an event depicted in the image of Ophiucus holding the serpent in the night sky.

A further clue to this association comes from the unlikely source of Geoffrey of Monmouth in his History of the Kings of Britain. Although a largely fictionalized work, it is clear that Geoffrey drew on elements of genuine Welsh tradition during the compilation of the text, confusing mythological characters with scarcely known, proto-historical figures. One of the kings mentioned is named Rhud Hudibras, 'the large stag of the wheel'. If the wheel is a metaphor for the revolving sky of the ecliptic, this must certainly be a reference to Cernunnos. The only story that Geoffrey relates concerning Rhud Hudibras was that he built the walls of Shaftesbury and was associated with a prophetic eagle. He was also the father of Bladud (who is etymologically identical to the Gaulish Ulatos Ateula) an alternative name for Esus/Lug.

Four important aspects relating to the story of Rhud Hudibras describes a myth in the region of the sky depicted on plate IV: the huge stag, Cernunnos; the wall of Shaftesbury, the Milky Way; the prophetic eagle, Aequila; and the fact that Bladud crashed into the temple of Apollo. All of these events may be described in terms of Esus's transformation into an eagle and his ascent along the Milky Way to release Maponus, the consequence of which was the hanging of Cernunnos, symbolizing the flowering of the mistletoe.

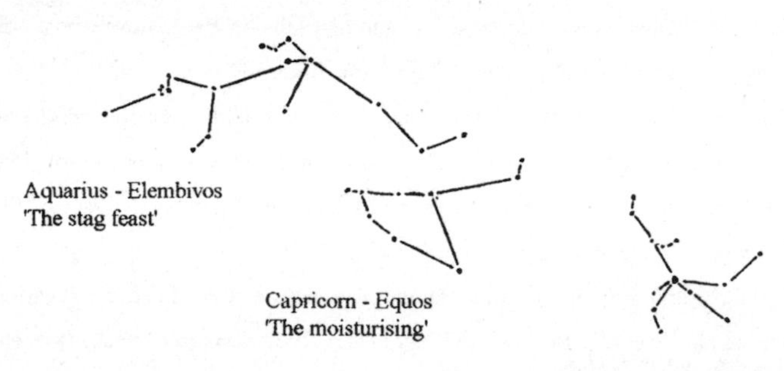


**FIG. 37.** *The constellations from Sagittarius to Aquarius.*

In the Welsh tale Culwych and Olwen, the hero had to locate the whereabouts of Mabon, of whom nothing was known other than it was he:

> *who was taken from his mother when three nights old from betwixt his mother and the wall, and it is not known where he is now, nor whether he is living or dead.*

The location of Mabon was eventually revealed by the oldest living animal, the salmon of Llyn Llyw, but he could only relate the following:

> *With every tide I go up along the river until I come to the bend in the wall at Caer Loyw, and there I found such distress that I never found its equal in all my life.*

The salmon was persuaded to ferry one of the heroes to the site of Mabon's imprisonment. On plate IV a similar event is depicted in the form of a man riding on the back of a salmon closely pursued by a lion: which is the lion of Esus/Ogronos chasing Cernunnos to his realm of the underworld. Looking again at the portion of the sky covered by the plate, we find that the lion is represented by the constellation of Hercules, the tail of the salmon by the Corona Boreales and the rider by Bootes. The story thus relates to three mythological events.

The first concerns the release of Mabon fought between the protagonists Esus and Cernunnos. The second refers to the death and rebirth of Cernunnos as the personification of the mistletoe plant. This is reflected in the Rig Veda by the relationship shared between Soma, the oblation of the sacrifice, and Agni, the consumer of the sacrifice as the Celtic Apollo. A symbiotic relationship that describes the Druidic conception of the seasonal cycles of the year, one in which balance could only be achieved by the seasonal sacrifice of the Dionystic god of the earth (and hence vegetation), Cernunnos, by the elemental gods Taranis, Esus and Teutates.

The third event describes the marriage of Cernunnos to the goddess as a metaphor for the mistletoe plant and the sacred mead. In terms of the divine hunt in the rites of sacral kingship, Cernunnos the stag reveals himself to the goddess in the guise of the beast of the chase, in which form he must copulate with her.

## Plate V

Proceeding anti-clockwise, plate V displays a military procession terminating in perhaps one of the most famous scenes on the cauldron, the immersion of a man head first into a vat. It has often been speculated that this represents the sacrifice propitiated to the god Teutates, as described by one of the medieval commentators of Lucan's Pharsalia. The scene is also apparently referred to on the Paris column with the names Smertrius, 'the immerser', and Cernunnos, 'the headfirst one', applied to the Celtic Mars and Dis.

If this plate relates to the next quadrant of the sky, we would expect to find some evidence of similarity between the images on the plate and the patterns of stars along the ecliptic. The first clue comes from the identical shape shared between the stars of Aquarius and the gigantic 'immerser' on the extreme left of the plate. This suggests that the composition includes the constellations of Sagittarius, Capricorn and Aquarius. If this is the case, Capricorn resembles the shape and location of the vat and victim, while Sagittarius can be seen in the quadruple image of the horseman pursuing the ram-horned serpent (see *Figure 37*).

## SAGITTARIUS/SIMIVISONNA

The lunar month of Simivisonna corresponds with the full moon rising in the constellation of Sagittarius. Meaning 'likened with bird song', the month alludes to the time when birds are in full song.

In classical mythology Sagittarius was the centaur Charon with drawn bow. The centaurs were said to be a hybrid race descended from Kentauros, 'the knowledgeable bull', who had mated with mares to sire the half-man, half-horse creatures. A similar story (recorded by the unknown author called the Pseudo-Plutarch) recounts how the goddess Epona was fathered by Pholoun Ivos Stellos, a man who preferred the favours of mares to that of women. The interpretation of his name suggests a ceremonial event rather than a person, meaning 'the evocation of the foal in the stars' – that is, the Celtic sky god as horseman was the father of Epona and represented the horseman of the constellation of Sagittarius. The 'Foal Feast' describes a ritual similar to that related by Geoffrey of Monmouth concerning the copulation of a petty king of Ulster with a white mare. This was an act performed during a coronation ceremony, suggesting a link to the rites of sacral kingship when a claimant was expected to mate with the goddess in her incarnation as a beast.

The imagery of the four horsemen chasing the ram-horned serpent along the top of plate V reflects an exaggerated motif of the mounted sky god riding down the snake-limbed creature, as depicted on the pinnacle of the Jupiter giant columns of eastern Gaul. The association of the sky god as a father of horses is also alluded to in Ireland where one of the surnames of the Dagdha was Eochaid Ollathair, 'the all father of horses'.

The four horsemen represent the victory of the mounted sky god pursuing the released Celtic Apollo as Belenus, an event marked by the resonance of bird song. In the Tain Bo a reference to horsemen and the power of bird song is made by the charioteer Loegaire as he describes his vision of the otherworld to his master Cu Chullain:

*At the door toward the west*
*On the side toward the setting sun,*

*There is a troop of grey horses with dappled manes*
*And another troop of horses, purple brown.*
*At the door towards the east*
*Are three trees of purple glass.*
*From their tops a flock of birds sing a sweetly drawn out song*
*For the children who live in the royal stronghold.*
*At the entrance of the enclosure is a tree*
*From whose branches there comes beautiful and harmonious music.*
*It is a tree of silver, which the sun illuminates.*
*It glistens like gold.*

The troop of horses refers to the mount of the sky god represented by the constellation of Sagittarius and the silver tree is a metaphor for the Milky Way, in the branches of which sing the birds of 'harmonious music'. These birds are none other than the three cranes of the transformed triple goddess. Two of the cranes are recognizable as the cruciform constellations of Cygnus and Aequila that lie above Sagittarius; the third crane may have possibly been identified with the constellation of Lyra.

The same myth is described in the Rig Veda:

*Two birds perch together on the same tree.*
*One feeds on the ripe fruit, the other looks away.*
*The birds sing of their knowledge of the immortal place,*
*Where the great controller of the earth imparts his wisdom to the uninitiated.*
*On the tree of ripe fruit the birds rest and feed upon the honey.*
*This is the food eaten by those who know the father.*

*Rig Veda I, 164, v 20-22*

These verses eloquently explain the mythology surrounding the cosmic tree of the Milky Way with the goddess residing in its branches as the three cranes. After her release from the head of the heavenly bull, the sweet fruit of Soma was produced, recognized by the Druids with the growth cycle of the parasitic mistletoe plant on the totem tree of the sky god, the oak.

## CAPRICORN/EQUOS

The next Gaulish month Equos covers the lunar period June/July when the full moon passes through the constellation of Capricorn. The name Equos, 'to moisten', alludes to the immersion sacrifice performed during this month, described in the imagery of Cernunnos, 'the headfirst

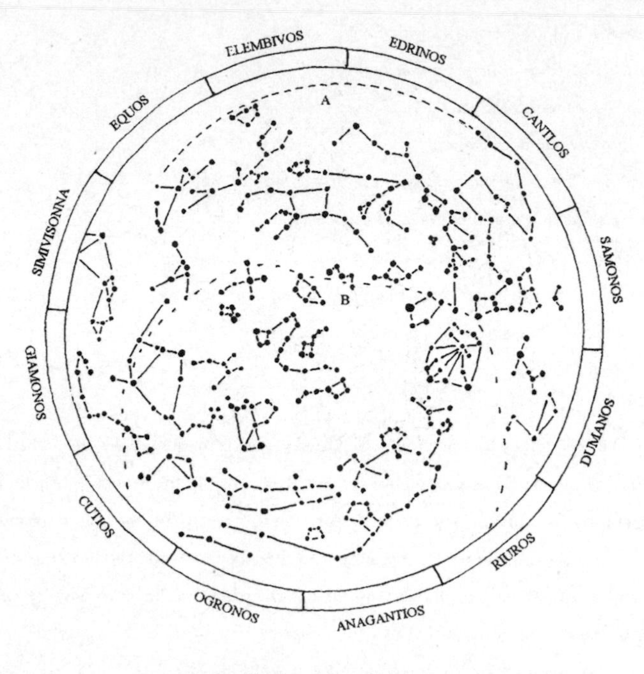


The two sacred celestial rivers
A The Eridanus flowing from Aquarius to Orion
B The Milkyway flowing from and to the head of the bull Cepheus

**FIG. 38.** *The cosmological significance of Eridanus.*

one', being immersed headfirst by Smertrius, 'the immerser', on plate V. This myth relates to the need for moisture during the month that contains the summer solstice. The immersion sacrifice would have taken place on day 15 of Equos, described on the Coligny calendar by the term Ganor, 'the consummation'.

## AQUARIUS/ELEMBIVOS

The constellation of Aquarius forms a distinctive inverted L-shape, which exactly mirrors the image of 'the immerser' on plate V. The next lunar month for July/August was called Elembivos, 'the evocation of the stag', denoting the veneration of the vegetation god during the season of harvesting. On one of the outer plates the imagery of Smertrius immersing Cernunnos as a stag is depicted by the god holding two stags, dangling head first. The myth refers to Smertrius preparing the mead of the goddess of sovereignty from the flowers of the mistletoe plant, a role evident in the surnames attached to the Celtic Mars in the epigraphy, such as Cocidius, 'the cook', and Briacus, 'the brewer', among others.

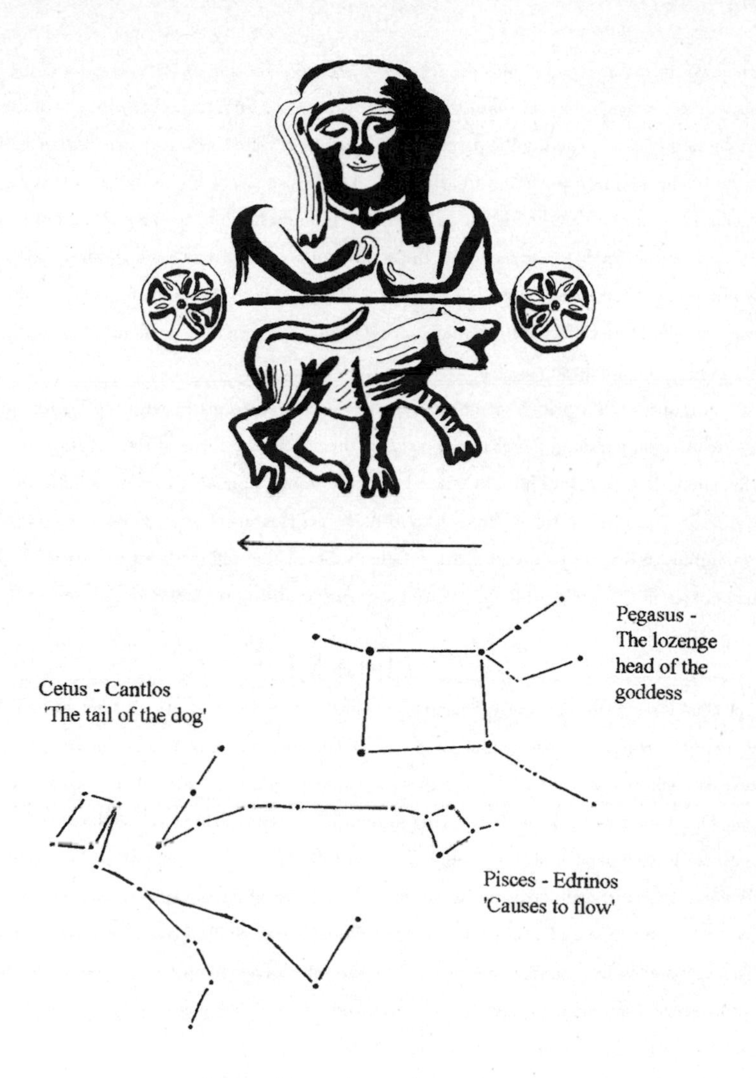


**FIG. 39.** *The constellations of Pisces to Aries.*

## THE LEGEND OF ERIDANUS

An interesting story from Greek mythology connects the constellations of Aquarius with that of Orion and concerns the formation of the river Eridanus, a celestial river like the Milky Way, which was said to emanate from the overflowing of Aquarius running:

> *under the feet of the gods, a river of tears that reaches at last the left foot of Orion.*
>
> *Aratus, Phaenommena*

The basis of the myth surrounds the legend of Phaeton, the son of Helios who, on discovering his true parentage, took control of the chariot of the sun. Unfortunately the beasts of the zodiac frightened Phaeton, causing the passage of the sun to deviate from its course, either falling too close to the earth or ascending too high into the heavens. Fearing a universal calamity, Zeus struck Phaeton with a thunderbolt and his body plummeted into the river Eridanus. In Plato's Timmaeus the myth is explained as 'the enthroning of Eridanus', which along with Auriga would one day take over the role of the Milky Way. That is to say, the passage of Eridanus from Aquarius to Orion reflected the same function in the southern celestial hemisphere as the Milky Way did in the northern (see *Figure 38*).

The imagery on plate V contains elements of the same myth, with the horseman as the Celtic sky god pursuing the chaotic power of the sun in the form of the ram-horned serpent (Belenus). Belenus is eventually tamed by the immersion of Cernunnos into the vat of Capricorn, causing it to overflow into the river Eridanus. The 3rd-century Greek writer Apollonius of Rhodes recorded that the Celts believed that the Eridanus was formed from the tears of Apollo, inferring that they shared a similar tradition regarding the origins of the river.

## Plate VI

The final inner Plate (VI) must therefore cover the area of the ecliptic not mentioned thus far, namely the constellations of Pisces and Aries. An observation of this sector of the night sky reveals a number of features that resemble the spatial composition of plate VI (see *Figure 39*).

The plate depicts the goddess being drawn along by the schematic rendering of a chariot, outlined by two petal-spoked wheels and a shaft following the base line of the bust figure of the goddess. The most distinctive constellation in this region of the sky is Pegasus, easily discernible by the four major stars that form an immense square with a tail of stars streaming to the right. This is matched by a similar line of stars to the left, which form part of the constellation of Andromeda. The spatial context of Pegasus closely resembles the distinguishing headdress of the goddess on plate V, which has two flanking tails.

If the head of the goddess is represented by Pegasus/Andromeda, then the shaft of the chariot would follow the pattern of stars that form Pisces. The circular cluster of stars on the far right of the constellation symbolize the wheel to the right of the shaft, while the left wheel is designated by the opposing cluster of circular stars formed at the tail end of the neighbouring constellation of Cetus.

### PISCES/EDRINOS

The lunar month covering the period August/September was known on the Coligny calendar as Edrinos, 'causes to flow'. This alludes to the consequence of the ritual immersion of

Cernunnos and the bringing of rains before the harvests were gathered in. In Gaelic this month was known as Iuchar, 'of the worm (snake)', in reference to the power of the sun as the ram-horned serpent.

## ARIES/CANTLOS

The last month on the Coligny calendar covers September/October and is named Cantlos, 'the tail of the dog', from the Irish form cainte, dog. On plate VI a dog is depicted below the goddess with its tail raised towards the left wheel, taking up the position of the rest of Cetus. Both Cantlos and its opposite month Cutios were associated with the two guardian hounds of the underworld who stood sentinel at the two equinoxes.

The imagery of plate VI is placed between the two constellations concerned with the legend of the Eridanus (its origin at Aquarius and its termination beneath the toes of Orion). This perhaps relates to a Celtic version of the myth in which the Celtic goddess played a role. A clue to this role may be found in the origin of the name Eridanus. A common appellation of the goddess was Danu or Donn, which not only survives in the insular sources but is also present in the names of the major Continental rivers, Danube, Dneiper and Donn. Eridanus may then actually translate as 'the plentiful of Danu'. If we compare this evidence with the account given by Apollonius that the Celts believed the Eridanus to have formed from the tears of Apollo, we may presume that the river was strongly associated with the mythology surrounding the ram-horned serpent. Indeed, when we look at the imagery of the Paris column, Smertrius (as Orion) holds up a headless ram-horned serpent, which matches the terminus of the constellation Eridanus itself. In the Rig Veda we find an interesting description of the goddess drawn along in her chariot, inspiring the same imagery as that depicted on the last inner plate:

> *Her head was in the sky and her chariot was the wind.*
> *The two luminaries were the two beasts which drew Sūrya to the house.*
> *The two bulls pulled together yoked as one by the chanted verse.*
> *She listened to the two wheels as they turned along the path of the sky.*
> *The two luminaries were the wheels of her carriage whilst the axle was made of the wind.*
> *Surya went to her husband borne aloft her chariot impelled along by the wind.*
> *Rig Veda 10, 85, v 10*

CHAPTER NINE

# THE SOUL OF THE DRAMA

Central to Celtic religion was the concept of sacral kingship, the observance of rites that seasonally re-enacted the threefold death of the Celtic Dis at the hands of the elements: a symbolic perception of the changing seasons and the effects they manifested on the life cycle of vegetation. The underlying principle of the doctrine was that the king represented the mortal consort of the goddess of sovereignty.

## The Divine Play

The inner plates of the Gundstrup cauldron depict the rising and setting constellations of the night sky. These are the celestial scenes of a divine play that were seasonally re-enacted in the rites of sacral kingship in description of the Druidic cosmological lore. Just as the stars rise and set in the heavens, so the plates of the cauldron were read from right to left, the anti-clockwise reading of a clockwise rotational movement.

To fully understand the mythological narrative it would be wise to heed the words of Aristotle when he proclaimed: 'The mythos is the soul of the drama.'

The soul is the order of the narrative, which in this instance describes the ordered procession of the stars of the ecliptic in their seasonal movement. The mythos is the reading of the individual constellations, which become the acted scene when the full moon passes through them. We are fortunate in that the evidence of the Gundstrup cauldron helps us to interpret the soul of the play, while the written text surviving on the Coligny calendar reveals the mythos.

The mythological traditions shared within many of the cultural branches of the Indo-European family comprise of three distinct themes: the maiden's tragedy, the hero's quest and the cosmic battle.

The maiden's tragedy relates to the goddess in her aspect of the desired virgin, who is seduced by a god (usually the sky god) and then abducted to the underworld while pregnant with the child of the former deity. The story of the maiden goddess was only a single act in a seasonal drama. The full narrative concerning the goddess was recognized by the Celts in three parts: the spring maiden, the mother of summer and the winter crone.

The child of the maiden was the champion of light, who in his youth has to undergo a series of tasks before ascending into his rightful place. This was the hero's quest and describes the exploits of the hero who protects the source of light during its seasonal orbit of the constellations of the zodiac. To the Celts, this was the Celtic Mercury who championed the dual nature of the Celtic Apollo symbolized by the two ram-horned serpents. At Beltene he releases the winter sun Mabon, who transforms into Belenus. At Samhain he prompts the release of the soul of Belenus and ferries it to the circumpolar region where it remains in captivity as Maponus.

The cosmic battle involves a fight between the deities of light and the powers of the underworld over the beneficial resources of the earth. In Ireland the Tuatha Dé Danann confront the cthonic Formorions at Samhain during the Second Battle of Mag Tured ('Plain of Towers'), led by Lugh/Esus and the Dagdha/Taranis. In the Welsh tradition the same battle is described in the Cad Goddeu ('the Battle of the Trees'), where the children of the goddess Donn (equivalent to the Irish goddess Danu) fight against the god of the underworld, Arawn/Ogmios, and his champion Bran. Bran is the Celtic Mars, his name derived from bran, 'torch' or 'firebrand' (a tool that Smertrius holds in his depiction on the Paris column). The battle was fought because Amaethon (Apollo) had stolen three enchanted animals from Arawn.

In the The Battle of the Trees the gods of light protected the identity of the goddess Achren, 'of the woods'. In a variant on the same myth recited in the Mabinogi Lleu's wife is called Blodeuwed, 'flowerface', for whom he is overcome by Goronwy (Cernunnos). This relates to the magical reanimation of foliage during spring when the trees come to life and take part in the cosmic battle that follows.

Before the Second Battle of Mag Tured, two Druidesses promised to enchant the formorions so that, '..the trees and stones and sods of the earth shall become a host against them'. In the Welsh version, it was Gwydion, 'the one of the wood', who was accredited with the magical act:

> *I was at Caer Nefenhir when grasses and trees moved off.*
> *Minstrals sang, warriors marched.*
> *Gwydion lifted his magic staff.*
>
> *Book of Taliesin 24, v 1-3*

Gwydion was the Celtic sky god and so is to be identified with the Dagdha and his wheeled fork, the staff representing the thunderbolt. That the trees were brought to life by the thunderbolt of the sky god suggests a link with the birth of the Celtic Apollo as Maponus. In Welsh tradition Mabon was born of Madron ('the mother') and Mellt ('lightening'). This metaphor refers to the return of Apollo from his winter captivity, heralding the revivification of plants in spring, also described as the return of Amaethon from the underworld.

## The Characters

Using the lists of deities described by Caesar and the Viromanduans with reference to the insular sources, the following six characters may be discerned from the mythological narrative:

(i) Jupiter/Taranis/Sucellus/Dagdha/Gwydion – sky god with wheel/heavenly bull.
(ii) Minerva/Belisama/Nantosuelta/Boann/Achren – earth goddess born of the flood.
(iii) Mercury/Esus/Lug/Lugh/Lleu – champion god of light and protector of the sun.
(iv) Apollo/Belenus/Maponus/Bile/Amaethon – the twin ram-horned serpents.
(v) Mars/Teutates/Smertrius/Nuada/Bran – protector of Dis.
(vi) Dis/Cernunnos/Ogmios/Oghma/Arawn – vegetation god symbolized by the mistletoe.

## The Plot

From the list of characters given above, a number of scenes or events can be interpreted using the evidence of the Gundstrup cauldron to place them into their seasonal order.

### PLATE I

The birth of the Celtic Minerva from the head of the heavenly bull. described in terms of Esus releasing the three cranes from the bull Tarvos Trigaranus. In Ireland, this is remembered in the myth of Boann and the formation of the River Boyne – a metaphor for the celestial river the Milky Way, known in Gaelic as 'the path of the white cow'.

In the flood, Boann was transformed into a crane – a cosmic event remembered in the names of the goddess that allude to major rivers, and in the name Nantosuelta, 'the river covered'. By the sky god she is the mother of the Celtic Apollo.

### PLATE II

The sacrifice of the white Apollonian bull (or the decapitation of the ram-horned serpent) by Smertrius. An offering to the sky god for the return of Cernunnos as the seed of the heavenly bull (mistletoe berry). The soul of Apollo Belenus returns along the Milky Way to the land of the north for the winter.

### PLATE III

The sky god Taranis hands over the broken solar wheel (representing the weakened power of the sun at the winter solstice) to Esus/Lug 'of the long arm'. The identity of Esus as the protector of the sun is shown by the bull-horned helmet taken from the hide of the slain

Belenus, the victim of the first Tarbhfess. In return for the burning of Cernunnos, the sky god gives Esus the solar disc to draw northwards.

**PLATE IV**

Esus and Cernunnos fight in the form of lions. Esus pursues Cernunnos who is eventually consumed when the mistletoe stops producing fruit. This is the consumption of the berry as the milk of the goddess at Oimlec. Cernunnos retreats to the underworld, (symbolized by the dormant cycle of the mistletoe plant). At Beltene the imprisoned Mabon is set free by Esus. This is achieved when Cernunnos is hanged from a tree and the mistletoe comes into flower during the month of sprouting.

**PLATE V**

The sky god, as horseman, pursues the uncontrollable power of the summer sun as the ram-horned serpent. Cernunnos, as the god of vegetation, is scorched from the heat and has to be immersed in the vat by his immortal twin Smertrius, an act of sympathetic magic appealing for the summer rains to protect the crops during the 'dog days'.

**PLATE VI**

The goddess drives across the sky in her chariot, bringing the desired rains that tame the power of Belenus until he is eventually overcome again by Smertrius when the cycle renews itself at Samhain. This is depicted on the Paris column by Smertrius lifting the decapitated ram-horned serpent.

## Survival of the Myth in Folklore

It would seem impossible that all traces of the mythological narrative could disappear from the cultural memory of the descendant peoples of the free pagan Celtic world. Despite the imposition of the interpretatio Romana, the Celtic religion was merely exorcized of the harsher elements of Druidic practice, allowing the more moderate sects to survive. These acceptable neo-Druids operated a milder form of devotion, rejecting the abhorrent rites of human sacrifice for the milder ritual observance of prophetic healing. They not only survived the Roman conquest but flourished in the spring sanctuaries dedicated to the Celtic Mars, Mercury and Apollo.

It was the rapid growth of the new religion known as Christianity that finally rang the death knell for the old Celtic religion. Even the gods and goddesses of classical Rome were doomed after the abrupt conversion of Constantine signalled the imperial adoption of the new religion. Throughout the 3rd century AD, Christianity took on an unprecedented growth in all the principal urban settlements across the empire. The movement not only followed the trade routes but also the administrative structure of the empire, where conversions to the new state religion were often rewarded with a rapid progression through the hierarchy. By the end of the 4th century the empire had become officially Christian, with any adherence to the pagan gods considered not only heretical but also potentially treasonous.

During the 4th century, the pagan religion was already retreating into the relative safety of the rural areas. Even there, temples were periodically torched by evangelical missionaries like Martin of Tours (who usually required the assistance of a military escort to carry out this divine duty). But old customs are hard to die and faithfulness to the old religion remained in isolated areas. At the beginning of the 6th century AD Caesarius, Bishop of Arles, reported:

> *We have heard that some of you make vows to trees, pray to fountains, and practice diabolical augury. What is worse, there are some unfortunate and miserable people who are unwilling to destroy the shrines of the pagans but even are not afraid or ashamed to build up those which have been destroyed.*
>
> *Caesarius of Arles, Sermons*

At about the same time the people living in the area west of Massif Central still openly practised prophetic healing:

> *In the territory of Javols there was a large lake. At a fixed time a crowd of rustics went there and, as if offering libations to the lake, threw into it linen cloths and garments, pelts of wool, models of cheese and wax and bread, each according to his means. They came with their wagons; they brought food and drink, sacrificed animals, and feasted for three days.*
>
> *Gregory of Tours, Glory of the Confessors*

Gregory of Tours also reported how at the end of the 4th century Simplicius, the Bishop of Autun, witnessed the annual pagan ceremony of the image of the goddess Berecynthia being drawn by an ox cart 'for the preservation of fields and vineyards'.

So despite the encroachment of Christianity, the old pagan customs continued to be exercised among the rustics, but not just randomly. Outside the church, there still existed an alternative hierarchy of religious advisors, who the Christian clerics collectively knew as the arioli (ariolus in the singular) from aras, 'altar'. These arioli continued to operate at shrines in rural areas, where not just partially converted people would resort but also members of the clergy themselves. The arioli were said to worship beside altars of hideous idols and dispensed their skills in the arts of divination and medicine, much akin to the filidh of later Christian Ireland. They were also said to be magicians, augurs, diviners and soothsayers who still practised animal sacrifices while making incantations to the old gods. So priests of the old religion continued to ply their trade despite the restrictions placed upon them in the Theodosian code of AD 438, which made it illegal for any citizen to consult with an ariolus.

In Ireland and Wales, many of the Druidic teachings that were not repugnant to the new Christian philosophy were preserved in the oral teachings of the filidh and the bards. But by the time they were first written by Christian scribes (from about the 6th century AD) their original religious meaning had almost inevitably become lost to doctrinal re-editing. The names and deeds of the old gods had given way to cycles concerning semi-historical kings, but were always remembered in some form or other in the psyche of rural folklore.

Elements of the mythological story described on the Gundstrup cauldron I believe are preserved, albeit in a rather vague manner, in the fairy tale of Jack and the beanstalk, and the folk customs surrounding the celebration of May Day.

As previously suggested in Chapter 4, Hellequens was the surviving folk memory of the Gaulish god Ogmios. Similarly, the story of Jack and the beanstalk describes the exploits of the solar hero Lug and his acquisition of various objects from the realm of the sky god. We know that the original character Jack is one and the same as Jack the giant killer, preserved in the early folklore of Cornwall. This Jack was said to have carried a hammer and to have worn a bull hide with horns. If we remember, Esus is depicted on plate III with a bull-horned helmet.

In the fairy tale Jack has to part with a cow to acquire some magic beans. If the magic beans were originally the berries of the mistletoe then this suggests an identical myth with that of Esus surrendering the white bull to Smertrius, which had to be sacrificed to procure the berry from the oak tree. Jack then has to climb the magic beanstalk to the realm of the giant in the clouds, a metaphor for Lug ascending the Milky Way to the heavenly bull to release the goddess as the three cranes. In the fairy tale the goddess is remembered as the goose or hen that laid the golden egg. In other accounts, Jack retrieves a singing harp, reminiscent of Lugh accompanying the Dagdha after the Second Battle of Mag Tured to return the harp from the Formorions – an allusion to the freeing of Apollo Maponus at Beltene. Jack then chops down the beanstalk, similar to the depiction of Esus chopping down the oak tree on the Paris column and the Trier stone relief.

The myth also survives in the rustic traditions celebrating the arrival of summer during the May Day (Beltene) festivities. Elements of the folk customs practised at this time follow a formula that strongly resembles the ritual depictions on plate V, with the processional carrying of a totem tree and the immersion of a character representing the spirit of vegetation. The formula is described thus:

(i) A tree is chopped down and carried by procession to a desired location.
(ii) The tree is then trimmed, erected and artificially adorned with foliage.
(iii) There is then a race to the tree (or up it) to select the youth who is to represent the May king, variously known as 'green George', 'Jack in the green' or 'the little leaf man'.
(iv) The youth is requested to give an abundant harvest with offerings of food.
(v) The youth is then dunked into water, earning the right to soak anybody else.

The traditions behind the maypole ceremony indicate the underlying belief in a god of vegetation, who reveals himself in the first blossom of spring and is then ritually immersed into water with requests of rains during the following dry months of summer to promote the crops and keep good pasture for cattle.

These events, carried out on a single day (Beltene), coincidentally describe the rituals named in the Coligny calendar and depicted on the Gundstrup cauldron for the following months of summer. Hence during Giamonos, 'of sprouting', the vegetation god Cernunnos reveals himself on May Day (Beltene) as the blossom of the mistletoe. The next month describes the subsequent transformation of the goddess into a bird in the month Simivisonna, 'bird like song'. Then during the month of Equos, 'the moisturizing', the vegetation god is dunked into water by Smertrius to bring about the much-needed summer rains. Finally Cernunnos is ritually consumed as the offering of first fruits (the vegetation god in his animal form) during the feast of Lugnesad, 'the produce of Lugh' – that is, Cernunnos is consumed as the personification of the mistletoe flower infused in the mead of the goddess.

The identification of the mistletoe flower as an ingredient of the mead may be evident on a silver decorative plaque, from Barkway in Hertfordshire, which is decorated in a trefoil design. The plaque was dedicated to Mars Toutates by one Tiberius Claudius Primus, offering an oblation of 'a tincture of wine'. The trefoil represents the flower of the mistletoe, which was used by the Celtic Mars in preparing the sacred mead of the goddess and was thus the offering to the god who performed the initial rite. (see *Figure 40*).

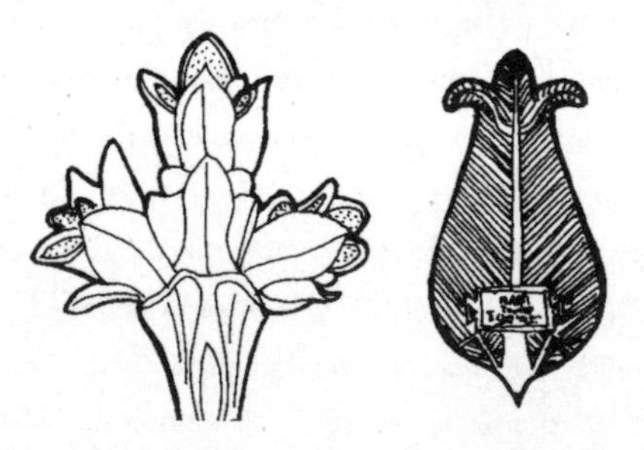

**FIG. 40.** *The mistletoe flower and the Barkway plaque.*

Lucan, in his Pharsalia, describes a number of legends that were attached to the rites performed at the sacred grove the Romans encountered near Marseilles:

> *Water also fell there in abundance from dark springs. The images of the gods, grim and rude, were uncouth blocks, formed of felled tree trunks. Legend also told that often subterranean hollows quaked and bellowed; that yew trees fell down and rose again, that the glare of conflagration came from trees that were not on fire; and that serpents twined and glided round the stems.*

The trees that were uprooted and rose again may refer to a ritual that involved the chopping down of a tree and its re-erection, similar to the setting up of the maypole. Indeed a marked characteristic of religious enclosures dating from the Late Iron Age is the presence of large timber-post-hole features set in the interior of the shrines. Some appear to be single large posts set up in the centre of the complex, others are arranged in a group – perhaps the construction of an artificial grove.

The allusion to trees appearing to be on fire might be explained if the leaves were artificial metallic ornaments, ceremonially suspended from the trees to catch the light of the sun or the glitter of fires. Evidence for such a practice could be suggested from the bronze leaves found in the sanctuary at St. Maur (Oise) and iron leaves with attachment rings from Villeneuvre-St Germain (Aisne). The legends recited by Lucan in describing the rites performed within the sacred grove ultimately share common elements with the later rural customs celebrating May Day.

## Evidence from Other Sources

In this book I have proposed a new theory for interpreting the inner plates of the Gundstrup cauldron, a theory based on the sequential order of rituals performed during the process of sacral kingship.

In order to corroborate these findings I have so far drawn on evidence from the insular sources and the accounts recorded by contemporary Greek and Roman writers, supported by references to the religious beliefs contained in the oldest Indo-European religious text, the Rig Veda. Apart from the ritual calendar from Coligny, the only other iconographical evidence I have concentrated on has been restricted to Gaulish coin issues and the Paris column. Now I would like to explore the evidence from other sources of Celtic art to find a recognizable formula of religious symbolism that hopefully supports my hypothesis thus far.

The first piece of evidence to examine is the engraved bronze and iron scabbard from Halstatt in Austria. Immediately it is possible to recognize the four horsemen depicted on plate

**FIG. 41.** *The Halstatt scabbard.*

**FIG. 42.** *Detail of pot from Sopron-Varishegy.*

**FIG. 43.** *Detail of pot form Sopron-Burgstall.*

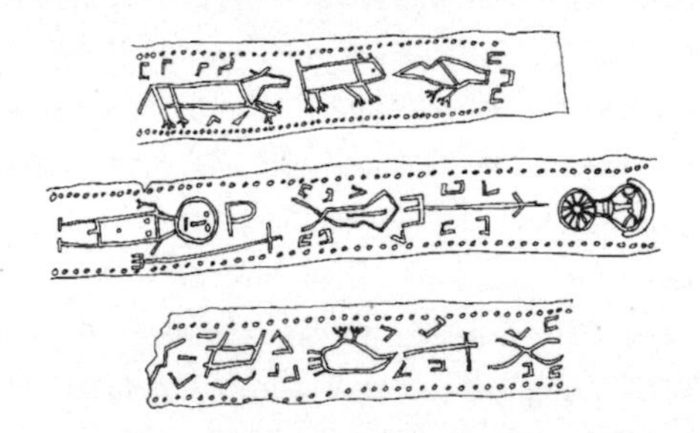

**FIG. 44.** *The Farley Heath sceptre.*

V of the Gundstrup cauldron. The image is bordered on both sides by the representation of Taranis handing over the wheel of the sun to Esus, featured on plate III of the cauldron. The significance of these two scenes only becomes apparent when we regard them as the constellations of Gemini/Dumanos ('silence') and Sagittarius/Simivisonna ('likened with bird song'), the two constellations placed at opposite positions in the sky (see *Figure 41*).

The next piece of evidence comes in the form of two pots dating from the 4th century BC from Hungary. The first pot is from Sopron-Varishegy. Following the images from right to left there is a sequence of events that corresponds to plates IV-VI on the Gundstrup cauldron. The narrative shows a stag (plate IV), a man riding a horse, two figures performing the immersion sacrifice (plate V) and the triple goddess (plate VI). The second pot, from Sopron-Burgstall follows the same section of the narrative, also read from right to left: a stag accompanied by other animals (plate IV), a mounted horseman with spear (plate V) and the goddess born aloft her wagon (plate VI). Both pots therefore seem to depict the constellations of the night sky between Beltene and Samhain (see *Figures 42* and *43*).

Both pieces of evidence so far date from the Halstatt phase (from circa early 7th century BC) suggesting that the cosmological lore expressed on the cauldron was already formulated during this period. To show that the mythological formula remained relatively unchanged during the ascendant period of Druid activity, we shall now turn to the evidence dating from the later La Tène period. Three more examples of the narrative can be confidently identified from this period in the form of two religious sceptres from Britain and the decorated pillar from Mavilly (Côte d'Or, France).

The terminal of a ritual sceptre was found among a hoard of religious bronzes at Willingham Fen in Norfolk, England. The images presented on the terminal shows the following reading from right to left: a triple-horned bull (plate II); the sky god standing on a head and an eagle perched on a wheel (plate III); the image of a dolphin/salmon (plate IV). From the Romano-British temple at Farley Heath (Surrey) comes a decorated sheet bronze sceptre binding displaying an entire sequence of stamped schematic figures. The narrative begins with the broken image of a bull with a bird at the terminal end (plate II). Next appears Esus in the guise of Vulcan with hammer and tongs, followed by the sky god with wheel and forked thunderbolt (plate III). Finally a stag is depicted alongside a hound and a bird (plate IV). (See *Figure 44*.)

The iconography depicted on the Mavilly pillar also follows the same narrative outlined on the cauldron. Dating from the reign of Claudius, the pillar describes a purely Celtic myth, though the characters are artistically classical in form. Unlike the Tiberian Paris column, the figures are not inscribed with names and may represent an attempt to express a Celtic religious narrative at a spring sanctuary during a period of increasing imperial intolerance towards Druidism (see *Figure 45*).

Reading from the top stone down, face A begins the narrative with Esus seated above the sky god, who has a bird perched on his right shoulder with the ram-horned serpent entwined about him. This would seem to refer to the birth of the Celtic Minerva, with the goddess transformed into a bird on the back of the sky god (represented on the Paris column as the heavenly bull Tarvos Trigaranus). The event was instigated by Esus, who rests his feet on the ram-horned serpent, similar to his image on plate III. Face A therefore corresponds to plates I and III of the cauldron, with any reference to the bull sacrifice on plate II remarkably absent, perhaps indicating a deliberate omission of the bloodier aspects associated with Druidic practices.

The entwining of the ram-horned serpent around the sky god reflects Lucan's statement concerning the legend of serpents gliding about the stems of trees in the grove near Marseilles. If we remember, Maximus of Tyre recorded that the Celts worshipped Zeus in the form of an oak. During Pax Romana the effigy of Taranis as an oak was evidently discontinued and replaced with an altar. Depictions of a ram-horned serpent entwined around such an altar can be found in Lypiat Park (Gloucestershire) and Mavilly (see *Figures 46* and *47*), with the same beast wrapped around a tree on the Lyon cup (see *Figure 48*).

Face B of the Mavilly pillar shows the descent of Esus into the underworld to retrieve the abducted Apollo. On the upper stone he is depicted as the victorious champion of light, while below him Cernunnos is seated holding a cup and accompanied by his hound (plate IV). The cup represents the mead of the goddess (which Cernunnos personified) and Esus stands in the background with his hands over his eyes as the goddess perches on the shoulder of Cernunnos, representing the rivalry between Lleu and Goronwy over the goddess. Face C describes the subsequent fate of the goddess. On the upper part of the face she is assimilated with the Roman goddess Fortuna, with cornucopia ball and wheel. The lower portion shows the goddess brandishing a torch and carrying the two Apollo serpents that she has gained from the underworld. The final face D depicts the goddess reproaching the advances of the bearded sky god above, while below she consorts with the Celtic Mars. In the background the ram-horned serpent slithers upwards, representing the spirit of Apollo Belenus ascending the Milky Way after the decapitation of the white bull by Mars Smertrius, thus reinitiating the whole sequence of seasonal events.

## The Outer Plates

Having suggested a plausible sequence for the inner plates based on the rites of sacral kingship and the order of constellations of the ecliptic they represented, the final task left to us is to attempt an interpretation of the depictions on the outer plates.

**FIG. 45.** *The Mavilly pillar.*

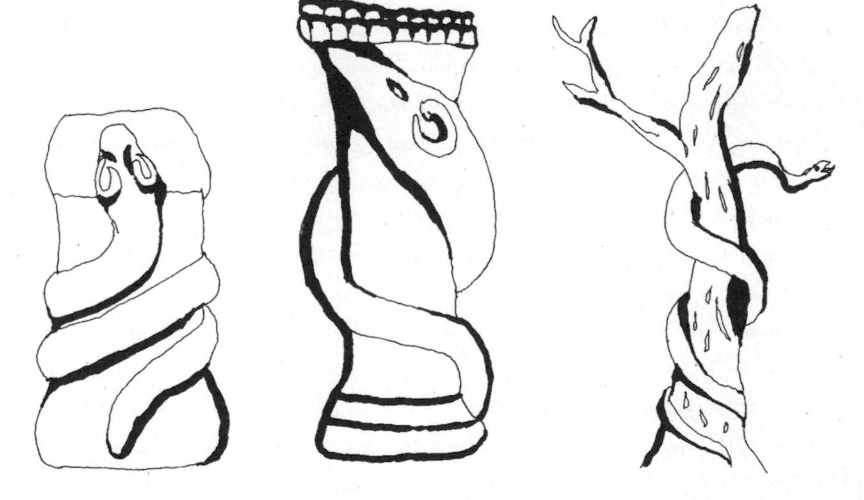

**FIG. 46.** *Altar from Lypiat Park.* **FIG. 47.** *Relief of altar from Mavilly.* **FIG. 48.** *Detail from the Lyon cup.*

It is difficult to form a coherent analysis since only seven of the original eight plates have survived in situ, but our first assumption must be that the outer plates support the narrative described on the inner plates. The composition of the plates also follows a uniform pattern: the large bust figure of a deity forms the focal point of a specific scene, while the borders portray images of events in miniature. In order to conform to the anti-clockwise reading of the inner plates from right to left, we must presume the outer plates were designed to be read from left to right (see *Figure 49*).

The first plate (A) in the sequence introduces the narrative with the three leading characters. At the centre of the plate is the large bust figure of the goddess. To her left is a clean-shaven youth wearing a torc, conforming to the image of Cernunnos without his antler attribute. To her right is a bearded god with a distinctive pendent, recognized on inner plate III as the sky god holding his distinctive wheel emblem. Hence the goddess is placed between the god of the underworld and the god of the sky. This links with the imagery on inner plates I and II, which describes the conception of the Celtic Dis as the seed of the heavenly bull and the birth of the Celtic Minerva from his head (see *Figure 50*).

Plate B introduces the two protagonists in the story. The bust figure of a bearded god wearing a torc is placed at the centre of the scene. On the left the Celtic Mars is depicted with his helmet, assuming the posture of a boxer or wrestler, which matches the equation made on the Paris column between Smertrius and Pollux. On the right Esus climbs a vine ascending to the otherworld (an image that resembles Jack (Lug) climbing the beanstalk), while below him Smertrius rides away on horseback. The scene reveals the Celtic Mars as champion of the underworld confronting Esus as protector of the Celtic Apollo, who ascends the Milky Way in pursuit of the spirit of Apollo Belenus, previously released by Smertrius's slaying of the white bull of Taurus. The bust figure in the centre probably represents the Celtic Mars (see Figure 51).

On plate C the bust figure of the goddess is portrayed with her arms folded, a posture of restriction. To her left Esus wrestles a lion, which, we surmised earlier, represents the Celtic Dis. To her right Esus climbs the vine again – having defeated Dis, he seeks the goddess in the underworld (see *Figure 52*).

Plate D reveals the bust figure of Esus holding up the two Apollonian serpents in the form of Hippocamps, while beneath him Cernunnos is devoured (see Figure 53). Plate E describes the transformation of the goddess into the form of a crane during the month of Simivisonna. Here she revitalizes Cernunnos with nourishment from her breast (see Figure 54). At the centre of plate F, Smertrius holds up the repeated image of Cernunnos (as the stag) by his hind legs. This mimics the headfirst immersion sacrifice described on inner plate V. This confirms the identity of the smaller figure being plunged into the vat as Cernunnos 'the headfirst one' (see *Figure 55*).

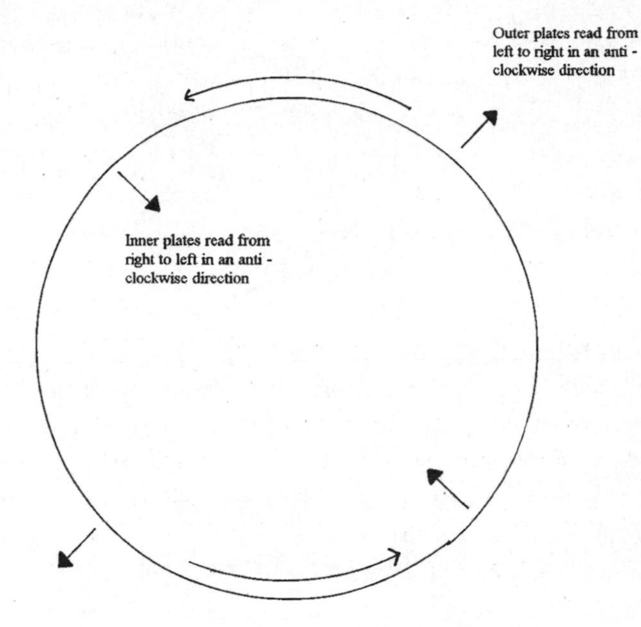


**FIG. 49.** *Reading direction of the inner and outer plates of the Gundstrup cauldron.*

**FIG. 50 (top):** *Outer plate (A).* **FIG 51 (bottom).** *Outer plate (B)*

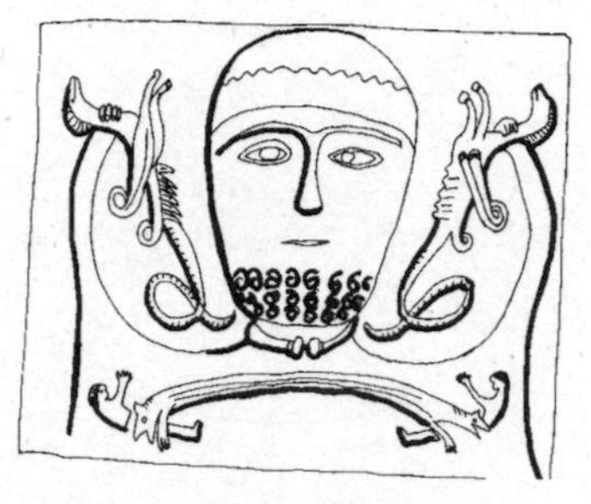

**FIG. 52 (top).** *Outer plate (C).* **FIG. 53 (bottom).** *Outer plate (D).*

**FIG. 54 (top).** *Outer plate (E).* **FIG. 55 (bottom).** *Outer plate (F).*

Finally, Plate G reveals the effects of the immersion sacrifice, symbolizing the rejuvenation of vegetation after the summer rains. Here Smertrius is the large bust figure at the centre of the scene, holding up the repeated image of the revivified Cernunnos, who is himself holding up a boar, the symbol of a martial victory. To the lower left of Smertrius, the hound reveals the identity of Cernunnos as the raised figure (similar to how the hound is depicted under the vat on plate V). At the bottom right of the plate the winged horse/griffin of Apollo Belenus retreats from the scene, symbolizing the waning power of the sun after the intense heat of the dog days (see *Figure 56*).

**FIG. 56.** *Outer plate (G).*

The position of the last plate can never be determined satisfactorily until we at least ascertain what was depicted on it, and so the story cannot be told with certainty from here. However, if we look at the same narrative depicted on the Mavilly pillar, the story ends with the goddess consorting with Smertrius prior to the bull sacrifice. On plate C, after the victory of Esus over Dis, the goddess appears with a double representation of the god. For the sake of composite balance, it would be tempting to speculate whether the last plate similarly marked the victory of Smertrius over Apollo, with his repeated image placed either side of the bust image of the goddess, possibly holding aloft the headless ram-horned serpent.

CHAPTER 10

# THE DRUIDIC LORE

When describing the ritual practices of the Druids most writers primarily draw on evidence from the classical and Irish sources, only cautiously approaching the rich supply of information provided by the traditions of Wales. Unfortunately the classical sources, although contemporary accounts, merely glance at the types of ritual performed. Even the most informative accounts, such as Pliny's treatise on the mistletoe rite, fail to explain the religious significance of Druidical acts. Instead they tended to concentrate on the more abhorrent rites involving human sacrifice, propitiated by a superstitious order of priests to satisfy their bloodthirsty gods. The emphasis on the barbaric nature of Druidism reflects the imperial policy of segregating and persecuting the renegade elements within the order, who failed to conform to Pax Romana.

I believe it is in the bardic tradition of Wales that much of the evidence for Druidic ritual practice is preserved, albeit embellished with later Christian symbolism. For this reason I shall draw specifically on the evidence presented in the enigmatic poems attributed to the Welsh poet Taliesin, who wrote during the 6th century AD, as a sample of just one of many bardic sources that are rarely cited.

Of the 58 poems ascribed to Taliesin, six in particular share a common theme in describing what appears to be the performance of a particular religious ritual, one that was preserved through oral transmission until it was first put into writing some time during the 10th century AD. The six poems we shall refer to are quoted in full in the Appendix (see page 193). They are: The Chair of Taliesin; The Ox-pen of the Bards; The Elegy of Uthyr Pendragon; The Spoils of the Deep; The Contention of the Bards; and The Battle of the Trees. When juxtaposed, the poems seem to relate an initiation rite that involves the taking of an oblation and the acquisition of poetic inspiration. This corresponds with the mysteries surrounding the goddess Ceridwen, 'the fair and loved', who was noted for possessing a cauldron from which 'awen', or poetic inspiration, could be obtained. The Druidical ceremony described in the six poems was held once a year, marking a pinnacle ritual event. It was intrinsically bound up with the concept of sacral kingship and involved the preparation of the mead of the goddess using mistletoe.

# Meet for a Sovereign

The last sentence in The Chair of Taliesin reveals the name of the ceremony, giving the first indication of the religious importance of the event: 'Meet for a Sovereign is the lore of the druids.' That is, a rite that was performed for the benefit of the king.

By cross-referencing the texts of the poems, I will now list the sequence of rituals in their apparent chronological order.

## SONG OF THE WESTERN CUDD

The Chair of Taliesin informs us that the ceremony commences with the lighting of a bonfire in honour of the god Dovydd ('of the water') among the assembly of those qualified to celebrate the mysteries. Then a bard who has knowledge of the 'Syweddydd' recites the 'song of the western cudd' within the stones. The term cudd means concealment, so we may suppose that the song is addressed to the setting sun as it descends below the western horizon into the sea, the realm of Dovydd.

In The Elegy of Uthyr Pendragon the same bard is referred to as the 'bardic proclaimer', the son and deputy of 'Hu with the expanded wings' – Hu being a corrupt form of Esus, whom we have encountered on Gaulish coin issues with the alternative name Ulatos Ateula. The bard is also called a Deon, or dean, a derivative of decan meaning 'of ten', suggesting that his office placed him in authority over 10 other bards. This bard then stands on a mound of stones, which we are told represents the earth, and recites 'the death song'. This is evidently an alternative name for the 'song of the western cudd', implying that the setting of the sun at the beginning of this ritual was regarded as the death of one aspect of the sun. So the ceremony would appear to address a particular mythological event.

The Ox-pen of the Bards describes that after putting on an excessive show, the bards assembled and began to sing while clutching their staffs. The staff was probably one of the three types of branch used to distinguish the grade of bard, much like the system used in Ireland among the filidh. The same song is mentioned in The Spoils of the Deep as 'the bardic lore', which is recited four times from the quadrangular enclosure:

*I will adore the sovereign, the supreme ruler of the land.*
*If he extended his dominion over the shores of the world,*
*Yet in good order was the prison of Gwair, in the inclosure of Sidhi.*
*Through the mission of Pwyll and Pryderi, no one before him entered it.*
*The heavy blue chain didst thou, O just man endure, and for the spoils of the deep,*
*Woeful is thy song; and till the doom shall it remain the invocation of the bards.*

The Spoils of the Deep then continues to describe how the cauldron is prepared at the same time the song is initiated:

*Am I not contending for the praise of the lore, if it were regarded,*
*Which was four times reviewed in the quadrangular inclosure:*
*As the first sentence, was it uttered from the cauldron,*
*Which began to be warmed by the breath of the nine maidens.*
*Is not this the cauldron of the ruler of the deep:*
*What is its quality?*
*With the ridge of pearls round its border,*
*It will not boil the food of a coward who is not bound by his sacred oath.*

'The nine maidens' refers to a sisterhood of nine virgin priestesses who specialized in the preparation of the potion of poetic inspiration. Most likely known as the Semnothoi or Semnitae, they wore black robes and worshipped the Celtic Dis as the Dionystic god of the mistletoe. The significance of the number nine and the lighting of the Beltene fires survived up until the 19th century in Wales, where the activity was left to nine youths. Early in the morning the youths would ascend a hill and cut a circular trench for a bonfire. Then they would collect wood from nine different trees and construct a frame, laying the wood crosswise over the trench. Each of the youths then took turns to ignite the fire, using two pieces of wood to create a spark. The one who could not ignite his piece of wood was singled out as the 'hag of Beltene' and probably represented the person who in times past would have been sacrificed in a similar fashion to one of the Semnitae described by Mela. The bonfire was known as the coel certh, or 'fixed assemblage', relating to the wooden frame that had to be ignited by the kindling wood, probably oak. The use of nine different types of wood reflects the tradition described in The Battle of the Trees (Cad Godeu), where Gwydion contrived the goddess Blodeuwed out of nine plants.

It is interesting to note that in a spurious work called the Barddas (a collection of Bardic lore edited during the 19th century, based on the works of a 16th-century bard), a similar practice is described in the use of Coelbrens or 'assemblages of wood'. They are described as finger-length blocks of wood (ebillion) with carved notches. The blocks were placed on a wooden frame known as a Peithynen, 'the elucidator', and turned so that the notches would join in various combinations, forming different letters. The turning mechanism was initiated by an 'axle-tree' called the Dasgubell Rhod, 'the wheel that plucks to the truth'. It would be tempting to think that the two rituals were related and described the myth behind the hidden identity of the goddess Achren ('of the woods') in the poem The Battle of the Trees.

The preparation of the mead and the incantation of the death song were addressed to the woefully imprisoned Gwair, 'the agitated one', an alternative name for Mabon/Maponus.

## THE AWAKENING

The second ritual is called 'the solemn festival between two lakes' in The Elegy of Uthyr Pendragon. A procession is led around the lakes, while the rest of the assembly invoke the 'gliding king', 'before whom the fair one retreats, upon the veil that covers the huge stones'. The 'gliding king' is the full moon rising to the east as the sun, 'the fair one', sets to the west. This rite is mirrored in The Chair of Taliesin, in which 'the silent proficient' animated 'the hero' by encouraging the bards 'to awaken the silent beholder, the bold illuminator of kings'. The 'silent proficient' appears to be another high-ranking bard who initiates another incantation to welcome the rising full moon, known variously as 'the hero', 'the gliding king', 'the silent beholder' and 'the bold illuminator of kings'.

## THE PREPARATION OF THE MEAD

The next stage of the ceremony involved the preparation of the oblation, which was variously perceived as the mead of the goddess of sovereignty, poetic inspiration, or 'the brine of Beli's liquor'. It is possible that the potion was an alcoholic beverage of mead or wine infused with a number of plants that had either religious importance or narcotic properties, or both. The Spoils of the Deep describes how the assembly stood on the walls of the enclosure:

> *in the island of the strong door, the twilight and the pitch darkness were mixed together,*
> *whilst bright wine was the beverage, placed before the narrow circle.*

'Strong door' was a widely used Irish pseudonym for the oak, while 'island' describes a demarcated area, perhaps denoting a kind of artificial grove formed from erected oak posts in the centre of the enclosure.

In The Chair of Taliesin a more detailed account of the procedure is given. A bard called 'the man of complete discipline' procures the 'mead of honour' and dedicates it to the god Dien. The offering comprises of assorted ingredients, listed as: wheat, honey, incense, myrrh, aloes, 'the gold pipes of Lleu', silver, 'the ruddy gem', berries, the foam of the sea and cresses. These plants are then washed in 'the fountain' before wort, 'the founder of liquor', is supplied by the assembly 'and a raised load secluded from the moon, of placid, cheerful vervain.'

## THE PROCESSION OF THE DRAGON

The next ritual involved the symbolic deposition of the oblation, which was apportioned into smaller vessels and placed into small pits, then covered with a cloth. The Elegy of Uthyr Pendragon describes the placing of the drink offering 'in the golden horns', but a more detailed account is given in The Chair of Taliesin, where 'priests of intelligence' and their assistants macerate and sprinkle the oblation before apportioning it into the smaller vessels (golden horns). There then followed:

> *the boat of glass in the hand of the stranger, and the stout youth with pitch and the honoured Segyffyg with medical plants from an exorcised spot.*

The 'boat of glass' was the smaller drinking vessel in which the potion was divided, the 'stout youth with pitch' was the brewer of the mead, and the Segyffyg – 'sickler' or literally 'the cutter by hand' – was the bard who collected the medical plants. Next The Elegy informs us that, 'the dragon moves around, over the places which contain vessels of drink offering.' The association of the dragon with the oblation re-emerges in the tale of Lludd and Llevelys, where the importance of concealing the oblation is tied to the transformation of the sun from Mabon into Beli.

## THE TAKING OF PLEDGES

This ceremony involved the taking of pledges between the bards, which ultimately decided if they were suitable to take the oblation. The poem The Chair of Taliesin describes how the bards form a procession, carrying primroses and the leaves of the 'Briw' (heather):

> *With the points of the trees of purposes and solutions and doubts, and frequent mutual pledges.*

That is, the pledges were taken when the adepts had been able to solve the doubts with the solutions offered by the trees of purposes. The Elegy of Uthyr Pendragon informs us that the cauldron would not boil the food of one who was not bound to an oath – that is, he could not take the pledge before the oblation because he could not solve the solution to a riddle with the trees of purposes.

Clues to what riddles must be solved by the bards are given in The Spoils of the Deep. Here we are informed of how the multitude stand on the walls of the enclosure 'with the ensign of the governor' and with 'trailing shields', ignorant of the meaning to the following triad of riddles:

*I On what day the stroke would be given, or*
*On what day the chief was appointed.*
*II What hour of the supreme day, Cwy would be born*
*and who prevented his going into the dales of the water; or*
*On what hour of the serene day the proprietor was born.*

*III. They know not the brindled ox, with the thick head band,*
*having seven score knobs in his collar; or*
*What animal it is which the silver headed one protects.*

## THE TAKING OF THE OBLATION

Once the pledges had been recited and confirmed, the initiated could then take the oblation. The Chair of Taliesin describes it in the following manner:

> *and with wine which flows to the brim, from Rome to Rosedd, and deep standing water, a flood which has the gift of Dovydd, or the tree of gold which becomes of a fructifying quality, when that brewer gives it a boiling, who presided over the cauldron of the five plants. Hence the stream of Gwion, and the reign of serenity and honey and trefoil and horns flowing with mead, meet for a sovereign is the lore of the druids.*

The poems inform us that five plants were used in the infusion. Wort is readily identifiable as the sweet liquor extracted from malted wheat, while vervain is cut during an auspicious phase of the moon. The 'gold pipes of Lleu' and the fructifying tree of gold probably refer to the mistletoe, which takes on a golden hue after being cut. Reference to the trefoil alludes to the mistletoe flower, which begins to bloom during the month of Giamonos when the Beltene festival occurs. The other two plants are merely described as berries and cresses. The berries of 'ruddy gem' might represent the rowan berry, a fruit recognized in the Irish tales as a food of the otherworld. In the tale of Diarmmuid and Grainne the rowan was described as one of the three foods of the gods. In the story of Fraoth it is a magical fruit guarded by a dragon which had the power to heal the wounded, add a year to a man's life and give the satisfaction of nine meals. The cresses could be any of the plants in the Cruciferae family, but possibly refer to the common garden cress.

## THE SACRIFICE

The Elegy of Uthyr Pendragon records the offering of a sacrifice after the oblation had been taken prior to sunrise:

> *Whilst the golden horns are in the hand,*
> *whilst the hand is upon the knife,*
> *whilst the knife is upon the chief victim.*

The Ox-pen of the Bards briefly mentions the macabre act with the proclamation:

> *Let the thigh be pierced.*

This sacrifice is a later bardic memory of the sacrifice offered to Esus, when the victims were suspended from a tree and ritually stabbed. I have previously suggested that this sacrifice probably occurred at Beltene for a number of other reasons. The few brief lines cited above seem to suggest the hypothesis may be justified.

## THE DAWN CEREMONY

The final ritual took place to greet the dawn and consisted of three distinct phases: the marking out of the stones; the declaration to the rising sun; and the closing feast. The Ox-pen of the Bards offers the most detailed account:

> *Let the rock before the billow be set in order at the dawn, displaying the countenance of him who receives the exile into the sanctuary, the rock of the supreme proprietor, the chief place of tranquility... Then let the giver of the mead feast cause to be proclaimed; I am the cell; I am an opening chasm; I am the bull Becr Lled; I am the repository of the mystery; I am the place of re-animation. I love the top of the trees, with the points well connected. And the bard who composes without meriting a repulse. But him I love not, who delights in contention. He who defames the adept shall not enjoy the mead. It is time to hasten to the banquet where the skilful ones are employed in their mysteries, with the hundred knots, the custom of our countrymen.*

The Elegy of Uthyr Pendragon closes with the final invocation:

> *Sincerely I implore thee, O victorious Beli, son of the sovereign Man Hogan, that thou wouldst preserve the honours of the honey isle of Beli.*

## The Quadrangular Enclosure

The quadrangular enclosure described in the bardic repertoire was usually called the Buarth Beirdd, 'the cattle pen of the bards'. This conforms with the evidence of such ritual sanctuaries in the archaeological record dating from the 4th century BC, found in both British and Continental contexts.

The boundaries to these sanctuaries were delineated by a simple ditch and bank, and were sometimes surmounted by a palisade on the inside. The interiors were kept clean of ritual debris such as bones and votive offerings, which were deliberately deposited in the surrounding ditch. At the sanctuary of Gournay-Sur-Aronde (Oise) the deposition of the bones in the ditches indicates the strict observance of a prescribed ritual formula: human bones were placed around the corners of the enclosure and cattle skulls were deposited on either side of the entrance. The different types of bone found suggests that a variety of animal were treated with particular religious discrimination; certain animals could be eaten during ritual feasts, while others were singled out for arbitrary sacrifice. Hence we find the best cuts of sheep and pig (like legs and shoulders), suggesting that these beasts were consumed on site. The remains of horses and cattle however, predominantly consist of skulls and vertebrae, indicating that the best cuts of the meat were consumed elsewhere.

The interiors to the sanctuaries had one of two types of structural activity at the centre. The first took the form of pits or post holes, which are usually interpreted as representing the socket holes that held large timber uprights or raised tree trunks – artificial groves like the 'island of the strong door' mentioned in The Spoils of the Deep. During the 3rd century BC the tradition of erecting small timber-structured shrines developed into the more complex constructions of the Gallo-Roman period. The later shrines consisted of an inner sanctum or cella, which contained holy objects or a spring. Around this was placed the ambulatory, so that ritual processions could take place around the sanctified place of the cella. The significance of an ambulatory in Druidic ritual practice emphasizes the importance of circumambulation. The poems of Taliesin describe no less then three such processions in one ritual festivity.

## A Beltene Ceremony

The ceremony described in the poems was an all-night vigil, starting with the descent of the sun as Gwair/Cwy and ending with its rising as Beli the next morning. This corresponds with the mythology surrounding the transformation of the weak winter sun into the stronger summer sun at Beltene. Diodorus describes the following account about the Hyperboreans, quoting from the Greek chronicler Hecataeus of Miletos:

*Leto was born on this island, and for that reason Apollo is honoured among them above all other gods. The account is also given that the god visits the island every nineteen years, the period in which the return of the stars to the same place in the heavens is accomplished. At the time of this appearance of the god, he both plays the cithara and dances the night through from the vernal equinox until the rising of the Pleiades, expressing in this manner his delight in his successes.*

The reference to Apollo dancing and playing the cithara from the end of March until the middle of May corresponds to the months of Cutios and Giamonos and incorporates the feast of Beltene. In Irish folklore it was said that the sun could be observed dancing at Whitsuntide, a possible allusion to the same phenomenon recorded by Diodorus. The ceremony of the poems was therefore synonymous with Beltene, celebrated when the full moon began to rise in Scorpio/Ophiucus when the sun was in Taurus/Orion.

The sun rising in the Pleiades is significant in that this is a cluster of stars situated within the constellation of Taurus. In the closing invocation of The Ox-pen of the Bards the bull Becr Lled is named as the place of reanimation – that is, the sun rising on the back of Taurus. This realization helps us to interpret the triadic riddle described in The Spoils of the Deep, which the bard was required to learn before he could take of the oblation.

The first riddle relates to what day of the year the stroke would be given for the king to be appointed, namely the serene day of Beltene. The next riddle asks at what hour of that day Cwy, the agitated one, will be born (that is the hour of sunrise on Beltene). The third and final riddle concerns the brindled ox with the thick headband and the seven-score knobs on his collar, the animal protected by the silver-headed one. This is the bull of Taurus, his headband being the cluster of stars known as the Hyades, while his collar is the Pleiades. The silver-headed one describes the moon, which represented the power of the Celtic Dis as god of the night in the same way that the sun represented Apollo. The importance of the timing of Beltene was the rising of the full moon in the constellation of Cernunnos as the serpent bearer – that is, holding aloft the Apollonian ram-horned serpent.

We know from the Coligny calendar that Samhain was celebrated during the three nights of the full moon, culminating on the 17th day of the month. In Ireland a similar tradition is recorded in relation to Beltene, in an account that tells of how the Milesians invaded the country on the 17th day of the moon. The Milesians were the descendents of Miled, the son of Bile (Beli), the basis of the myth referring to the arrival of Belenus during the full moon.

The 9th-century Cormac's Glossary describes the rites performed by the Druids at Beltene, when two bonfires were lit and cattle were driven between them in a ritual act of purification. In view of the evidence so far, this ceremony might reflect a type of sympathetic magic, the passage of the cattle driven between the flames being symbolic of the bull or ox of Taurus bearing the re-born sun at dawn on the first day of summer.

More clues to the rites of Beltene can be extracted from the famous poem sung by Amergin, 'of the wonderful mouth'. It is an often-cited poem full of enigmatic symbolism, which I believe relates to the Irish equivalent of the Beltene ceremony we have analysed in the poetic repertoire of Taliesin. It is important to note that Amergin was a Druid and that he recited the song when he first stepped foot on Ireland during Beltene, on the 17th day of the moon:

*I am the wind that blows over the sea,*
*I am a wave of the ocean;*
*I am the murmur of the billows;*
*I am the ox of seven combats;*
*I am the vulture upon the rock;*
*I am a ray of the sun;*
*I am the fairest of plants;*
*I am a wild boar in valour;*
*I am a salmon in the water;*
*I am a lake in the plain;*
*I am the craft of the artificer;*
*I am a word of science;*
*I am the spear point in battle;*
*I am the god that creates in the head of man the fire of thought,*
*Who is it that enlightens the assembly upon the mountain, if not I?*
*Who telleth the ages of the moon, if not I?*
*Who showeth the place where the sun goes to rest, if not I?*

The first six lines refer to the dawn ritual described in The Ox-pen of the Bards, where the stone is set 'beyond the billow', but here the rock has a vulture perched on it. The ox must be Taurus, with the epithet 'of seven combats' referring to the seven stars attached to his collar, the Pleiades. 'The fairest of plants' is the fructifying tree of gold otherwise called the 'golden pipes of Lleu' in The Chair of Taliesin. The boar in the next line relates to the sacrificial victim offered to Esus, the boar evidently replacing a human offering as pigs are usually hung when slaughtered. In The Battle of the Trees the sacrifice of the boar is also described:

> *The slaying of the boar; its revealing and hiding... the surrender of many limbs upon the tongue of my blade.*

The slaying of the boar and the cutting of its limbs is testified in the archaeological record from the large quantities of pig joints discovered deposited in the ditches surrounding ceremonial enclosures.

The next two lines of the song allude to the festivity between two lakes. In The Battle of the Trees the salmon is replaced by the speckled snake or adder on the hill (the hill represents the mound mentioned in The Elegy of Uthyr Pendragon). The Druids were known as the Naddred, 'the adders' by the later bards, a fact further identified in The Battle of the Trees with a description of their distinctive red cloaks.

The rest of Amergin's song relates to the taking of pledges among the gathered assembly. The 'spear point in battle' refers to the sprigs of the trees of purposes in The Chair of Taliesin, used effectively in the discourse over the triadic riddle. The artificer is the inspired bard and the mountain is the mound of stones that represents the world. Here the chief bard, 'the silent proficient', addresses the assembly with his knowledge of the rising and setting motions of the sun and moon.

## The Dragon and the Mead

In the tale of Lludd and Llevelys we come across a striking theme that directly relates to the ritual called 'the procession of the dragon' in the Welsh poems, where the oblation is ceremoniously deposited into small pits around 'the narrow circle'.

In the story a fearful scream resounds throughout the country on the night before Beltene every year. Llevelys advises Lludd to locate the two dragons responsible by digging a pit in the middle of the kingdom. He was then told to place mead into the pit and cover the top with a silk cloth. When the dragons become intoxicated, the king should imprison the dragons in a stone coffer and re-bury them at Dinas Emrys in Snowdonia. Four parts of the story associate it with the ritual 'the procession of the dragon':

(i) Both occur on the Eve of May/Beltene.

(ii) The scream of the dragons is reminiscent of the woeful cry of the imprisoned Apollo Maponus. This emphasizes the link between the dragons or snakes with the two-ram horned serpents.

(iii) In the ritual the mead is placed into pits around the narrow circle at the centre of the sanctuary – that is, the cella, around which the procession is made. In the story this is reflected by Lludd digging a pit at the centre of the kingdom and placing the mead into it.

(iv) The dragon in the ritual is moved over the place of the deposition as opposed to Lludd transferring them to Dinas Emrys.

A clue to the meaning of the myth is found in the iconography surrounding the cult of Cernunnos, explaining the symbolic relationship between the mead and the dragons and why they are intoxicated. The identification of Cernunnos as the Celtic Dis is a crucial clue to the puzzle. The initial finding of the two dragons underground suggests that they are in the realm of Dis, imprisoned in the underworld. Although captive, the dragons were well treated by Cernunnos, who is often depicted feeding the two ram-horned serpents from his lap. This helps us to understand why Caesar particularly identified him with Dis, the god of the beneficial aspects of the earth, whose seasonal death and consumption in the mead ensured the transformation of Apollo.

The story of Lludd and Llevelys gives us some insight into the original myth relating to the roles of the Celtic Mars and Mercury. The character Lludd is identical to Nudd/Nuada (or Mars Nodens), the divine twin of Dis who was also envisaged as his father through his role in maintaining the seasonal rebirths of his brother. The question of the identity of Llevelys in the Celtic pantheon is not as straight forward.

The Irish sources offer a possible clue. In The Second Battle of Mag Tured, the King of the Tuatha Dé Dananns, Nuada, steps down in favour of the more able champion, Lugh. This reflects the same relationship between Lludd and Llevelys, the Celtic Mars relying on the support of the Celtic Mercury. So Llevelys represents Lugh or Lleu. If this is correct, the name Llevelys might originally have been Lleu-elys, 'Lleu who announces' (from the Latin elicio), a title perhaps demonstrative of his role in discovering the whereabouts of the imprisoned Maponus.

## THE MYSTERY OF THE HUNDRED KNOTS

In The Ox-pen of the Bards we are informed that during the banquet that followed the dawn invocation, the 'mystery of the hundred knots' was performed.

Allusions to this ritual are also made in *The Elegy of Uthyr Pendragon*:

*Have not I destroyed a hundred forts?*
*Have not I slain a hundred governors?*
*Have I not given a hundred veils?*
*Have I not slaughtered a hundred chieftains?*

*And in The Spoils of the Deep:*

*I have gained a hundred spoils...*
*I have slept in a hundred islands,*
*I have dwelt in a hundred forts.*

Combined, these cryptic references appear to describe the exploits of the Celtic Apollo. The number one hundred is used to symbolize his frequent passage across the heavens.

The giving of a hundred veils and the sleeping in a hundred forts refer to the setting of the sun to the west, while the slaying of a hundred governors and chieftains, and the acquisition of spoils, is indicative of the triumphant sun rising from confinement in the underworld.

In the first section of The Elegy of Uthyr Pendragon the account of the hundred knots is interwoven with the story concerning the origin of the cauldron in the underworld. Here the Celtic Dis is called Gorlasser, 'the exhausted giant', the 'protecting prince in darkness, to him who presents my form at both ends of the drinking vessel'.

Gorlasser is also mentioned in the Welsh Triads along with his wife, Haearnwedd, 'she who is rich in iron', the parents of the three bravest men of the island of Britain. Haearnwedd is named after her cauldron, thus equating her with the goddess Ceridwen and her Pera (cauldron) in which 'awen' was brewed. The connection between Gorlasser and the cauldron is also described in the Mabinogi's tale of Branwen. In this tale we are told of how the King of Ireland first saw the cauldron near a mound by 'the lake of the cauldron'. It was carried on the back of a giant called Llassar Llaeasgyvnewid (Gorlasser) demonstrating why the giant was 'exhausted'. His wife is described as having the power to give birth every six weeks to a fully armed warrior who had great prowess in battle, an attribute reminiscent of the three sons of Haearnwedd.

We must now consider in what way the mystery of the hundred knots is tied in with the origins of the cauldron. The first rational observation to make would be that the term 'knots' implies the ritual of tying and untying. As regards the Beltene ceremony, this can only refer to the imprisoned Mabon, who was bound and fettered. So logically the last ritual act performed in the ceremony symbolizes the release of the Celtic Apollo from his bondage in the underworld prior to sunrise.

The cauldron was believed to have originated in the underworld. In the tale of Pywll, Arawn is described as possessing just such a cauldron. The hypothesis is also supported by the fact that after the ritual was completed, the vessel was symbolically returned to the infernal regions following the closing feast. Archaeological evidence shows that in the La Tène period the practice of ritually depositing cauldrons into lakes, springs and marshes was commonplace throughout the Celtic world. The manner in which they were deposited suggests two types of ritual tradition. The larger and more elaborate cauldrons tended to be deliberately dismantled before deposition, an act that symbolically killed the object in this world in preparation for its transference to the otherworld. The other form of deposition required the vessel to be buried intact, usually with a hoard of iron objects either in or around it.

Evidence for the breaking of cauldrons is also found in the Welsh sources. In The Chair of Taliesin we are informed of how the cauldron burst after the bard had tasted the three drops of potion that had contained poetic inspiration, rendering the rest of the brew poisonous. Similarly, in the tale of Branwen the cauldron is also broken into four pieces. Both accounts point to the belief that once the potion had been consumed in the ceremony, the receptacle had to be returned to the underworld as a reciprocal offering for the release of Mabon from his captor.

The sentiment of the ritual indicates the importance placed on secrecy surrounding the inner mysteries of the oblation, a theme common to many stories concerning Beltene and the use of the cauldron. In the tale of Branwen the otherworldly cauldron had the ability to reanimate the dead but they could not speak. In The Chair of Taliesin the consort of Ceridwen was Tegid Voel, 'the bald silent one', the Celtic Dis identified with the bald and aged Ogmios/Cernunnos/Gorlassar. The reference to silence alluded to the secrecy that the initiated were expected to observe after taking the mead of poetic inspiration.

CHAPTER ELEVEN

# THE BATTLE OF THE TREES

Although the subject of The Battle of the Trees is encompassed in the Beltene rites discussed in the previous chapter, the complexities attached to this particular subject are such that it requires a whole chapter of its own.

In The Chair of Taliesin we are informed of the ritual concerning the taking of 'mutual pledges', consisting of a circumambulatory procession in which the bards carried 'the trees of purposes, solutions and doubts'. These trees, or branches, appear to have served both a mystifying and a meaningful function related to a system of divination using wood. Their use was similar to the application of the ogham tree alphabet by the Irish and the Coelbrens by the bards of Wales, the latter showing a strong resemblance to the alphabetical characters inscribed on the Farley Heath sceptre (see *Figures 57* and *58*). The ritual use of this system was ultimately bound up with the mystical meaning of trees, which I believe described a cosmological story that survives in the text of Taliesin's enigmatic poem, The Battle of the Trees (Cad Godeu)

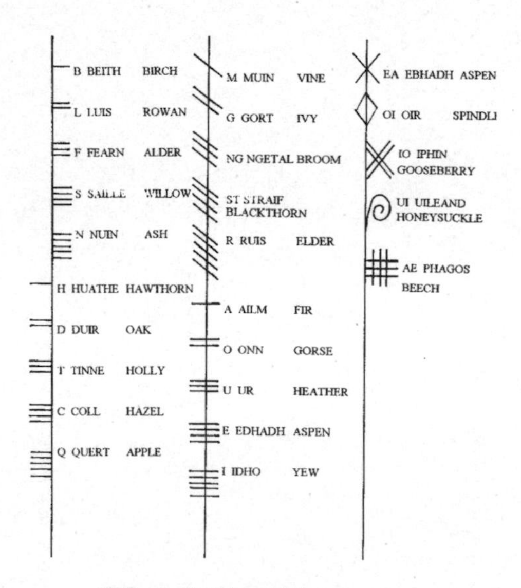


**FIG. 57.** *The Ogham alphabet.*

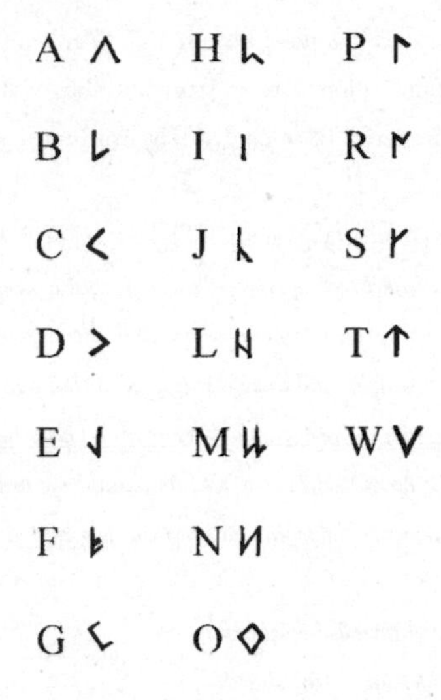


FIG. 58. *The bardic Colbrens and the script on the Farley Heath sceptre.*

## The Triad and the Englyn

There are three references to the battle of the trees in the medieval Welsh sources: an excerpt from the Triads, an englyn (verse) fragment, and the poem attributed to Taliesin. All three texts refer to the battle as an event rather then a ritual, which suggests that the ceremony was based on a well-known mythological event that was commonly believed to have instigated the use of trees for divinatory practice. Indeed, the name of one of the principal characters in the myth was Gwydion, 'the one of the trees', denoting his particular association with the story. Remember, also, that the Welsh term Gwydd and the Irish Fid were interchangeable words meaning both 'tree' and 'letter', demonstrating at the very least an early association between the name of a tree and its application in the formation of an alphabet.

The first reference, in Triad 84, describes the battle as being one of the three most futile battles that had ever occurred in the island of Britain. Futile because it was regarded as a battle fought between compatriots:

> *One of them was the Battle of Godeu. It was brought about by the cause of a bitch, together with the roebuck and the plover.*

The second text is a larger account published in the 17th-century Welsh antiquarian journal *Mynyvian Archaeology*. The publication date is late, but the content is generally accepted as representing the surviving fragment of an englyn that was once part of a larger medieval poem.

> *These are the englyns that were sung at the Cad Godeu, or as others call it, the battle of Achren, which was on account of a white roebuck, and a whelp, and they came from Annwn, and Amaethon ap Don brought them. And therefore Amaethon ap Don and Arawn, king of Annwn, fought. And there was a man in that battle, who unless his name were known could not be overcome, and there was on the other side a woman called Achren, and unless her name were known her party could not be overcome. And Gwydion ap Don guessed the name of the man, and sang the two englyns following:*
>
> *"Sure footed is my steed impelled by the spur;*
> *The high sprigs of alder are on thy shield;*
> *Bran art thou called, of the glittering branches.*
> *Sure hoofed is my steed in the day of battle:*
> *The high sprigs of alder are in thy hand;*
> *Bran thou art, by the branch thou bearest,*
> *Amaethon the good has prevailed".*

This extract gives us more information than the few details contained in Triad 84, though they both seem to have shared a common source. The englyn does omit the plover as one of the animals abducted from the underworld, while the Triad fails to mention any of the characters involved in the story. The general theme of the myth surrounds the abduction of three animals from the world of the Celtic Dis, Arawn ('the silver tongued') by Amaethon. In reprisal for the abduction, Arawn raised an army under his champion Bran, while Amaethon was supported by the gods Gwydion and Lleu. The latter is mentioned as participating in the battle in another context, where he is alluded to as Huan ap Don, from Hu/Esus.

The allusion to understanding the names of the man and the woman on each side was the apparent aim of the battle. Bran was recognized by Gwydion by the sprig of alder he carried. The identity of the woman was not betrayed but her name Achren, 'of the woods', suggests that she too could be recognized if her tree sprig was likewise identified. The battle was therefore a war of words, where the names of trees were used to disclose hidden meaning. In ritual terms, the battle was a mythological precedent whereby bards would use sprigs of different trees in a religious discourse. This ritual is to be identified with the taking of mutual pledges in The Chair of Taliesin, where the trees of purposes were used to settle solutions and doubts. A cryptic discourse associated with the triadic riddle described in *The Spoils of the Deep* (the spoils being the three animals that Amaethon abducted from the underworld).

Among the Romans the term 'elicio' was used to describe the policy of acquiring the secret names of foreign gods, affording spiritual domination to complement the physical subjugation of conquered peoples. Elicio actually means 'to denounce' and, as previously mentioned, was used as an epithet for Lleu in the tale of Lludd and Llevelys, where Lleu-elys denounced the location of the two screaming dragons at Beltene.

In the Triads we are told of two types of interrelated rituals concerning the hiding and revealing of sacred bones as talismanic charms. The first was ancudd, 'to reveal' or 'disclose' and the second was cudd, 'to conceal' or 'hide'. The Chair of Taliesin describes how the Beltene ceremony commenced at dusk with the 'song of the western cudd', a reference to the setting sun as Mabon during the night of the ceremony. This is the concealing act of the ritual. The ancudd or 'revealing' must then logically apply to the rising of the sun the next morning as Beli. In The Ox-pen of the Bards, the rising of Beli was celebrated as being in the place of tranquility, the bull Becr Lled (Taurus).

If the englyn fragment does contain elements of bardic tradition, we should expect to find some reference to the cudd or ancudd of the sun during Beltene. Our only clues come from the identification of the six characters described – the same number of deities who existed in the Gaulish pantheon according to both Caesar and the two Viromanduans. If my theory concerning the identification of a Druidic zodiac on the inner plates of the Gundstrup cauldron is correct, we should be able to apply that evidence to an interpretation of the religious symbolism used in the englyn.

Thus Amaethon ascending from the underworld with his spoils alludes to the sun rising as Apollo Belenus on 1 May. In The Ox-pen of the Bards, the location of his rising was identified as Taurus in the form of the bull Becr Lled, the bull of seven combats in the song of Amergin and the bull with the thick headband in *The Spoils of the Deep*.

In the englyn fragment the only mythological act disclosed to us is that Gwydion is the mounted sky god who reveals the identity of Bran because of his sprig of alder – also called a 'glittering branch'. I contested previously that the name Bran comes from a word meaning 'torch' or 'firebrand', in allusion to the tool he is depicted holding. On the Paris column Smertrius (the Celtic Mars) clutches just such a firebrand as he wrestles with a headless ram-horned serpent. In Britain Mars was also equated with the alder (as Bran is in the englyn) in an inscription dedicated to the god Mars Vernostonus, 'of the illuminating alder' – a reference to the glittering branches of Bran in the myth. So if Bran is to be identified with Smertrius, we have an astronomical observation of the sun rising above the raised arm of Orion.

The disclosure of the sun is described in terms of Gwydion riding on his steed as he reveals the identity of Bran. This reflects a constant theme in Celtic iconography, where the mounted sky god accompanies the serpentine Apollo. On the Jupiter giant columns of eastern Gaul, the sky god rides behind a snake-limbed creature, rendering the same narrative depicted on plate V of the cauldron where the four horsemen pursue a ram-horned serpent. According to my interpretation of the narrative, this represents the Celtic sky god as the constellation of Sagittarius. The mythological meaning would then be understood as the sun rising in Orion/Taurus as the full moon sets between Ophiucus and Sagittarius.

The englyn fragment also relates to the hidden identity of the lady Achren, 'of the woods', who represents the goddess. The only information we have concerning her is that she is on the side of Gwydion, Lleu and Amaethon, against the forces of Arawn and Bran. An unexpected clue to her identity comes from a description of the first use of ogham contained in the Irish book of Ballymote. Here Lugh is warned that his wife was in danger of being abducted to the underworld:

> *Your wife will be carried away from you seven times into the Underworld or to some other place, unless she is guarded by birch.*

In the ogham alphabet, the letter 'B' was symbolized by the birch tree. If we relate the cryptic clues given in the englyn fragment, the abductor would be Bran and the abductee Achren, the wife of Lleu. In the Mabinogi the wife of Lleu is recorded as Blodeuwed, 'flowerface', so named because of the nature of her creation by Gwydion and Math:

> *So they took the blossoms of the oak, and the blossoms of the broom, and the blossoms of the meadow-sweet, and fashioned from them a maiden, the fairest and most graceful that man had ever saw.*

'Achren' was a title rather than a name, describing that she too was to be identified by a sprig of wood. But unlike Bran, her identity is unfortunately not revealed. In order to discover her tree symbol, we must once again look to the Irish evidence for the first use of ogham.

Birch is one notch in ogham. The account states that this was written seven times to reveal the message about the abductor and abductee. The abductor was known to be Bran, revealed by the three notches of the alder. The remaining four notches must therefore denote the identity of the abductee, the goddess (see *Figure 59*). In ogham the letter 'S' is written by four notches revealing the goddess as the tree of that letter, Saille, the willow. Saille/Salis, is cognate with the name of the goddess as Sulis (who is equated with Minerva on at least three inscriptions from Britain and Gaul). Hence, the wife of Lleu was seasonally abducted by her lover Goronwy/Cernunnos.

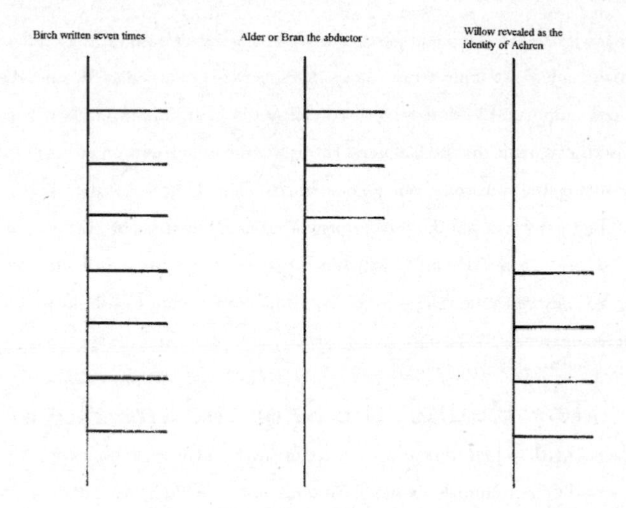


**FIG. 59.** *Birch written seven times.*

As the ogham alphabet was invented by Oghma, the logical conclusion would be that the Celtic Dis was represented by the birch, the first letter of the script. Also the book of Ballymote tells us that the goddess was protected if she was guarded by birch, the tree of the god of the underworld giving her a talismanic shield against his champion. The silver bark of the birch may have been alluded to in the name of the god as Arawn, 'the silver tongued', expressing the initial use of ogham confined to strips of birch bark.

Another enigmatic poem recorded in Mynyvian Archaeology refers specifically to the birch as the tree of the god of the underworld and the oak as that of the sky god. The poem is entitled Tribam Milwr, 'the procession of the kindred':

*Saplings of the green-topped birch, which will draw my foot from the fetter.*
*Repeat not your secret to a youth.*
*Saplings of the oak in the grove, which will draw my foot from the chain.*
*Repeat not your secret to a maiden.*
*Saplings of the leafy oak, which will draw my foot from prison.*
*Repeat not your secret to a babbler.*
*Golden princes with their horns are heard, cold is the breast plate, full of lightening air,*
*briefly it is said, true are the tree sprigs.*

The details contained in the poem particularly address the release of Mabon from his chained imprisonment, which we know from *The Spoils of the Deep* occurred at Beltene. We are also told that the oak is important in disclosing or revealing the Celtic Apollo, a fact that must be kept secret from youths, maidens and babblers. The 'golden princes with their horns' are the initiate bards who drink the oblation from golden horns (The Elegy of Uthyr Pendragon), having understanding of the true-speaking tree sprigs that are 'the trees of purpose' in The Chair of Taliesin. The 'breast plate' (Irish; lorica) was a generic term for a protective charm, and the 'lightening air' describes the disclosure of Bran's identity by the Celtic sky god as Gwydion in the englyn fragment.

## The Hound, the Stag and the Plover

Having discussed the characters involved in the myth, we must now turn to the religious importance of the three animals abducted from the underworld by Amaethon, namely the white roebuck, the whelp bitch and the plover. Previous attempts at explaining their symbolic meaning have centred on the theme of animals acquired from the underworld by a divine hero for the benefit of mankind: the hound for hunting, the stag for game, and the plover for its association with the bringing of rain. If Amaethon was the Celtic Apollo, his emergence from the underworld with the three animals describes a celestial event; the sun (Amaethon) rises to the east at dawn as the stars (the three animals) descend in the west. The understanding that the battle of the trees took place as part of the Beltene ceremony is crucial to our deciphering the symbolism surrounding the three animals, thus giving us an exact place in time from which to work.

If the Gundstrup cauldron's iconography does identify a lost Druidic zodiac the sequence of constellations setting at dawn during Beltene should reveal the three animals.

On analysis, the three consecutive months surrounding Beltene on the Coligny calendar correspond with the three animals mentioned in the Triad extract and the englyn fragment. The bitch is the hound of Cu-tios, 'the house of the hound', representing the constellation of Libra. The white roebuck is the stag-antlered god Cernunnos, represented in the constellation Ophiucus, the month of Giamonos or 'sprouting'. The next month is Simivisonna, 'likened with bird song', in allusion to the plover, the goddess transformed into a bird. This corresponds to the full moon in Sagittarius when the mounted sky god as Gwydion denounces the identity of Bran/Orion as the place where the sun will rise on Beltene morning, the plover represented by the constellation of Cygnus.

## The Battle of the Trees (Cad Godeu)

I will now attempt to tackle the perplexing poem attributed to Taliesin, breaking it down into sections to afford commentary and hopefully direction. The first section describes the series of transformations that Taliesin has had to undergo in his role as the embodiment of poetic inspiration:

*I have taken on many forms, before a better state assumed.*
*I was a sword's slender tongue, I shall see by its gleam.*
*I was a raindrop from the sky.*
*I was a glittering star.*
*I was a word in a book, I was conceived in that book.*
*I was the light of a torch, for a year and a day.*
*I was a bridge that spanned, three score rivers.*
*I was an eagle in flight.*
*I was a boat on the sea.*
*I was a smiter in battle.*
*I was an infant's swaddle string.*
*I was a hand-wielded sword.*
*I was a protecting shield.*
*I was a harp's plucked string, for a year in which to sing, amidst the bubbling waters.*
*I was a sprig in the fire, I was a tree in a thicket.*
*In all forms I have assumed.*

The next passage describes a foreboding of the approaching battle and the vision of a beast, which probably represents the Apollonian ram-horned serpent:

*I have fought though weak, before the numerous fleets, of the chief of the Britons, in the battle of Godeu Brig.*
*Unseeing bards proclaimed, warning of the beast, of ferocious temperament, and its screaming head.*
*From the back of its throat and the depth of its tongue;*
*Another battle had begun.*
*Upon the beast's limbs are a hundred claws, a speckled crested serpent, to scorch the skin, of a hundred woeful souls.*

The numerous fleets are the masts of the ships of Bran's invasion of Ireland. In the Tale of Branwen we are told how the invading host were spotted by Irish sentinels, who reported the spectacle to their king in the following terms:

> *... a wood was growing in the sea, and beside the wood a mountain ridge in the middle of it, and two lakes, one at each side. And wood and mountain moved towards the shore...*

As we shall soon discover, this reveals the location of the Beltene ceremony described in the poems of Taliesin. The mountain ridge was the sacred mount of Snowdon and the two lakes are those that stretch out in the wooded valley of Nant Gwenant on its southern slopes. The movement of the fleet and the mountain describes the growing shadows cast by the rising sun on the morning of the ceremony. In the sheltered valley we come across the sanctuary of Dinas Emrys, the site where the two dragons were concealed by Lludd. As Lludd is identical to Bran (the Celtic Mars), the concealment refers to the setting of the sun in the constellation of Orion at the beginning of the ceremony. The masts of the invading fleet are the tree sprigs carried by the bards preparing to perform the ritual of 'the trees of purposes'. The beast described in the above passage is none other then the Apollonian serpent Beli, who is transformed as a result of the ceremony and purifies the skin of the initiated with his warm rays. This was the site of Godeu Brig, 'the exalted trees'.

The next section of the poem deals with the formation of the trees into their order of battle or, more precisely, the ritual sequence in which the different tree sprigs are used in the discourse relating to the triadic riddle described in *The Spoils of the Deep*. The poem continues:

> *I was at Caer Fefynedd, where the trees and grasses moved, understood by outsiders, the warriors were confused; at the renewal of conflicts, that Gwydion had composed.*
> *Appealing to the sky, for the saviour's deliverance, the all-powerful lord, if only he responded.*
> *By magical craft and charms, the chief trees were arrayed.*
> *The warriors were stricken, ignorant of how to fight.*
> *The trees grasped hope, for they were enchanted, surrounded the camp fires, to give no respite.*
> *Three together is best,*
> *They encircled in content, one of them related, the story of the flood, another of the execution, and one of the reckoning to come.*

In the original text the saviour and the execution are given as the person of Christ and his crucifixion, a later rendering of the Celtic Mercury as the hero and the hanging sacrifice that was offered to him. The basic theme of the ritual seems to follow this pattern: The site is called Caer Fefynedd, 'the enclosure of the swarm', in reference to it being surrounded by the circumambulatory procession of bards carrying their tree sprigs. These are the 'outsiders' who have understanding of the trees and the triadic riddle. The 'warriors' are the uninitiated bards who repose by the campfires, awaiting their induction into the mysteries. Then three of the outsiders approach the warriors about the triadic riddle.

One of the riddles, 'the reckoning', relates to the day of reckoning, which probably does not reflect the biblical event but rather the Druidic conception of the apocalypse. Strabo recorded the cosmological belief held by the Druids that at some time or other the souls of man and the universe will be destroyed by fire and water. In *The Spoils of the Deep* this is described as the mystery surrounding the brindled ox or the constellation of Taurus, in which sign the sun sets at dusk into the western sea. The second riddle concerns the 'execution', termed in *The Spoils of the Deep* as the day on which the stroke is given and the chief is appointed. The final riddle concerns a flood and should correspond with the riddle described in *The Spoils of the Deep* as 'the hour in the serene day' Cwy would be born and who prevented him from going into the water.

The next section of the poem deals with the sequence in which the different tree sprigs are used during the ceremony. The first tree is the alder, the tree of Bran that was recognized by Gwydion in the englyn fragment. This possibly relates to the riddle concerning the flood, as Bran was the son of the sea, 'ap Llyr', and Amaethon is prevented from returning to his realm by the intercession of Gwydion. The next tree is the willow, the tree of the goddess Achren, and relates to the riddle concerning the reckoning. The goddess was envisaged as transforming into a water bird after the cataclysmic flood, as in the legend of Boann. In the englyn fragment she is represented by the plover (the bird that brought forth rain). In Gallic tradition, she is the crane associated with the heavenly bull Tarvos Trigaranus from whose head she was born. The last of the first three trees is the rowan (luis in ogham), which I believe represents Lleu/Lugh, to whom the sacrifice is offered during the ritual. The sequence follows thus:

*Alders in the front row, the hostility they began, willow and rowan behind them, but slower to begin.*
*The plum tree had, the love of man lost; with vigour had earned it, much like the medlar.*
*Hordes of spectres hid, in the shade of the bean; the raspberry committed, an unripe fruit disdained.*
*Thriving under shelter, the ivy was in season with the privet and the honeysuckle.*
*The gorse was battle proven, from the black cherry's rebuke.*
*Decidedly but slow the birch began to stir, through no lack of valour, but because of its girth.*

*The fir appeared to be, a strange and savage tree.*

*Of the majestic pine, I gave much praise to its prowess in battle, before kings it is raised.*

*Its vassals are the elms, which yielded not a pace but from a great distance, delivered to its aim.*

*The hazel famed in wisdom, the apple likewise made, the yew a dowry had in berries its due paid.*

*The blackthorn and the mulberry; both chieftains proud in war the beech alone did prosper, whilst others moved before.*

*The dark green holly, with courage it abounds with prickly limbs around it, hands departed.*

*The poplars well endured, though battered in the fray, the ferns were badly plundered like the brooms and their spray.*

*The hawthorn was in a frenzy, until finally constrained.*

*The heather gave respite, placed people at their ease before the reed had arrived and swiftly gave chase.*

*The oak began to turn, the sky and earth did shake, against the foe his name declared, strong door post in his wake.*

*Bound together and contained, the elder was consumed in flame, other trees were cast aside, due to holes they had sustained.*

*The vine stirred in a fury, with violence it dispensed.*

*The ash was dark and cruel, when the chestnut quietly withdrew.*

The poem now changes theme and describes the effects of the battle, first in terms of an apocalyptic destruction by fire and water, then the beginning of a new order in the aftermath:

*There will be great darkness, the mountain will quake, there will be a purifying fire, but first a great wave, with cries born in its wake.*

*The top of the beech will sprout, from a withered state anew.*

*The tops of the oak were strangled, the great door uttered a groan.*

*The apple was of a happier nature, nurtured beside the rock.*

After the 'reckoning' the strength of the oak is replaced by the beech and the apple. The tree of the Celtic otherworld of Avallach (or Avalon) thrives as the symbol of the reborn Apollo.

The next section covers the creation of the goddess described in seasonal allegory as the rebirth of Blodeuwed and the preparation of the mead:

*My flesh and blood neither, of mother or father formed: but from nine kinds of nature,*

*from the fruit of fruits, from the fruit of the divine, from mountain primrose blossom,*
*from the buds of trees and shrubs, from the soil of the earth.*
*By Math was I contrived, from the blossom of nettles and the water of the ninth wave.*
*Gwydion enchanted me, great tree of the Britons, before I was immortal.*
*From many mysteries, from Math and his learned kind, from the excellence of splendour, from the golden mead.*

The poem then describes the various faculties expected of the bard, interlaced with ritual procedures that the adept must undergo during the taking of the pledge:

*Half consumed by flames the king revealed to me, knowledge of the stars, of stars before the earth was I born.*
*Renowned bards by tradition, recite the epics of their land.*
*I played in the twilight, I shared the enclosure with Dylan of the sea, reclined between two royal knees:*
*The storm's stream descended, from the sky to the deep, like two blunt spears, let loose violently.*
*Four score hundred verses, of neither old nor young; the poems from me parted, upon their pleasure sung.*
*Of nine hundred songs are known, about the blood stained sword, noble direction will inspire me, the lord rewards with knowledge.*

The next few lines discuss the sacrifice, which originally would have been the hanging execution propitiated to Esus:

*The slaying of the boar; its revealing and concealing, with wisdom and words.*
*The splendid light, its numerous rays that shower fiery embers from the sky to the deep.*
*I was a speckled snake on the hill; I was an adder in the lake; I was a dim lit star; I was the weight of a dew drop.*
*Red is the colour of my cloak.*
*Before four score clouds,*
*I foresee without duress, the fate of all who envisage this, the surrender of many limbs upon the tongue of my blade.*

Reference to the adder alludes to the Druids, who were known to later medieval bards as the Naddred, or 'adders', the red cloak being part of their garb, overlapping a white tunic. The hill is the mound of stones, which represents the earth from where the opening recitation of the death song took place.

The last few lines close with a description of the sky god Gwydion, mounted on his steed, followed by an introduction to the mysteries of the hundred knots:

> *Noble is the yellow-maned steed, but a hundred paces his stride, my pale coloured mount is swifter than a bird, for it cannot overtake me, between the shore and the sea.*
> *I am proven in fields of blood, a hundred spoils gained, the gems of my ring are red, the edge of my shield is gold.*
> *My equal has not been born, to confront me in the ford; excepting Goronwy, from the dale of Edrywy.*
> *Long and white are my fingers, I was a herdsman long ago, across the earth I wandered, before I became learned.*
> *I have travelled far and wide, I have made the circuit, I have slept in a hundred islands, I dwelt in a hundred enclosures.*
> *O knowledgeable druids, of Arthur they divined, or was it I they proclaimed, and the execution of the hero, the imminent day of reckoning, and the story of the flood.*
> *With my golden charm set in gold, I am offered royalty, I am the feat of splendour, born from the craft of the Feryllt.*

After the description of the hundred knots we are told of how the Druids sought the knowledge of Arthur. If it was Lleu/Esus who is referred to, then Arthur may translate as ar-taur, 'the one before the bull', in allusion to the god's depiction in the circumpolar stars standing before the heavenly bull Tarvos Trigaranus. The triadic riddle is then described, closing with the importance attached to the feryllt for the successful completion of the ritual.

CHAPTER TWELVE

# THE SACRED CENTRE

Caesar informs us in De Bello Gallico that the Druids of Gaul held an annual assembly in the forest of the Carnutes 'at a consecrated spot'; a location they regarded to be the centre of Gaul. During this assembly the Druids met in conclave under the guidance of an arch Druid who 'held chief authority amongst them'. The function of the assembly appears to have been judicial, settling private and public disputes pertaining to issues of inheritance, succession, territory and crime. We are also told of how a new arch Druid was usually elected to the primacy at the death of his predecessor, although at times this was resolved by force of arms when the Druids 'of pre-eminent standing' could not acquire a clear mandate in the election.

## The Cosmological Division of the Land

In Ireland the division of the land into five provinces appears to follow a precedent reflected in cosmological lore, which describes the partition of the cosmos into four parts, placed around a fifth sacred point. Indeed, the Irish word for province, coigdh, means 'fifth'. The fact that such a cosmological belief was held I believe remains preserved in both the Irish sources and in the description of Ireland supplied by Ptolemy, the 2nd-century AD geographer.

In the Irish Lebor Gabala Erenn ('The Book of the Invasions of Ireland'), a sequence of mythological invasions are listed, which describe the cosmological significance of the number five. The development of Ireland during each successive invasion describes the geographical changes brought on the landscape in terms of the clearing of the plains and the formation of lakes – a metaphor for the creation of the universe.

The first invasion was under Cessair, the daughter of Bith ('life'), the son of Noah. The biblical connection with Noah is evidently a later Christian interpolation based on the connection of the myth with a cosmic flood, which ended this settlement phase. The Druidic conception of an apocalyptic deluge is recorded by both Strabo and the triadic riddle of *The Spoils of the Deep*, and refers to the myth surrounding the inundation of the goddess in the creation of the cosmic river. In Ireland, therefore, Cessair is another name for the goddess Boann, the wife of the Dagdha, and equivalent to the Gaulish divine couple Nantosuelta and

Sucellus. The name Cessair possibly translates as 'she who has yielded' – that is, surrendered to the waters of the cosmic river.

The second invasion was under Partholon, 'the divider', so called because he cleared four plains and created seven lakes from the one great primordial plain that existed after the flood. The division of four may then refer to the ordering of the seasons in the year, with Partholon representing the transitory nature of the Celtic Apollo as the power of the sun. The creation of seven lakes relates to a lunar reckoning of time, being the seven days of a lunar week.

The third invasion was instigated by Nemedh, 'the encloser', who was said to have cleared 12 plains and created four lakes. The 12 plains would thus represent the 12 constellations of the ecliptic in which the procession of the sun is enclosed, while the four lakes describe the four principal quarter phases of the moon.

The last two invasions describe a proto-historical record of later Celtic settlements on the shores of Ireland. The arrival of the Tuatha Dé Dananns marked the beginning of the fourth invasion. These were the gods of the Irish tales, the pantheon of gods who surround the goddess Danu, identical to the Brythonic goddess Donn. Although this possibly does not relate to a physical invasion, it does suggest the imposition of a new order of gods of a particularly British and Gaulish nature. The final invasion surrounds the arrival of the Milesians who drove the old gods into the underworld and redefined the central province of Midhe, a later account of the collapse of paganism before the arrival of Christianity.

Geoffrey of Monmouth gives an alternative account of the division of the universe in his Vitae Merlini. Although Geoffrey's historical detail is spurious, he did base his works on the concurrent Brythonic tradition. In one account he describes how Telgesianus (Taliesin) taught Merlin about the creation of the universe out of four elements, the division of the land into five parts and the threefold partition of the heavens.

A further piece of evidence for a cosmological precedent describing the division of the land into five comes from Ptolemy's geographical account of Ireland during the 2nd century AD. The details contained in his description not only confirm the division of Ireland into five provinces at this point in time but also confirm the age of the Ulster cycle as dating back to a late La Tène oral tradition. Using the names of the five provinces and their ritual centres from the Irish sources, we find that Ptolemy's account shares more than just a passing resemblance:

| Direction | Province | Ritual Centre | Tribe |
|---|---|---|---|
| North | Ulaidh/Ulste | Emain Macha/Regia | Volunti |
| West | Connacht | Rath Chruachan/Regia | |

| Direction | Province | Ritual Centre | Tribe |
|---|---|---|---|
| South | Mumhan/Munster | Sidhedhruim/Ivernis | Iverni |
| East | Laighin/Leinster | Dun Ailinne/Dunon | Dumnoni |
| | | | |
| Middle | Midhe/Meath | Tara/Laberos | |
| Centre | Uisneach/Macolicon | | |

Although the earliest texts of the Ulster cycle date from the 10th century, the style of writing and language suggests they were based on a source predating the 7th century. Even here, the historical details that the narratives contain indicate they were recounting tales from a much earlier period preserved in oral tradition.

There are three reasons for supposing the Ulster cycle to have been in existence prior to its earliest surviving format. First, the tales are ostentatiously pagan with no reference to Christian customs. Second, the cycle describes the political structure of Ireland as consisting of only five provinces, a condition that predates the 4th century AD when the greater province of Ulster was dissolved into three separate kingdoms. Third, the heroes of the tales are termed eirr or 'charioteers'. The chariot as a weapon of engagement was already out of use in Gaul for at least a generation before Caesar's conquest in the mid-1st century BC. In Britain the importance of chariots survived until the 3rd century AD, when the Picts employed them to carry out swift raids on the relatively unprotected region south of Hadrian's wall. In Ireland the latest use of chariots dates from about the same period.

The Ulster cycle describes Ireland as consisting of five political provinces, each with a royal seat, which were not so much residencies as uninhabited ritual sanctuaries used only for ceremonial functions. This fact has been confirmed by archaeology, where no evidence of occupational debris has been found on any of the excavated royal enclosures.

Looking at the table above, we may observe how both the evidence from the Ulster cycle and Ptolemy testify to the fivefold division of Ireland dating from at least the later phase of the La Tène period.

## Totem Trees and Screaming Stones

Uisneach, unlike the other five tribal centres, was entirely a religious site with no political bias shared with the other provinces. In Ptolemy's description Uisneach is called Macolicon ('the place of gathering together') and is located in the true centre of Ireland, much akin to the consecrated spot of the Gaulish Druids in the territory of the Carnutes. At Uisneach the Druids (and later the filidh) met under their elected leader once a year, during Beltene. This was the Mordhail Uisnigh, 'the great assembly of the naval'. The use of the term 'naval' suggests a similar cosmological belief shared with the Greeks, that the centre of a country was considered to be an omphalos that connected the earth with the realm of the sky.

At Uisneach all five provinces of Ireland converged on a large outcrop of stone (about the size of a house) known as 'the stone of divisions', the sacred naval of the entire country. As the Druids gathered there at Beltene, 'the stone of divisions' possibly served as the mound of stones described in the poems of Taliesin, which we are told represented the earth during the ritual.

In the Irish Dinnschenchas we are told how all the fires of Ireland were extinguished on the eve of Beltene and could only be rekindled by Druids from the sacred fire lit during the ceremony held at Uisneach. Caesar informs us that the Druids were exempt from taxation but does not give any details about their ability to impose religious taxes. Hence at Uisneach, Druids were taxed the price of a pig and a sack of corn to acquire a torch from the Beltene fire. In the poems of Taliesin, the pig was the object of sacrifice, which replaced the ritual of hanging victims offered to Esus.

Other aspects of the ritual observed at Uisneach included the driving of cattle between two bonfires, which I believe re-enacts the rising of the sun in the constellation of Taurus on the morning of Beltene, and the activity surrounding one of the five sacred trees (bile) situated there. The ash of Uisneach was the bile of the Midhe (Meath). However, the kings or high kings of Meath were supposedly inaugurated beneath the bile at Tara. A discrepancy suggesting that the bile had to be seasonally carried between the two centres. A ceremony similar to that portrayed on plate V of the Gundstrup cauldron where a procession of warriors carry a tree at the point of their spears. The natural assumption must therefore be that the bile was a moveable totem, a kind of maypole that was transported in ceremonial procession to the royal enclosure at Tara to re-enact the inauguration of the king every Beltene.

The Dinnschechas describes the five sacred trees of Ireland:

> *The tree of Ross and the tree of Mugna and the ancient tree of Dathi and the branching tree of Uisenech and the ancient tree of Tortu, five trees are those. The tree of Ross is a yew, the renown of Banbha, the spell of knowledge and the king's wheel, a princes right, a straight firm tree, a firm strong god. Now the branchy tree of Belach Dathi is an ash… Now the tree of Mugna is an oak; three crops it bore every year: apples, goodly, marvellous, and nuts, round red, and acorns, brown ridgey. The tree of Tortu was an ash… Due northward fell the ash of Uisenech.*

Lucan possibly alludes to the ceremonial carrying of biles when he recited the legends surrounding the sacred grove felled by Caesar near Marseilles. In the legend he describes how yews were felled and mysteriously rose again – that is, the raising and planting of totem poles.

In the above account of the sacred trees, the tree of Mugna was said to bear three types of fruit: apples, nuts and acorns. This may refer to the dressing of the trees with foliage and fruits, in the same way that maypoles were originally decorated.

Archaeological evidence for such a ceremonial practice has come to light at Emain Macha (Navan Fort, County Armagh), the royal seat of Ulaidh or Ulster. The ritual complex consists of two internal circular structures placed within a bank and ditched enclosure. Site A to the west is now a ploughed out banked enclosure. Site B to the east is extant however, and consists of a mound surrounded by a bank. Excavations of site B revealed the existence of a timber-framed circular structure, 40 metres in diameter, made up of four concentric rings of regularly spaced post-holes. This uniformity is only interrupted by a widened passage extending from the entrance (to the west), leading to the centre. At the centre a post-hole was discovered, some 5.5 metres in diameter, which contained the remains of an oak post sunk to the depth of 2.8 metres. The tree rings preserved on the stump indicate that the tree was felled when it was 200 years old, and when erected possibly stood some 13 metres high.

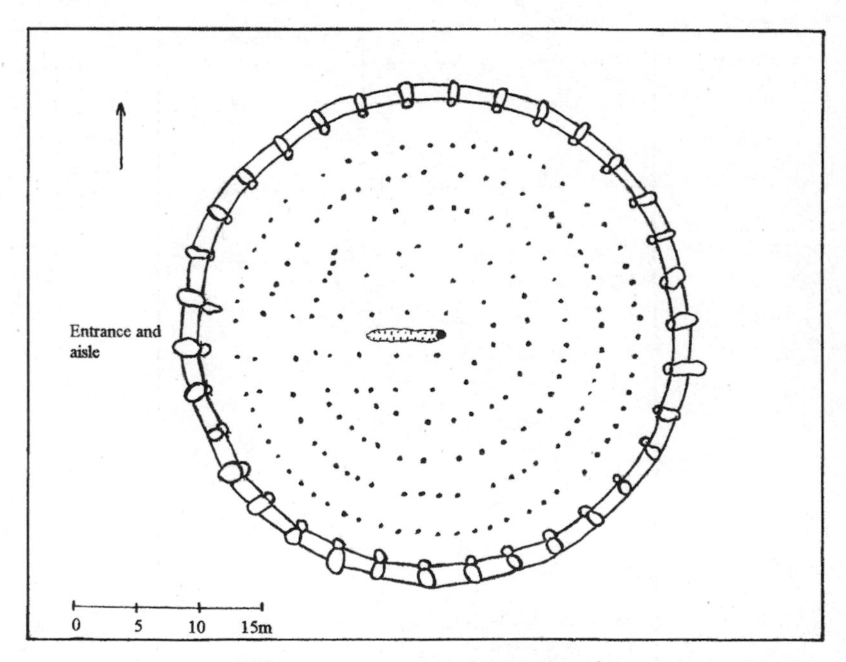


**FIG. 60.** *Site plan of Emain Macha, the royal seat of Ulster.*

What is significant is the remains of a sloping ramp dug into the side of the post-hole in the direction of the widened passage and entrance (see *Figure 60*). The fact that the central post was not apparently erected until after the completion of the building suggests that it served no structural function. The widened passage and the sloping ramp into the post-hole indicate the presence of a ritual that involved the raising and lifting of an oak post. It could be that these are the remains of the oak of Mugna, the sacred bile of the province of Ulaidh, left in situ after its 'felling' with the arrival of Christianity.

The royal seat of Tara in Meath is a ceremonial complex consisting of some 40 monuments. The focal point of the site is the Rath na Riogh, 'the fort of kings', an enclosure of 5.9 hectares bounded by a bank and internal ditch similar to that found at Emain Macha. At the centre of the enclosure stands a conjoined ring work comprising a bank and ditched mound to the west, known as Tech Cormac ('the house of Cormac'), and a ringed sub-enclosure to the east, called the Forradh ('the royal seat'). (See *Figure 61*.)

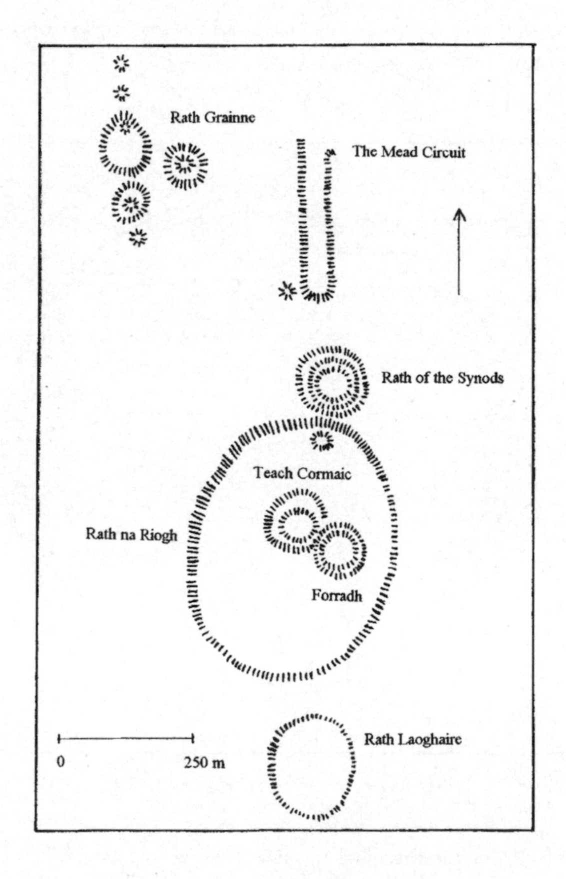


**FIG. 61.** *Site plan of Tara, the royal seat of Midhe.*

The legendary Lia Fial, 'the stone that betrays', still stands on the Tech Cormac, indicating that this part of the monument was related to the final trial endured by the royal candidate prior to his inauguration. Here he stood before the stone and touched it. If it screamed aloud, it betrayed the nominee as the true and rightful king. The function of the Forradh is suggested by its name as the place where the king sat beneath the bile of Meath – that is, the tree of Uiseneach, which must have been ritually carried to the site.

The relative positions of these two ritual sites – a mound and a ring work within a banked and ditched enclosure – resembles the two monuments present at Emain Macha. They are described in Taliesin's poems in the form of the mound of stones and the narrow circle. As the 'song of the western cudd' was sung on the mound, this may give us a clue to the true meaning of the Lia Fial screaming aloud – namely that the king touches the stone prior to sunset on Beltene Eve.

The ceremonial centre of Connaught was situated at Cruachain, a site demonstratively different to the comparative seats of Ulster and Meath. The ceremonial complex here consists of 49 separate earthworks arranged in rows and avenues known as the Religh na Righ, 'the royal cemetery'. The complex focuses on the largest mound of the group called the Rath Cruichain, the royal seat of the legendary queen of Connaught, Mebdh, the personification of the goddess of sovereignty. The word Rath means both 'fort' and 'wheel', which is interesting since the mound of Rath Cruachain was constructed in the shape of a petalled wheel, with sloping lobed banks radiating around the circumference of the monument. The association between the wheel and the site of the inauguration of kings is not altogether surprising, considering that the wheel brooch was the most important ornament in the king's regalia – the badge of his office, so to speak.

The second largest mound in the group is the mound of Daithi, the supposed burial site of one of the last kings to rule at Tara prior to the arrival of St. Patrick. Surmounting this mound is a 7 feet-high standing stone similar to the Lia Fial of Tara, which is 6 feet high. Perhaps this represents another Lia Fial, which was used during the inauguration rites for the kings of Connaught. The name Daithi also suggests that the bile of Belach Dathi may have been situated here.

The bile of Leinster was the tree of Ross and was probably located in the royal seat at Dun Ailinne (County Kildare). Similar to the enclosure at Tara, this precinct is oval in shape with a bank and internal ditch enclosing some 13 hectares. In the last phase of the site the focal point of ritual activity surrounded a circular feature on a low-lying mound towards the centre of the sanctuary. The function of the site is unclear, other than evidence that burning had taken place. This was of a ceremonial nature as no occupational debris or evidence of a hearth were found during excavations. The circle was surrounded by a ring of large posts and regularly spaced pits around the outside of the perimeter wall. The poems of Taliesin describe the placing of the apportioned mead in similar pits around the narrow circle, leaving us with the tempting hypothesis that an identical ritual was performed here (see Figure 62).

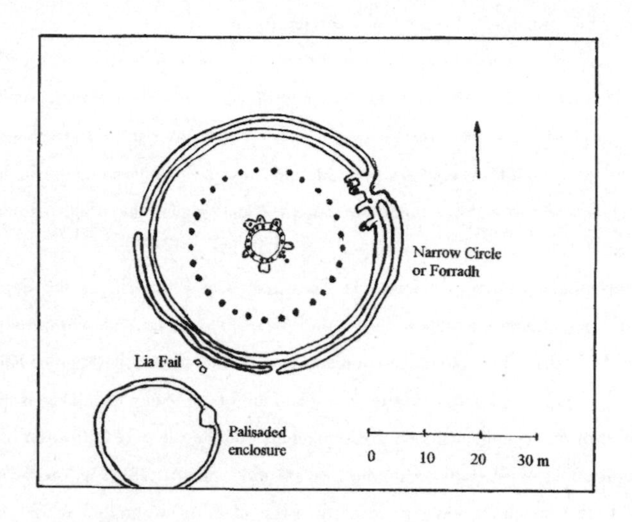


**FIG. 62.** *Site plan of Dun Ailinne, the royal seat of Leinster.*

The royal seat of the fifth and last province, Munster, was situated on the site of the old Cathedral in Cashel (County Tipperary), on the famous rock that overlooks the market town. The royal precinct was formally known as Sidhruim, 'the ridge of the mound', prior to the building of a stone fort or 'cashel' on the site during the 5th century. The original name alludes to the presence of a mound comparative to the mounds situated in all the other provincial centres. In the grounds of the ruined cathedral a stone cross rests on a granite block, on which all the kings of Munster were said to have been crowned since their conversion to Christianity. Local legend has it that this was the true Lia Fial, but most probably it was one of several Lia Fial, its function as a speaking stone becoming redundant when St. Patrick converted Oengus, the last pagan king of Munster, who promptly built the fort on the sacred enclosure and reused the stone as a throne.

Thus there appears to be three Lia Fial still located in their ritual contexts, namely those of Tara, Cruachain and Cashel. The stone of Emain Macha may have stood in site A, where the remains of a large socket-hole was uncovered in the epicentre of the ring work. At Dun Ailinne to the south west of the mound, in an area disturbed by post-Iron Age activity, the remains of two pieces of granite lay on the ground beside a widened pit. This is just outside a small, circular, palisaded structure, contemporary with the structure on the mound. Could this be what is left of the Lia Fial of Leinster? Wrenched from its palisade enclosure and left lying on the ground where it was later quarried. Its sacred importance had been forgotten along with the rituals that were once performed around it.

## 'The Chosen Father'

The cosmological division of Ireland into fifths was completed with the spiritual seat placed in the geographical centre of the country at Uisneach, 'the naval'. In Caesar's description of Gaul he mentions the annual assembly of the Druids, which was convened in the territory of the Carnutes at a location that was also perceived to be the centre of Gaul. This would appear to be the composite equivalent of the annual meeting of the Irish Druids at the Mordhail Uisnigh held during Beltene.

The Coligny calendar informs us that the Gauls held their own version of the Feis Temhra ('the feast of Tara'), which met every third year. On the calendar this event was referred to with the name of the intercalary month Ciallos Buis ('the gathering together').

This assembly was evidently different to the annual meeting in the territory of the Carnutes and as it was probably associated with the rites surrounding a high king, its possible location was in the territory of the neighbouring tribe, the Aedui. At the time of Caesar's conquest of Gaul, the Aedui were the principal political force in the country. Under their king, Divitiacus, who was also a Druid, the Aedui expediently sided with the Roman cause against a coalition of tribes who were under the tutelage of their traditional enemy, the Arverni.

If Divitiacus was the high king of Gaul then the equivalent of Tara would have been held at the sanctuary in the principal oppidum of the Aedui, Bibracte. A clue to this hypothesis lies in Ptolemy's description of Ireland, where Tara is named as Laberos, 'the place of booking'. The name Bibracte has an almost identical meaning – 'the place of direction from the book'. The use of the word 'book' probably relates to the activity of recording accounts, which Caesar informs us was practised by the Druids (who used Greek letters for the purpose). It must also be noted that the Coligny calendar was found within the tribal territory of the Aedui.

The assembly site of the Druids in the territory of the Carnutes is usually believed to have been located in the vicinity of Chartres. However, the principal oppidum of the Carnutes before the Roman invasion was located near Cenabum (Orléans), situated on the northern most bend of the river Loire. The location of the assembly in this vicinity is perhaps indicated by the testimony of Caesar himself.

In books VII and VIII of De Bello Gallico, the Gaulish revolt of 52 BC is described in detail. The revolt was instigated by the meeting of tribal leaders 'in secluded woods' in the proximity of Cenabum. The discussions culminated with the delegates representing the Carnutes declaring they would strike the first blow against the Romans. The other tribal leaders applauded the declaration and 'stacked their military standards together', a solemn act that bound military alliances between tribes in the presence of the Celtic Mars as Camulos, 'of the pile'.

The revolt began with the Carnutes attacking the Romans at Cenabum. The leaders of the offensive were the Carnutian king Conconnetodumnus, and one Gutuater. Gutuater, 'the chosen father' is a title rather than a name and alludes to the arch Druid of the assembly situated near Cenabum. Hence we find a power struggle erupting in Gaul between the pro-Roman Divitiacus and a confederation of tribes bound in opposition under his religious rival, Gutuater, and his political rival Vercingetorix, king of the powerful Arverni.

The revolt was inevitably short-lived and was crushed the following year. Caesar went to extraordinary lengths to capture Gutuater, who had gone into hiding. He was eventually found and surrendered by his own people. The angst felt by the legionaries was such that the protection of Caesar himself was ineffective. Gutuater was flogged to death and beheaded, a demonstration of how political activists amongst Druids would be dealt with in the future.

In the aftermath of the revolt the site of the assembly was probably moved to Bibracte, where it was reformed into a collegium. Tacitus records that the collegium of Bibracte was later moved to Augustodunum (Autun) which was established by the emperor Augustus in 12 BC. In the same year, Augustus reformed the administration of Gaul with the creation of a new provincial council at Lugdunum (Lyon), to be held annually on 1 August – the old Druidic feast of Lugnesad. This was a ploy aimed at extinguishing the political independence of the Druids once and for all. The religious emphasis of the native Lug was replaced with the cult of the living emperor and significantly the cult was first presided over by the chief priest of the Aedui, who was quite possibly the Gutuater of the Druidic college that still existed in Autun at that time. But the days of the Druidic college were numbered and was most likely dissolved during the persecution of Claudius. Evidence for the location of the college at Autun is found on two inscriptions from the city. Both were offered to the god Anvallus 'the unveiled one' by an officiating Gutuater.

The folk memory of the Gaulish sacred centre apparently lived on in bardic lore, from which Geoffrey of Monmouth drew one of the supposed prophecies of Merlin in the Vitae Merlini: 'A marvellous maid will come from the Nemus Cenutum for the healing of nations.' Nemus Cenutum was a later corruption of Nemus Cenabum, 'the grove at the place of communion'.

# The Place of Dragons

Sacred centres existed in both Ireland and Gaul. Evidence that other such centres existed is supported by Strabo's reference to a comparative site in Galatia. During the 3rd century BC, some 20,000 Galatae crossed into Asia Minor at the request of the king of Bythinia. After a period of consolidation the Galatae created their own tribal territory founded on the sacred centre of Drunemeton, 'the oak grove', where the Galatian council convened to celebrate the re-unification of the three tribes. With the existence of extra tribal ritual centres occurring apparently wherever the Celts settled, one must assume that similar assemblies must have taken place on the British mainland. In the Ravenna Cosmography two possible sites are cited at, Medionemeton, 'the middle grove' in the region of the Antonine wall; and Vernemeton, 'the great grove', located at Willoughby in Nottinghamshire. In the Welsh tale of Lludd and Llevelys the importance of two other sites are described in reference to the discovery and concealing of the two screaming dragons.

The first site is Oxford, which Lludd discovered to be the exact centre of his kingdom where the two dragons were concealed. A possible location for this site is the ritual complex situated on the summit of Lowbury Hill (Oxfordshire). Long regarded as a site of religious importance dating from at least the 1st century AD. Here there are several earthworks including a rectilinear enclosure and a mound similar to those described in the poems of Taliesin . Excavations have also revealed the presence of irregularly spaced shallow scoops dug into the chalk which have been interpreted as either sockets for raised tree trunks or the replanting of trees to create an artificial grove.

After revealing the dragons, Lludd transported them in a stone coffer to Dinas Emrys in north Wales. The historical importance of this area to the Druids is confirmed by Tacitus, who recorded the siege and fall of the last Druidic stronghold on the island of Mona (Anglesey). The presence of Druids in this locality was substantiated in 1943 with the discovery of over 150 metal objects found ritually deposited in the lake of Llyn Cerrig Bach. The assortment of items had come as far a field as Ireland, the south west of England and Yorkshire. The styles of the objects reveal that votive offerings had taken place over three centuries, right up until the Roman assault of the island during the middle of the 1st century AD.

The story of Lludd describes the ritual transportation of the two dragons from the sacred centre at Oxford to another sacred enclosure at Dinas Emrys during Beltene. This resembles the supposition I made earlier about the bile of Uisneach having to be carried from the sacred naval to the seat of the high king at Tara, also during Beltene. This indicates that the same ritual connection existed between Oxford/Uisneach and Dinas Emrys/Tara. Only in the Welsh account the totem tree is replaced with the two dragons, which we may assume to be religious metaphors for the sun.

The actual object transported would also have been a totem tree, which represented the two serpents. In his description of the sacred grove near Marseilles, Lucan mentions the tradition that serpents twined themselves about yew trees that were raised and set during the ceremony. The Celtic name for the Yew was Eburos, from eb-uros, 'the burning that recedes' or more accurately 'slow to burn'. So the yew was apparently chosen as the totem tree of the Celtic Apollo because it could withstand the heat of fire. The serpents of Lucan's account may describe what the Romans actually observed at the grove, religious images of the Celtic Apollo (as the ram-horned serpents), entwined around his sacred tree.

The religious importance of the area around Dinas Emrys is also alluded to by Plutarch in his description of the Celtic 'land of the dead', which he states was situated beyond an impassable wall on the western extremity of Britain. If by 'the land of the dead' Plutarch is describing a region of profound sanctity, then the impassable wall may well have been the chain of mountains that expand across Snowdonia enclosing Eyri, 'the royal area'. Furthermore, Plutarch informs us that the land of the dead could be reached from the shores of northern Gaul in an hour, perhaps misinterpreting his sources in describing the passage across the Menai strait between the island of Anglesey and the Welsh mainland.

In the Black book of Carmarthen Dinas Emrys is described as lying beneath the 'panting cliffs of Snowdon' where a community of druids was maintained:

> *'Upon the road from the promontory of Lleyn to the part of the coast which is opposite Mona.'*

The 9th-century Welsh historian Nennius informs us that Dinas Emrys was named after the 5th-century king Ambrosius Aurelianus. This site is situated in the valley of Nant Gwynant to the south of Mount Snowdon, in an area generically known as 'the forest of Snowdon'. The name of the enclosure prior to Ambrosius's possession was Dinas Ffaraon, 'the fort of the beacon'. The early 15th-century bard, Rhys Goch Eyri, described an alternative legend to that of the two dragons, identifying the head of Ambrosius as the item buried at the site:

> *'... to the crag where is the head of the son of Fendigaid, a blade of grass in the course of battle, in the darkness of the oak hidden in the forest of Ffaraon on a cold rock in Eyri... where I was reared.'*

In the Welsh genealogies Ambrosius was the brother of Uthyr Pendragon, 'the victorious head of the dragon'. We might see here the later synthesis of ideas surrounding the myth of the decapitation of the ram-horned serpent as the Celtic Apollo. Geoffrey of Monmouth's

Ambrosius Aurelianus corresponds to the king called Aurelius Ambrosianus by the 6th-century historian Gildas. Aurelius is also given the title Gwledig Emrys, 'the chief of Emrys' in other Welsh sources. This suggests that Aurelius acquired the title Emrys/Ambros from the name of the fort rather then visa versa. The name Emrys stems from em-righ, 'the giving of kingship', describing the original function of the site in relation to the rites of sacral kingship.

## The Knowledge of the Feryllt

In the last line of The battle of the trees reference is made 'to the craft of the Feryllt', a title that apparently addressed a particular kind of Druid. The importance of the Feryllt is also alluded to in the alternative name for Dinas Emrys as Dinas Ffaraon. Their title stems from pher-syllu, literally 'to gaze at lights' making them 'the light gazers'. In the story of Taliesin, the goddess Ceridwen consulted from 'the book of Feryllt' during the preparation of awen. From this book she learned the timing of when to add specific ingredients to the brew based on astronomical calculations. The potion was said to take a year and a day to prepare. A clue to the date when the potion was prepared and consumed comes from The Contention of the bards:

> *'... my original country is in the region of the summer stars... I have been three periods in the prison of Arianrhod... For a year and a day in stocks and fetters...'*

Taliesin, 'radiant brow' is the Celtic Dis. Before he accidentally consumes three drops of the potion he was called Gwion Bach. Gwion is the Welsh equivalent of the Irish god Fion, who like Taliesin, gained poetic inspiration from an accidental splash of potion.

The preparation of the potion took place at Beltene and was initiated by events observed in the summer stars by the Feryllt, that is the movement of the sun and moon through specific constellations heralding the opening and closing phases of the ritual. The opening of the ritual is described in The Elegy of Uthyr Pendragon:

> *'Whilst the sanctuary earnestly invoke the gliding king, before whom the fair one retreats, upon the rock that covers the huge stones.'*

The full moon rises to the east as the sun has set to the west. The Ox-pen of the Bards describes how the closing ritual is initiated at dawn:

> *'Let the rock beyond the billow be set in order at the dawn, displaying the countenance of him who receives the exile into his sanctuary. The rock of the supreme proprietor, the chief place of tranquility.'*

If the Feryllt marked the timing of ceremonies and Dinas Emrys was the sanctuary referred to in the six poems of Taliesin, we should expect to find some conformity shared between the geographical details given in the texts and the topography around the enclosure. Our first two clues relate to the rising and setting position of the sun cited in the two verses above (See *Figure 63*). Looking to the north west of the enclosure an outcrop of rock known as Craig Wen terminates on a sloping ridge. In English the name of these rocks translate as 'the steep rock of the fair one'. From Dinas Emrys the sun would set behind these rocks on the eve of Beltene, indicating that this could be the site of the 'huge veiled rock'. From the enclosure a narrow ridge leads off to the north-east towards a gap between two outcrops of rock called Hafod-y-Porth, 'the portal of Summer'. In The Ox-pen of the Bards we are told that the rock was set beyond the billow before dawn. The term billow usually describes a large wave but in this instance may refer to the narrow ridge. The portal set beyond it corresponds to the position of sunrise on Beltene day.

Remembering that the sun rises in the constellation ofTaurus at the time of the celebration, we find the following clues hidden in the enigmatic language of *The Spoils of the Deep*:

> *'Against him will be lifted the bright and gleaming sword; and in the hand of the sword bearer shall he be left; and before the entrance of the gate of hell, shall the horns of light be burning.'*

The first part of the extract describes the setting of the sun above the sword raised by the right arm of Orion/Smertrius, into whose hands he is left during the nightly vigil. Then at dawn the regenerated sun rises between the gates of hell (Hafod-y-Porth) born before the horns ofTaurus.

## Ar-Taur and the Greal of Rebirth

The last stanza of each verse in *The Spoils of the Deep* describes a myth concerning the descent of Arthur into the Underworld and returning with its spoils, in this case the release of Cwy/Mabon. The myth of Arthur is often associated with the legend of attaining the Holy Grail and conjures up the idea that the theme of the poem describes a similar tale about Arthur acquiring the cauldron of the goddess Ceridwen. In this instance the character of Arthur in later medieval narratives was based upon a mythological forebear, a god familiarly invoked as Artauros, 'the one before the bull. We are informed that excepting seven, no others returned from the sanctuary with Arthur. The sanctuary is referred to by the following descriptive names in each verse:

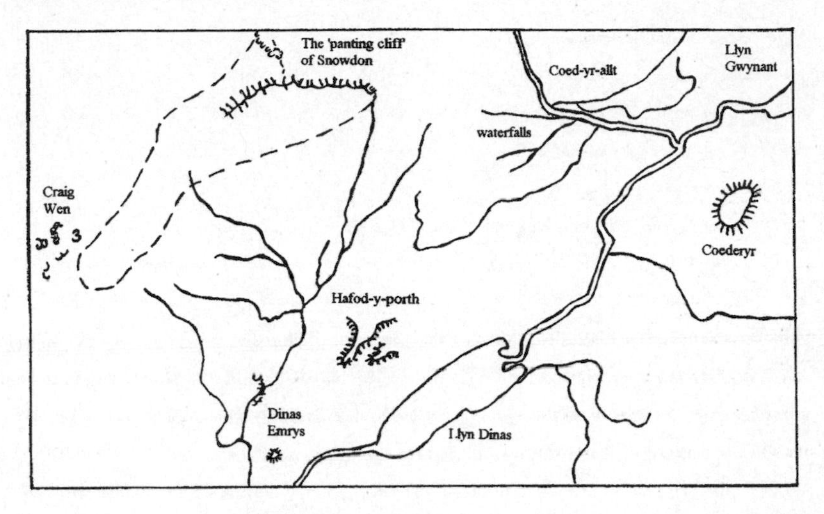


**FIG. 63.** *The environs of the Nant Gwynant Valley.*

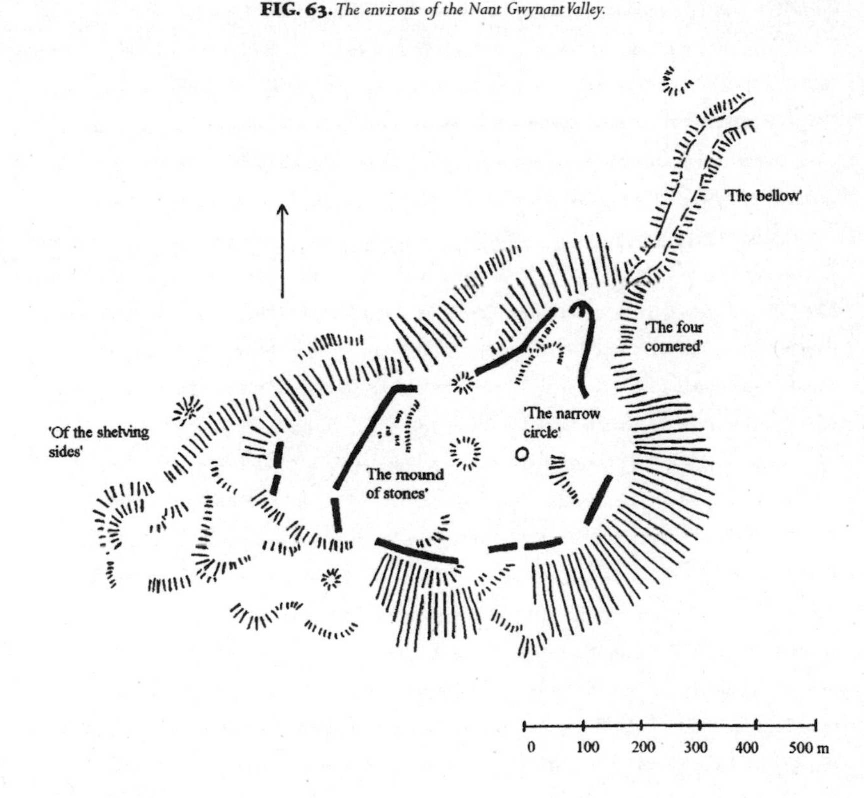


**FIG. 64.** *Site plan of Dinas Emrys.*

*Caer Sidhi; 'of the mound'*
*Caer Vediwid; 'of the wise ones'*
*Caer Rigor; 'of the royal'*
*Caer Golur; 'of the hidden'*
*Caer Vandwy; 'of the lofty'*
*Caer Ochren; 'of the shelving'*
*Caer Pedryvan; 'of the four corners'*

Three of the names specifically allude to the function of the site in performing the Beltene ritual, namely the assembling of 'the wise ones' (the bards) to find 'the hidden one' (Mabon) and thus endorse the rule of 'the royal one' (the high king). The other four names describe the physical appearance of the enclosure. Dinas Emrys is built on the summit of a hill (lofty), has terraced platforms on the western and southern slopes (shelving), has a rectilinear shape (four cornered) and has a mound located towards the centre (Sidhi). (See *Figure 64*.)

In the centre of the enclosure a mound overlooks a swampy hollow where excavations revealed the concentration of occupational activity during the dark ages. This was when the site lost its ritual importance and was transformed into a defended settlement. Within this area is a circular earthwork (usually interpreted as a pool) corresponding with the only other internal feature described in the poems, the 'narrow circle' where the libation was placed.

Further up stream from the enclosure lies a hill situated between the two lakes called Coed-eryr, 'the area of assembly'. This is possibly the site of the 'solemn festivity round the two lakes' described in the poems. Just to the north of the hill on the other side of the river, a stream descends from Snowdon and forms a waterfall at Coed-yr-allt, 'the other assembly place'. This could be the fountain where the priests of intelligence ceremoniously washed the ingredients of the potion after they had been collected by the 'sickle cutter'.

It was the release of Amaethon from the underworld that formed the basis for the celebration of Beltene, his ascension marking the victory of the gods of light and the ascension of the first day of summer. In The Elegy of Uthyr Pendragon Cernunnos/Dis is recognized as Gorlasser 'of the sky', who, as the constellation of Ophiucus was 'a protecting prince in darkness', the place where the full moon rose above the horizon. He gave the tremendous sword to Henben (Orion/Bran), with his raised arm pulling down the sun at dusk on Beltene eve, an act described as a rite of purification corresponding to Arawn giving Bran the alder branch in the Battle of the Trees. This event occurred when Haearndor 'moved with toil to the top of the hill'. Haearndor ('rich in iron') was the goddess as the personification of the cauldron. So as the sun sets in Orion the cauldron is ritually carried to the mound for the preparation of the mead.

In the Welsh Triads Gleissar is the husband of Haearnwedd and father of the three bravest men in Britain: Gruddnei, 'born of the gruel'; Henben, 'old head'; and Edenawg, 'the winged one'. As we have observed, Henben was the Celtic Mars/Smertrius associated with the beheading of the Apollonian ram horned-serpent. Edenawg is readily identified as Hu 'of the expanded wing', otherwise known as Lleu/Esus or Ulatos Ateula. The final character is the Celtic Apollo himself, reborn at Beltene after the libation of the goddess had been consumed by the high king and the initiated assembly.

The name 'gruel' stems from the Irish greal, the food contained in the cauldron of the Dagdha. This was the basis for the later Christianized myth surrounding king Arthur and the search for the holy grail. The greal or mead of the goddess brewed in her cauldron was replaced with the legendary chalice that Jesus used during the last-supper. The god Ar-Taur, 'the one before the bull', was renamed Arthur and relegated to the status of a heroic king. Ar-Taur was Esus who climbed the cosmic tree to procure the mistletoe, 'the golden pipes of Lleu'.

## The Fountain of Knowledge

In Ireland the myth concerning the mead of inspiration was cryptically remembered in the story of the Fountain of Knowledge, alternatively known as Connla's Well. This was a sacred spring identical to Nechtan's Well in the myth of the goddess Boann and the formation of the river Boyne. In the Irish tale of Cormac and The Land of Promise we find the following description of the fountain:

> *'Then he sees in the garth a shinning fountain, with five streams flowing out of it, and the hosts in turn drinking from its waters. Nine hazels of Buan grow over the well. The purple hazels drop their nuts into the fountain, and the five salmon which are in the fountain sever them, and send their husks floating down the streams. Now the sound of the falling of those streams is more melodious then any that men sing.'*

The Land of Promise was the Otherworldly kingdom of Manannan Mac Lir, and was situated under the ocean. Manannan later explained the vision of the fountain to Cormac:

> *'The fountain which thou sawest, with the five streams out of it, is the fountain of knowledge, and the streams are the five senses through which knowledge is obtained. And no one will have knowledge who drinketh not a draught out of the fountain itself and out of the streams. The folk of many arts are those who drink of them both.'*

Cormac is then given two magical tools, the essential religious accessories of a Druid: a silver branch 'for music and delight' and a golden cup which discerns 'between truth and falsehood' by breaking into three pieces. The branch was the staff of office and the cup was his personal vessel to be used only when taking of the sacred mead. This was the golden horn that the bards of Wales placed before the narrow circle during the Beltene ceremony as described by Taliesin.

The Fountain of Knowledge was a metaphor for the cauldron, which brewed the mead of poetic inspiration during the festivities of Beltene. This itself represented the celestial head of the bull where the Milky Way flowed out and across the sky descending to the ecliptic. The nine hazels of Boann are the nine stars of the constellation of Cepheus, which surround the source of the celestial river. A number replicated with the sisterhood of nine maidens whose duty it was to prepare the mead and tend the fires of the cauldron during the ceremony. The fruit of the 'nine hazels' was the seed of the heavenly bull, a metaphor for the flowers and the berries of the mistletoe religiously prepared by the nine maidens (the semnothoi). Finally, the five salmon, which consumed the nuts of the hazel, were the five planets known throughout the ancient world, namely Mercury, Venus, Mars, Jupiter and Saturn. The five streams were the orbits that they followed along the ecliptic.

In the Irish tale of Sinend, we find another description of the fountain in an almost identical myth to that surrounding Boann, only this time Sinend is drowned and the river formed was the Shannon.

> *'Sinend, daughter of Lodan Lucharglen, son of Ler, out of the land of promise went to Connla's Well which is under the sea, to behold it. That is a well at which are the hazels and inspirations of wisdom, that is, the hazels of the science of poetry. And in the same hour their fruit and their flowers and their foliage break forth, and these fall on the well in the same shower, which raises on the water a royal surge of purple. Then the salmon chew the fruit, and the juice of the nut is apparent on their purple bellies. And seven streams of wisdom spring forth and turn their again.'*

In this account seven streams are described as rising from the fountain, apparently including the orbits of the sun and the moon to the five other planets mentioned previously. In this instance the name of the source is Connla's Well and appears to suggest a link with the Irish story of the Connla bull. The bull was the possession of a hag who had transformed three brothers into the shape of a crane. The charm could only be broken with the blood of the slain bull. The mythological precedent seems to describe the same religious formula encountered with the transformation of the goddess from and into the shape of a crane and the slaying of the heavenly bull.

The ritual significance of 'the fountain of knowledge' is supported by the layout of the internal features found in a number of Celtic sanctuaries. The earliest type of internal feature dating from the early La Tène usually consisted of a number of pits placed around a larger central pit. This formula of ritual architecture continued into the Roman period with the development of the distinctive Celtic fana. The fanum had two principal constituents to its plan, reflecting a distinctly Celtic form of ritual observation. The design of the internal features describe the performance of a circumambulatory rite. The central pit of the earlier temples gave way to the enclosed cella of the later fana. This was the place where the most sacred objects were kept and the most solemn rituals performed. Just as the large central pit in the earlier La Tène shrines was enclosed by a ring of smaller pits, the cella was likewise surrounded by an ambulatory, a sheltered portico defining the processional walk around the fanum. In both instances we may assume the continuation of a specific ritual observance.

A good example of such an array of pits comes from Gournay in Picardy. These pits were dug in three groups of three, surrounding the central ditch on three sides, suggesting a tradition continued with the development of the later fana where we find that the cella was also built on three sides with the fourth side open to the east.

The next question must then be to deduce what the ceremony entailed and when it occurred. Fortunately archaeology has retrieved a few clues from the ritual sanctuary of Gournay. Here the central pit appears to have been the temporary repository for the bones of slaughtered oxen. The oxen were apparently slaughtered elsewhere in the sanctuary, decapitated by a sword blow. The heads were then interred in the ditch surrounding the entrance while the rest of the beast was dragged to the central pit where it remained for approximately six months (or until all of its flesh had fallen off the bone). After this period the pit was then ritually cleared of bone leaving behind the remains of tendons.

The oxen were initially sacrificed during Samhain when the full moon entered Taurus, the bones were then left in situ in the central pit until they were exhumed six months later, at Beltene. In the poems of Taliesin we noted that during the Beltene ceremony a number of circumambulatory rituals were performed. One in particular was called 'the procession of the dragon'. Here, they marched in procession around the central pit known as 'the narrow circle'. The dedication of this rite to the dragon suggests that it was an act of worship performed in honour of the ram-horned serpent or the Celtic Apollo. At Gournay, the Celtic Apollo was slain in his guise as a white bull, a Gallic tradition also recorded by Pliny. The nine surrounding pits would then have been equivalent to the places where the bards deposited their drinking vessels during the celebration. So, just as the dragons were revealed at Beltene in Wales, in Gaul the bones of the bull slain at Samhain were exhumed and paraded around the central pit to commemorate the release of Maponus from the underworld and his transformation into Belenus.

This was in essence the re-enactment of the myth displayed in the stars of the circumpolar region. The nine pits were the sockets for the seasonally erected posts that formed an artificial grove replicating the nine stars of Cepheus, the head of the heavenly bull. The central pit contained the oak post of the Celtic sky god himself. When the post was lifted between Samhain and Beltene, a bull was sacrificed and placed in its socket. This was a particularly Gallic interpretation of the Irish legend of the fountain of wisdom, the spring surrounded by the nine hazels of Boann, the source of the celestial river the Milky Way.

# APPENDICES

## POEM 1: THE CHAIR OF TALIESIN

*I am he who animates the fire, to the honour of the god Dovydd,*
*on behalf of the assembly of associates, qualified to treat of mysteries:*
*A bard with the knowledge of Sywedydd, when he deliberately recites*
*the inspired song of the western cudd, on a serene night amongst the stones.*

*As to loquacious glittering bards, their encomium attracts me not,*
*when moving in their course; admiration is their great object.*
*And I am a silent proficient, who addresses the bards of the land:*
*It is mine to animate the hero; to persuade the unadvised;*
*to awaken the silent beholder, the bold illuminator of kings.*

*I am no shallow artist, greeting the bards of the household,*
*like a subtle parasite; the ocean has a due profundity !*
*The man of complete discipline has obtained the mead of honour,*
*in every nightly celebration, when Dien is propitiated*
*with an offering of wheat, and the suavity of bees,*
*and incense and myrrh, and aloes from beyond the seas,*
*and the golden pipes of Lleu, and cheerful precious silver,*
*and the ruddy gem, and the berries, and the foam of the ocean,*
*and cresses of a purifying quality, laved in the fountain,*
*and a joint contribution of wort, the founder of liquor,*
*supplied by the assembly, and a raised load secluded from the moon,*
*of placid cheerful Vervain.*

*With priests of intelligence to officiate on behalf of the moon,*
*and the concourse of associated men, under the open breeze of the sky,*
*with the maceration and sprinkling, and the portion after the sprinkling,*
*and the boat of glass in the hand of the stranger,*
*and the stout youth with pitch, and the honoured sickle cutter,*
*with medical plants from an exorcized spot.*

*And bards with flowers and perfect convolutions,*
*and primroses, and the leaves of the Briw,*
*with the points of the trees of purposes, and solution of doubts,*
*and frequent mutual pledges; and with wine which flows to the brim,*
*from Rome to Rosedd, and deep standing water,*
*a flood which has the gift of Dovydd, or the tree of gold*
*which becomes of a fructifying quality, when that brewer gives it a boiling,*
*who presided over the cauldron of the five plants.*
*Hence the stream of Gwion, and the reign of serenity,*
*and honey and trefoil, and horns flowing with mead:*
*Meet for a sovereign is the lore of the druids.*

### POEM 2 THE OX-PEN OF THE BARDS

*Gliding with rapidity were my thoughts,*
*over the vain poetic art of the bards of Britain,*
*who labour to make an excessive show at the solemn meeting,*
*with sufficient care hammer out a song.*
*I require a staff in unity with the bardic lore,*
*as for him who knows not the oxpen of the bards,*
*may fifteen thousand overpower and afflict him at once !*

*I am a skilful composer; I am an clear singer: I am a tower:*
*I am a druid: I am an architect: I am a Vate: I am a serpent:*
*I am love: In the social banquet will I indulge.*
*A bard am I not doting upon superfluous trifles.*
*When a master sings, his song will be close to the subject.*
*He will not be searching for those remote wonders.*
*Shall I then admit these, like men suing for garments,*
*without a hand to receive them; like men toiling in the lake, without a ship!*

*Boldly swells the stream to its high limit.*
*Let the thigh be pierced in blood.*
*Let the rock beyond the billow be set in order at the dawn,*
*displaying the face of him who receives the exile into his sanctuary.*
*The rock of the supreme proprietor, the chief place of tranquility.*

*Then let the giver of the mead feast cause to be proclaimed:*

*I am a cell; I am the opening chasm; I am the bull Becr Lled;I am the repository of the mystery; I am the place of re-animation.*

*I love the tops of the trees, with the points well connected,*

*and the bard who composes without meriting a repulse;*

*But him I love not, who delights in contention.*

*He who traduces the adept shall not enjoy the mead.*

*It is time to hasten to the banquet where the skilful ones*

*are employed in their mysteries, with the hundred knots;*

*the custom of our countrymen.*

*The shepherds of the plains, the supporters of gates,*

*are like persons marching to battle without their clan.*

*I am the bard of the hall; I am the stock that supports the chair;*

*I shall succeed in impeding the progress of the loquacious bards.*

## POEM 3: THE ELEGY OF UTHYR PENDRAGON

*Behold me, who is powerful in the tumultuous din;*

*who would not pause between two hosts without blood.*

*Am I not called Gorlassar the aetherial ?*

*My belt has been a rainbow, enveloping my foe.*

*Am I not a protecting prince in darkness,*

*to him who presents my form at both ends of the bowl?*

*Am not I a plower like Kawyl ?*

*Between two hosts I would not pause, without blood*

*Have not I protected my sanctuary, and with the aid of my friends,*

*caused the wrathful ones to vanish?*

*Have not I shed the blood of the indignant,*

*in bold warfare against the sons of the giant Nur?*

*Have not I imparted, of my guardian power,*

*a ninth portion, in the prowess of Arthur?*

*Have not I slain a hundred governors?*

*Have not I given a hundred veils?*

*Have not I slaughtered a hundred chieftains?*

*Did I not give to Henben the tremendous sword of the enchanter?*
*Did I not perform the rites of purification,*
*when Haearndor moved with toil to the top of the hill?*

*I was subjected to the yoke of my affliction;*
*but commensurate was my confidence;*
*the world had not existence, were it not for my progeny.*
*I am the bard; as for the unskillful encomiast,*
*may his lot be amongst the ravens, and eagles, and birds of wrath!*
*May utter darkness overwhelm him,*
*when he supports the square band of men, between two fields!*

*It was my will to ascend into heaven from the eagle,*
*to avoid the homage of the unskillful.*
*I am a bard; of seven score musicians,*
*I am the master of the harp, the pipe, and the crooth.*
*I am the mighty enchanter, privileged on the covered mount.*

*O Hu with the expanded wings has been thy son,*
*thy bardic proclaimer, thy deputy.*
*O father Deon: My voice has recited the death song,*
*where the mound representing the world, is constructed of stonework.*
*Let the countenance of Prydain, let the glancing Hu attend me!*
*O sovereign of heaven, let not my message be rejected!*

*With solemn festivity round the two lakes;*
*with the lake next to my side; with my side moving round the sanctuary;*
*whilst the sanctuary earnestly invokes the gliding king,*
*before whom the fair one retreats,*
*upon the veil that covers the huge stones; whilst the dragon moves round,*
*over the places which contain vessels of drink offering;*
*whilst the drink offering is in the golden horns;*
*whilst the golden horns are in the hand;*
*whilst the hand is upon the knife; whilst the knife is upon the chief victim;*
*Sincerely I implore thee, O victorious Beli, son of the sovereign Manhogan,*
*that thou wouldst preserve the honours of the honey isle of Beli.*

## POEM 4 THE SPOILS OF THE DEEP

*I will adore the sovereign, the supreme ruler of the land.*
*If he extended his dominion over the shores of the world,*
*yet in good order was the prison of Gwair, in the inclosure of Sidi.*
*Through the mission of Pwyll and Pryderi, no one before him entered into it.*
*The heavy blue chain didst thou, O just man, endure:*
*and for the spoils of the deep, woeful is thy song,*
*and till the doom shall it remain in the bardic prayer:*
*Thrice the number that would have filled Prydwen, we entered into the deep;*
*excepting seven, none returned from Caer Sidi.*

*Am I not contending for the praise of the lore, if it was regarded,*
*which was four times reviewed in the quadrangular inclosure!*
*As the first sentence was it uttered from the cauldron,*
*which began to be warmed by the breath of nine virgins.*
*Is not this the cauldron of the ruler of the deep! What is its quality?*
*With the ridge of pearls round its border,*
*it will not boil the food of a coward,*
*who is not bound by his sacred oath.*
*Against him will be lifted the bright gleaming sword;*
*and in the hand of the sword bearer shall he be left:*
*and before the entrance to the gate of hell,*
*shall the horns of light be burning:*
*And when he went with Arthur in his splendid labours,*
*excepting seven, none returned from Caer Vediwid.*

*Am I not contending for the honour of a lore that deserves attention!*
*In the quadrangular inclosure, in the island with the strong door,*
*the twilight and the pitchy darkness were mixed together,*
*whilst bright wine was the beverage placed before the narrow circle:*
*Thrice the number that would have filled Prydwen, we embarked upon the sea,*
*excepting seven, none returned from Caer Rigor.*

*I will not redeem the multitude with the ensign of the governor.*
*Beyond the inclosure of glass, they beheld not the prowess of Arthur.*
*Thrice twenty hundred men stood on its wall;*

*it was difficult to converse with its sentinel.*
*Thrice the number that would have filled Prydwen went forth with Arthur;*
*excepting seven, none returned from Caer Golur.*

*I will not redeem the multitude with trailing shields.*
*They knew not on what day the stroke would be given,*
*nor what hour in the serene day, Cwy would be born,*
*or who prevented him going into the dales of Devwy.*
*They know not the brindled ox with the thick head band,*
*having seven score knobs in his collar.*
*And when we went with Arthur, of mournful memory;*
*excepting seven, none returned from Caer Vandwy.*

*I will not redeem the multitudes with unguarded mouths.*
*They know not on what day the chief was appointed;*
*on what hour in the serene day the proprietor was born;*
*or the animal it is which the silver headed one protects:*
*When we went with Arthur into the mournful conflict;*
*excepting seven, none returned from Caer Ochren.*
*Monks congregate like dogs in their kennel, wrangling with their instructors.*
*Is there but one course to the wind; but one to the water of the sea!*
*Is there but one spark in the fire of boundless energy.*

*Monks congregate like wolves, wrangling with their instructors.*
*They know not when the darkness and the dawn divide;*
*nor what is the course of the wind or the cause of its agitation;*
*in what place it dies away or on what region it expands.*
*the grave of the saint is vanishing from the foot of the altar;*
*I will adore the sovereign, the great supreme.*

## POEM 5 THE CONTENTION OF THE BARDS

*Primary chief bard am I to Elphin,*
*and my original country is the region of the summer stars;*
*Idno and Heinin called me Merddin,*
*at length every king will call me Taliesin.*

*I was with my lord in the highest sphere,*
*on the fall of Lucifer into the depth of hell.*
*I have borne a banner before Alexander;*
*I know the names of the stars from north to south;*
*I have been in the stars at the throne of the distributor.*

*I was in Canaan when Absalom was slain;*
*I conveyed Awen to the level of the vale of Hebron;*
*I was in the court of Don before the birth of Gwydion.*
*I was the instructor of Eli and Enoch;*
*I have been winged by the genius of the splendid crozier.*

*I have been loquacious prior to being gifted with speech;*
*I was at the place of the crucifixion of the merciful son of god;*
*I have been three periods in the prison of Arianrhod;*
*I have been the chief director of the work of the tower of Nimrod.*
*I am a wonder whose origin is not known.*

*I have been in Asia with Noah in the Ark,*
*I have witnessed the destruction of Sodom and Gomorrah;*
*I have been in India when Rome was built;*
*I am now come here to the remnant of Troia.*
*I have been with my lord in the manger of the ass.*

*I strengthened Moses through the water of Jordan;*
*I have been in the firmament with Mary Magdalene;*
*I have obtained the muse from the cauldron of Ceridwen;*
*I have been a bard of the harp to Leon of Lochlin.*
*I have been on the White Hill in the court of Cynvelyn.*

*For a day and a year in stocks and fetters,*
*I have suffered hunger for the son of the virgin,*
*I have been fostered in the land of the deity,*
*I have been teacher to all intelligences,*
*I am able to instruct the whole universe.*

*I shall be until the day of doom on the face of the earth;*
*And it is not known whether my body is flesh or fish.*
*Then I was for nine months in the womb of the hag Ceridwen;*
*I was originally little Gwion, at length I am Taliesin.*

# BIBLIOGRAPHY


D' Arbois de Jubainville, H., *The Irish Mythological Cycle*, Dublin, 1903.

Bromwich, Rachel, *TrioeddYnys Prydein*, Cardiff University Press, 1961.

Brunaux, J.L., *The Celtic Gauls Seaby*, 1988.

Chadwick, Nora, *The Celt*, Penguin, 1961.

Chadwick, Nora, *The Druids, University ofWales Press*, 1966.

Davies, Edward, *The Mythology and Rites of the British Druids*, London, 1809.

Davies, John, *The Celts*, Cassell, 2000.

Dinneen, Patrick. S., *Irish-English Dictionary*, Dublin, 1927.

Dumezil, G., *Les Dieux des Indo-Européens*, Paris, 1952.

Duval, Paul-Marie, *Les Dieux de la Gaule Payor*, 1957.

Duval, Paul-Marie, *'Observations Sur le Calendrier de Coligny'*, Etudes Celtiques 10, 1963.

Edwards, H. J, *Caesar: De Bello Gallico*, Loeb Library, 1917.

Esperandieu, E., *Recuil General des Bas Relief; Statues et Bustes de la Gaul* Romaine, Paris, 1907.

Grant, M., *Tacitus: The Annals of Imperial Rome*, Penguin, 1956.

Graves, Robert, *Lucan Pharsalia*,Penguin, 1956.

Graves, Robert, *Suetonius: The Twelve Caesars*, Cassell, 1957.

Graves, Robert, *TheWhite Goddess*, Faber, 1961.

Green, Miranda. J., *Dictionary of Celtic Myth and Legend*,Thames & Hudson, 1992.

Green, Miranda. J., *Exploring the World of the Druids*,Thames & Hudson, 1997.

Griscom., *Geoffrey of Monmouth: Historia Regum Brittaniae,* London, 1929.

Griffiths, R.T.H., *The Hymns of the Rig Veda*, Delhi, 1973.

Jones, Gwyn & Thomas., *The Mabinogion*, Everyman Library, 1950.

Kendrick,T.D., *The Druids*, London, 1927.

King, John, *The Celtic DruidsYear*, Blandford, 1998.

King, John, *Kingdoms of the Celts*, Blandford, 2000.

Mac Cana, Proinsias, *Celtic Mythology*, Hamlyn, 1968.

Macdonell, A.A., *A Vedic Reader for Students*, Oxford, 1917.

Matthews, John, *The Druid Source Book*, Blandford, 1997.

Matthews, John, *The Bardic Source Book*, Blandford, 1998.

Matthews, John, *The Celtic Seers Source Book*, Blandford, 1999.

O'Donovan, John, *Cormac's Glossary*, Calcutta, 1868.

O'Flaherty, W.D., *The Rig Veda*, Penguin, 1981.

Olmsted, G.S., *The Gundstrup Cauldron*, Latomus, 1979.

Parry, J.J., *Vita Merlini*, University of Illinois Press, 1925.

Piggot, Stuart, *The Druids*, Thames & Hudson, 1975.

Rolleston, T.W., *Myths and Legends of the Celtic Race*, London, 1919.

Ross, Anne, *Pagan Celtic Britain*, Routledge & Kegan Paul, 1967.

Spence, Lewis, *The Mysteries of Britain*, Rider, 1932.

Strachan, A., *An Introduction to Early Welsh*, Manchester, 1937.

Thevenot, E., *Divinities et Sanctuaires de la Gaule*, Fayard, 1968.

Thomas, E.J., *Vedic Hymns*, London, 1923.

Tierney, S.S., *'The Celtic Ethnography of Posidonius'*, Proceedings of the Royal Irish Academy, 1960.

Williams, I., *Canu Aneirin*, Cardiff, 1961.

# INDEX